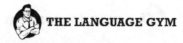 **THE LANGUAGE GYM**

SPANISH
SENTENCE BUILDERS
TRILOGY

A lexicogrammar approach
Beginner to Pre-Intermediate

PART I

THE LANGUAGE GYM

About the authors

Gianfranco Conti taught for 25 years at schools in Italy, the UK and in Kuala Lumpur, Malaysia. He has also been a university lecturer, holds a Master's degree in Applied Linguistics and a PhD in metacognitive strategies as applied to second language writing. He is now an author, a popular independent educational consultant and professional development provider. He has written around 2,000 resources for the TES website, which have awarded him the Best Resources Contributor in 2015. He has co-authored the best-selling and influential book for world languages teachers, "The Language Teacher Toolkit" and "Breaking the sound barrier: Teaching learners how to listen", in which he puts forth his Listening As Modelling methodology. Gianfranco writes an influential blog on second language acquisition called The Language Gym, co-founded the interactive website language-gym.com and the Facebook professional group Global Innovative Language Teachers (GILT). Last but not least, Gianfranco has created the instructional approach known as E.P.I. (Extensive Processing Instruction).

Dylan Viñales has taught for 15 years, in schools in Bath, Beijing and Kuala Lumpur in state, independent and international settings. He lives in Kuala Lumpur. He is fluent in five languages, and gets by in several more. Dylan is, besides a teacher, a professional development provider, specialising in E.P.I., metacognition, teaching languages through music (especially ukulele) and cognitive science. In the last five years, together with Dr Conti, he has driven the implementation of E.P.I. in one of the top international schools in the world: Garden International School. This has allowed him to test, on a daily basis, the sequences and activities included in this book with excellent results (his students have won language competitions both locally and internationally). He has designed an original Spanish curriculum, bespoke instructional materials, based on Reading and Listening as Modelling (RAM and LAM). Dylan co-founded the fastest growing professional development group for modern languages teachers on Facebook, Global Innovative Languages Teachers, which includes over 12,000 teachers from all corners of the globe. He authors an influential blog on modern language pedagogy in which he supports the teaching of languages through E.P.I. Dylan is the lead author of Spanish content on the Language Gym website and oversees the technological development of the site. He completed the NPQML qualification in 2021 and is now planning to pursue a Masters in second language acquisition.

Acknowledgements

We would like to thank our editors, Paloma Lozano García and Jaume Llorens, for their tireless work, proofreading, editing and advising on this book. They are talented, accomplished professionals who work at the highest possible level and add value at every stage of the process. Not only this, but they are also lovely, good-humoured colleagues who go above and beyond, and make the hours of collaborating a real pleasure.

Our sincere gratitude to all the people involved in the recording of the Listening audio files: Ana del Casar, Paloma Lozano García & José Luis Larrosa. Your energy, enthusiasm and passion comes across clearly in every recording and is the reason why the listening sections are such a successful and engaging resource, according to the many students who have been alpha and beta testing the book.

In addition, Dylan would like to thank his eagle-eyed students Shweta Nair and Sam Sajan for their insights and feedback during the editing phase of this book.

Our sincere thanks to Simona and Stefano for their ongoing support, since the very beginning of the Sentence Builder books project. Some important structural elements in this book, such as the inclusion of a listening element at the start of every unit, are inspired by their excellent work as lead authors of the Primary Sentence Builders series.

Finally, our gratitude to the MFL Twitterati for their ongoing support of E.P.I. and the Sentence Builders book series. In particular a shoutout to our team of incredible educators who helped in checking all the units: Aurélie Lethuilier, Joe Barnes-Moran, Jérôme Nogues, Anneliese Davies, Ana del Casar, Ester Borin, Simona Gravina, Christian Moretti, Ryan Cockrell and Roberto Jover Soro. It is thanks to your time, patience, professionalism and detailed feedback that we have been able to produce such a refined and highly accurate product.

Gracias a todos,
Gianfranco & Dylan

DEDICATION

For Catrina
-Gianfranco

For Ariella & Leonard
-Dylan

Introduction

Hello and welcome to the first 'text' book designed to be an accompaniment to a Spanish, Extensive Processing Instruction course. The book has come about out of necessity, because such a resource did not previously exist.

How to use this book

This book was originally designed as a resource to use in conjunction with our E.P.I. approach and teaching strategies. Our course favours flooding comprehensible input, organising content by communicative functions and related constructions, and a big focus on reading and listening as modelling. The aim of this book is to empower the beginner-to-pre-intermediate learner with linguistic tools - high-frequency structures and vocabulary - useful for real-life communication.

What's inside

The book contains 14 macro-units which concern themselves with a specific communicative function, such as 'Describing people's appearance and personality', 'Comparing and contrasting people', 'Saying what you like and dislike' or 'Saying what you and others do in your free time'. Each unit includes:

- a sentence builder modelling the target constructions;
- a set of listening activities to model and input-flood the target language
- a set of vocabulary building activities which reinforce the material in the sentence builder;
- a set of narrow reading texts exploited through a range of tasks focusing on both the meaning and structural levels of the text;
- a set of translation tasks aimed at consolidation through retrieval practice;
- a set of writing tasks targeting essential writing micro-skills such as spelling, functional and positional processing, editing and communication of meaning.
- a "Bringing it all together" section to recycle and interleave the target language seen in previous units

At the end of each term, there is also an End of Term - Question Skills unit. These units are designed to model asking and answering the key questions which have been studied throughout the term. This is also an additional opportunity for structured production as students move towards routinising the language and producing spontaneous speech by the end of the term.

Listening files

These can be accessed by going to **language-gym.com/listening** – access is free, and you can also share this link with students if you want to set a listening homework.

Each sentence builder at the beginning of a unit contains one or more constructions which have been selected with real-life communication in mind. Each unit is built around that construction <u>but not solely on it</u>. Based on the principle that each E.P.I instructional sequence must move from modelling to production in a seamless and organic way, each unit expands on the material in each sentence builder by embedding it in texts and graded tasks which contain both familiar and unfamiliar (but comprehensible and learnable) vocabulary and structures.

The point of all the above micro-units is to implement lots of systematic recycling and interleaving, two techniques that allow for stronger retention and transfer of learning.

Gianfranco and Dylan

 THE LANGUAGE GYM

SENTENCE BUILDERS TRILOGY
PART 1 - TABLE OF CONTENTS

 THE LANGUAGE GYM

TERM 1 – OVERVIEW

This term you will learn:

Unit 0 - Register routine: saying how you are
• How to say your name
• How to say how you are feeling

Unit 1 - How to introduce yourself and say how you are
• How to say your name and age
• How to say someone else's name and age

Unit 2 - How to say when your birthday is
• When your birthday is
• Numbers from 15 to 31 / Months
• Where you and another person are from

Unit 3 - How to say where you live and are from
• What your apartment or house is like and where it is
• Renowned cities and countries in the Hispanic world

Unit 4 - How to talk about subjects & teachers (OPTIONAL)
• Adjectives for describing people
• Masculine/feminine agreements

Unit 5 - How to talk about free time - likes / dislikes
• Three key verbs: hacer / jugar / ir
• Activities that go with those verbs

KEY QUESTIONS

- ¿Cómo te llamas?	*What is your name?*
- ¿Cómo estás hoy?	*How are you today?*
- ¿Cuántos años tienes?	*How old are you?*
- ¿Cuándo es tu cumpleaños?	*When is your birthday?*
- ¿Tienes hermanos o hermanas?	*Do you have any brothers or sisters?*
- ¿Cómo se llama tu hermano/hermana?	*What is your brother/sister called?*
- ¿Cuántos años tiene?	*How old is he/she?*
- ¿Cuándo es su cumpleaños?	*When is his/her birthday?*
- ¿De dónde eres?	*Where are you from?*
- ¿Dónde vives?	*Where do you live?*
- ¿Qué asignaturas estudias?	*What subjects do you study?*
- ¿Cuál (**no**) te gusta? ¿Por qué?	*Which one do you (**not**) like? Why?*
- ¿Te gusta el español? ¿Por qué?	*Do you like Spanish? Why?*
- ¿Qué te gusta hacer en tu tiempo libre?	*What do you like to do in your free time?*

In this unit you will learn:

- How to introduce yourself
- Key questions: "¿Cómo te llamas?" and "¿Cómo estás hoy?"
- How to say how you are feeling
- How to express your mental state

Hola, soy Olga, ¿cómo te llamas?

¿Cómo estás hoy?

Me llamo María

¡Bien, gracias!

UNIT 0
EPI Register Routine

¿Cómo te llamas? *What is your name?*	Me llamo *My name is*	Carlos María
¿Cómo estás hoy? *How are you today?*	Estoy bien, gracias *I am well, thanks*	
¿Qué tal? *How's it going?*		

					MASC	FEM
Hola *Hello* **Buenos días** *Good morning* **Buenas tardes** *Good afternoon* **Buenas noches** *Good evening /* *Good night*	**hoy** **estoy** *today I* *am*	**fenomenal** *great* **muy bien** *very well* **bien** *well* **regular** *so-so*	**pero** **estoy** *but* *I am* *(feeling)* **porque** **estoy** *because* *I am* *(feeling)*	**bastante** *quite* **un poco** *a bit* **muy** *very*	**aburrido** *bored* **cansado** *tired* **emocionado** *excited* **enfadado** *angry* **enfermo** *sick* **estresado** *stressed* **feliz** *happy* **nervioso** *nervous* **tranquilo** *calm* **triste** *sad*	**aburrida** **cansada** **emocionada** **enfadada** **enferma** **estresada** **feliz** **nerviosa** **tranquila** **triste**
Adiós *Goodbye* **De nada** *You're welcome* **Gracias** *Thank you* **Mucho gusto** *Nice to meet you* **Vale** *OK*		**mal** *(feeling)* *bad* **muy mal** *(feeling)* *very bad* **fatal** *(feeling)* *awful*				

***Author's note: "Estoy"** means **"I am"**. It is often used to talk about how you are feeling or how you are.*
***"Estoy mal/fatal"** should thus be translated as "I am <u>feeling</u> bad/awful"- not "I am a bad/awful person".*

1. Break the flow: draw a line between each word

a. ¿Cómotellamas?

b. Hola,mellamoPablo

c. ¿Cómoestáshoy?

d. Buenosdías,hoyestoyfenomenal

e. Hoyestoybastantecansado

f. Estoyunpocoenfadado

g. ¡Estoymuycontenta!

2. Faulty echo

a. ¿Cómo te llamas?

b. Me llamo Carlos

c. Buenos días, ¿cómo estás?

d. Buenas tardes, estoy fatal

e. Estoy muy tranquilo

f. Hoy estoy fenomenal, gracias

g. Mucho gusto

3. Arrange in the correct order

and quite calm	
Today I am great	
What is your name?	
Good morning	**1**
My name is Carlos	
because I am very happy	
And you, how are you today?	

4. Fill in the blanks

a. ¿C___ t_ l_____?

b. ¿C___ e____ h__?

c. B_____ d___

d. B____ _____s

e. B____ ____s

f. H__ e____ m__ b___

g. H__ e____ m__

h. E____ m__ f____

5. Listen and fill in the gaps

Paco: Hola, ¿cómo te _____?

María: _____, me llamo María

Paco: Mucho gusto María ¿Cómo estás _____?

María: Hoy estoy _____ porque estoy muy _____. ¿Y tú?

Paco: ¡Qué bien! Yo estoy _____ porque estoy bastante _____, gracias

María: Vale Paco, mucho _____.

Paco: Encantado ☺

tranquilo	feliz	bien	hoy
fenomenal	llamas	gusto	hola

6. Listen and fill in the grid in Spanish

		How are they?	Why?
e.g.	Paco	Muy bien	Feliz
a.	José		
b.	Tomás		
c.	Paloma		
d.	Dylan		
e.	Ana		

Unit 0. EPI Register Routine: VOCABULARY BUILDING

1. Match

Estoy bien	I am (feeling) bad
Estoy mal	I am sad
Estoy regular	I am happy
Estoy fatal	I am well
Estoy fenomenal	I am stressed
Estoy cansado	I am so-so
Estoy feliz	I am (feeling) awful
Estoy estresado	I am great
Estoy triste	I am tired

2. Faulty translation: some are correct!

a. Estoy feliz: I am stressed

b. Estoy cansado: I am happy

c. Estoy bien: I am well

d. Estoy estresado: I am sad

e. Estoy triste: I am tired

f. Estoy mal: I am (feeling) bad

g. Estoy regular: I am so-so

h. Estoy fatal: I am (feeling) awful

i. Hoy: now

j. Buenas tardes: Good afternoon

3. Break the flow

a. Estoybienporqueestoyfeliz

b. Estoymalporqueestoynerviosa

c. Estoymuybienporqueestoytranquila

d. Estoymuymalporqueestoyestresada

e. Estoymalporqueestoytriste

f. Estoymalporqueestoyenfadada

g. Estoyregularperoestoycansada

4. Fill in the gaps

a. _____, ¿cómo te _____?

b. Me llamo Paco, mucho _____.

c. _____ gusto, ¿cómo estás _____?

d. _____bien, gracias. ¿Y _____?

e. Estoy bien _____

f. …pero estoy un poco _____

mucho	tú	estoy	cansado	hola
hoy	llamas	gusto	hola	gracias

5. Broken words

a. H_____ ¿c_____ t__ l_____ ?
Hi, what's your name?

b. M_ l_____ L____, m_____ g_____
My name is Lily, nice to meet you

c. ¿C_____ e_____ h___?
How are you today?

d. H____ e_____ b_____ b_____, g_____
Today I am quite well (good), thanks

e. E_____ r_____, p_____ e_____ u_
p_____ e_____
I am so-so because I am a bit stressed (f)

6. Complete with a suitable word

a. _____, me llamo _____

b. ¿Y tú, cómo te _____?

c. ____ llamo Paco. Mucho _____.

d. _____ gusto, ¿_____ estás hoy?

e. _____ bastante bien, _____

f. ¿Y ____? ¿Cómo estás _____?

g. Hoy estoy mal porque estoy muy _____

h. Estoy _____ porque estoy feliz

i. Estoy muy bien _____ estoy tranquilo

THE LANGUAGE GYM

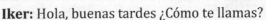

Olga: Hola, buenos días. ¿Cómo te llamas?
María: Hola, me llamo María, ¿y tú?
Olga: Me llamo Olga. ¿Cómo estás hoy María?
María: Estoy fenomenal, gracias. Estoy feliz y emocionada. ¿Y tú?
Olga: Hoy estoy regular.
María: ¿Por qué? ¿Qué te pasa?
Olga: Estoy muy cansada y un poco estresada. Gracias por preguntar.
María: De nada.
Olga: Vale, María, mucho gusto.
María: Igualmente *(likewise)*, mucho gusto.
Olga: Adiós, María.

Iker: Hola, buenas tardes ¿Cómo te llamas?
Joaquín: Hola, me llamo Joaquín, ¿y tú? ¿Cómo te llamas?
Iker: Me llamo Iker. ¿Cómo estás hoy Joaquín?
Joaquín: Estoy muy mal.
Iker: ¿Por qué? ¿Qué te pasa?
Joaquín: Estoy muy enfadado y un poco triste también *(too)*. ¿Y tú?
Iker: Ay, ¡lo siento! *(sorry!)* Yo estoy bastante bien hoy, gracias por preguntar. Estoy muy tranquilo.
Joaquín: Me alegro *(I'm glad)*.
Iker: Vale, Joaquín, encantado de conocerte.
Joaquín: Mucho gusto. ¡Adiós, Iker!

1. Find the Spanish for the following items in the Olga and María's dialogue

a. Hello, good morning.

b. What is your name?

c. My name is María

d. How are you today?

e. I am great, thank you.

f. I am so-so

g. Why?

h. What's up?

i. I am very tired

j. ...and a bit stressed

k. Thanks for asking

l. You're welcome

m. OK

n. Nice to meet you

o. Likewise

p. Goodbye

2. Answer the following questions about Olga and María

a. How is María feeling today?

b. What two reasons does María give to explain how she is feeling?

c. How is Olga?

d. What two reasons does Olga give to explain how she is feeling?

3. Find someone who...

a. ...is feeling very tired

b. ...is feeling very bad

c. ...is feeling quite well

d. ...is feeling a bit sad

e. ...is feeling great

f. ...is feeling a bit stressed

g. ...is feeling very calm

h. ...is feeling happy and excited

THE LANGUAGE GYM

Unit 0. EPI Register Routine: WRITING

1. Faulty translation: spot and correct (in the English) any translation mistakes you find below

a. Me llamo Dylan — *Your name is Dylan*

b. ¿Cómo te llamas? — *What are your llamas?*

c. ¿Cómo estás hoy? — *What are you today?*

d. Estoy regular — *I am great*

e. Estoy muy feliz — *I am a bit happy*

f. Estoy un poco estresado — *I am very stressed*

g. Estoy muy mal — *I am (feeling) very well*

h. Estoy fenomenal — *I am OK*

i. Estoy bastante cansado — *I am quite tiring*

j. Mucho gusto — *Many gusts*

2. Translate into English

a. Hola, ¿cómo te llamas?

b. ¿Cómo estás hoy?

c. Me llamo Pedro

d. Estoy bastante bien, gracias

e. ¿Y tú?

f. Estoy muy bien

g. Hoy estoy muy tranquilo

h. Hoy no estoy bien

i. Estoy muy feliz

j. Estoy triste y enfadado

3. Anagram challenge: unscramble the words and then translate

a. soBeun ídas

b. eBanus redtas

c. ¿moCó setás?

d. Etyos tetris

e. oytEs lifez

f. ¿oCóm et mallas?

g. yEtso istret

h. toyEs mefenonal

i. stEoy umy faendoda

j. choMu gotsu

4. Translate into Spanish

a. Hello

b. Good morning

c. Good afternoon

d. How are you today?

e. What's your name?

f. I am very well, thanks. And you?

g. I am so-so because I am a bit sad

h. I am very happy and calm

i. I am angry and nervous

j. I am a bit tired

 **THE LANGUAGE GYM**

UNIT 1
Talking about my age

In this unit you will learn:

- How to say your name and age
- How to say someone else's name and age
- How to count from 1 to 16
- A range of common Spanish names
- The words for brother and sister

Tengo diez años

Tengo un año

Tengo seis años

Tengo quince años

UNIT 1
Talking about my age

¿Cómo te llamas?				*What is your name?*			
¿Cuántos años tienes?				*How old are you?*			

Me llamo *I am called*					**tengo** *I have**	un	1	**año** *year*
Mi hermano *My brother*	**se llama** *is called*	Alejandro Antonio Arantxa Belén Carlos Diego Emilia Felipe Isabel José Julián María Paco Roberto	**y** *and*	**tiene** *he/she has***	dos	2	**años** *years*
					tres	3	
					cuatro	4	
					cinco	5	
					seis	6	
					siete	7	
					ocho	8	
					nueve	9	
Mi hermana *My sister*					diez	10	
					once	11	
					doce	12	
					trece	13	
					catorce	14	
					quince	15	
					dieciséis	16	

Soy hijo único *I am an only child (m)*   **Soy hija única** *I am an only child (f)*

Author's note:

* The number "uno" becomes "un" when it goes before a masculine noun. E.g. "Tengo un hermano".
** In Spanish, we use the verb "to have" for age. So, we say "tengo diez años" to say how old we are, even though it means, literally "I have ten years". There are a few Latin languages (e.g. Italian/French) that do this :D

 THE LANGUAGE GYM

1. Fill in the blanks

a. Me __ __ __ __ __ Alejandro.

b. Tengo __ __ __ __ __ años.

c. Tengo __ __ __ hermanos.

d. __ __ hermano mayor se __ __ __ __ __ Roberto.

e. Mi __ __ __ __ __ __ __ menor __ __ llama Julián.

f. ¿Cómo __ __ llamas?

g. ¿Cuántos __ __ __ __ tienes?

2. Break the flow: draw a line between each word

a. M e l l a m o A n t o n i o

b. T e n g o q u i n c e a ñ o s

c. M i h e r m a n o s e l l a m a J u l i á n

d. M i h e r m a n a s e l l a m a A r a n t x a

e. ¿C u á n t o s a ñ o s t i e n e s ?

f. M i h e r m a n o s e l l a m a F e l i p e

g. ¿C ó m o t e l l a m a s ?

3. Arrange in the correct order

I am thirteen years old	
Arantxa is fifteen years old	
My name is Tomás	**1**
My sister is called Arantxa	
I have a brother and a sister	
My brother is called Fernando	
Fernando is fourteen years old	

4. Spot the differences and correct the text

a. Te llamo Ana.

b. Tengo once años.

c. Tengo dos hermanas.

d. Mi hermano mayor se llama Pepe.

e. Mi hermano mayor se llama Roberto.

f. Paco tiene catorce años.

g. Roberto tiene ocho años.

h. ¿Cuántos años tengo?

5. Complete with the missing letters

a. Me llam__ Pedro

b. Soy d__ España

c. Tengo quin__e años

d. No tengo hermano__

e. …pero tengo un__ hermana

f. Mi hermana se llam__ Arantxa

g. Arantxa tien__ doce a__os

h. Y tú ¿Cómo t__ llamas?

i. ¿Cuántos años tiene__?

6. Spot the missing words and write them in

a. me llamo Pedro.

b. Soy España.

c. Tengo trece.

d. Tengo un hermano una hermana.

e. Mi hermano llama Roberto.

f. hermana se llama Isabel.

g. Roberto catorce años.

7. Listen, spot and correct the errors

a. Tengo catorce año

b. Me llama Carlos

c. Mi hermano se llamo Pablo

d. Tengo dos hermano

e. Tengo uno hermano y una hermana

f. ¿Cuánto años tienes?

8. Listen and fill in the grid

	Age	Brothers	Sisters
a. María			
b. José			
c. Paco			
d. Arantxa			
e. Dylan			
f. Amparo			

9. Faulty translation: spot the translation errors and correct them

a. Her name is Andrea.

b. I am from Argentina.

c. I have three brothers.

d. My older sister is called Amparo.

e. My younger sister is called Luana.

f. Amparo is ten.

g. Luana is fourteen.

h. I am eleven.

10. Translate the sentences you hear into English

a.

b.

c.

d.

e.

f.

g.

h.

i.

11. Narrow listening: gap-fill

Me llamo _____ . Soy de Barcelona, en _____ . En mi familia hay cuatro personas: _____ madre, mi padre y mis _____ hermanos. Mi hermano _____ se llama Miguel y mi hermano _____ se llama Paco. Miguel tiene _____ años y mi hermano Paco tiene _____ años. Y tú, ¿cómo te _____? ¿_____ años tienes?

llamas	Antonio	menor	mi	seis
mayor	quince	España	cuántos	dos

12. Narrow listening: gapped translation

(a) My name is _____ . I am from _____ in Spain. In my family there are _____ people: my mother, my father, my _____ brother, my _____ brother and myself. **(b)** My _____ brother is called _____ . He is _____ years old. **(c)** My _____ brother is called Antonio. He is _____ years old. How about you, what _____? How _____?

How_____?

Unit 1. Talking about my age: VOCABULARY BUILDING

1. Match

un año	seven years
dos años	four years
tres años	five years
cuatro años	six years
cinco años	eleven years
seis años	ten years
siete años	twelve years
ocho años	nine years
nueve años	two years
diez años	eight years
once años	one year
doce años	three years

2. Complete with the missing word

a. Tengo _____ años   *I am fourteen years old*

b. Mi hermano ___ llama Felipe   *My brother is called Felipe*

c. Me _____ Diego   *My name is Diego*

d. Mi hermano _____ dos años   *My brother is two*

e. Mi hermana tiene _____ años   *My sister is four*

f. _____ llamo Ana   *My name is Ana*

cuatro	tiene	se
me	catorce	llamo

3. Translate into English

a. Tengo tres años

b. Tengo cinco años

c. Tengo once años

d. Tiene quince años

e. Tiene trece años

f. Tiene siete años

g. Mi hermano

h. Mi hermana

i. Se llama

4. Broken words

a. Ten____ *I have*

b. Me lla____ *my name is*

c. Mi herm_____ *my sister*

d. Qui____ *fifteen*

e. Dieci_____ *sixteen*

f. On____ *eleven*

g. Nu____ *nine*

h. Cato_____ *fourteen*

i. Do____ *twelve*

5. Rank the people below from oldest to youngest as shown in the example

Miguel tiene quince años	1
María tiene trece años	
Francisco tiene dos años	
Pablo tiene cuatro años	
Alejandro tiene un año	
Roberta tiene cinco años	
Arantxa tiene nueve años	
Marta tiene tres años	

6. For each pair of people write who is the oldest, as shown in the example

A	B	OLDER
Tengo once años	Tengo trece años	B
Tengo tres años	Tengo seis años	
Tengo once años	Tengo doce años	
Tengo quince años	Tengo trece años	
Tengo catorce años	Tengo once años	
Tengo ocho años	Tengo nueve años	
Tengo once años	Tengo siete años	

Unit 1. Talking about my age: READING

Me llamo Nico. Soy argentino. Tengo doce años y vivo en Buenos Aires, la capital de Argentina. Tengo un hermano que se llama Antonio. Antonio tiene catorce años.

Me llamo Marco. Soy italiano. Tengo trece años y vivo en Roma, la capital de Italia. Tengo un hermano que se llama Robbie. Robbie tiene quince años.

Me llamo Marine. Soy francesa. Tengo diez años y vivo en París, la capital de Francia. Tengo una hermana que se llama Fabienne. Fabienne tiene once años. También tengo un hermano que se llama Pierre. Pierre tiene ocho años.

Me llamo Kaori. Soy japonesa. Tengo siete años y vivo en Tokyo, la capital de Japón. Tengo una hermana que se llama Yoko. Yoko tiene trece años. También tengo un hermano que se llama Hiroto. Hiroto tiene diez años.

Me llamo Ramón. Soy español. Tengo diez años y vivo en Madrid, la capital de España. Tengo una hermana que se llama Bárbara y un hermano que se llama Paco. Bárbara tiene cinco años. Paco tiene nueve años.

1. Find the Spanish for the following items in Nico's text

a. I am Argentinian

b. I am called

c. the capital

d. in Buenos Aires

e. who is called Antonio

f. I am twelve

g. is fourteen

2. Answer the following questions about Ramón

a. Where is Ramón from?

b. How old is he?

c. How many siblings does he have?

d. What are their names?

3. Complete the table below

	Age	Nationality	How many siblings	Ages of siblings
Marco				
Nico				
Ramón				

Me llamo Hans. Soy alemán. Tengo catorce años y vivo en Berlín, en Alemania. Tengo dos hermanos. Mi hermano mayor se llama Patrick y mi hermano menor se llama Philip. Patrick tiene dieciséis años y Philip tiene quince años.

4. Hans, Kaori or Marine?

a. Who is from Germany?

b. Who has an 11-year-old sister?

c. Who is 11?

d. Who has an older sister?

e. Who has a 15-year old brother?

 THE LANGUAGE GYM

Unit 1. Talking about my age: TRANSLATION

1. Faulty translation: spot and correct (in the English) any translation mistakes you find below

a. Me llamo Patricia: *Her name is Patricia*

b. Tengo dos hermanas: *I have two brothers*

c. Mi hermana se llama Marta: *My mother is called Marta*

d. Mi hermano tiene cinco años: *My sister is 5*

e. Tengo quince años: *I am five*

f. Mi hermano tiene ocho años: *My brother is seven*

g. No tengo hermanos: *I don't have a sister*

h. Tengo dieciséis años: *I am 17*

i. Tengo doce años: *I am 13*

j. Se llama Juan: *My name is Juan*

2. Translate into English

a. Mi hermano se llama Juan.

b. Tengo quince años.

c. Mi hermano tiene seis años.

d. Mi hermana se llama Mariana.

e. Tengo siete años.

f. Vivo en Madrid.

g. Mi hermana tiene catorce años.

h. Tengo un hermano y una hermana.

i. María tiene doce años.

j. Arantxa tiene nueve años.

3. Translate into Spanish

a. My name is Paco. I am six.

b. My brother is fifteen years old.

c. I am twelve.

d. My sister is called Arantxa.

e. I am fourteen.

f. I have a brother and a sister.

g. My name is Felipe and I am fourteen.

h. My name is Gabriel and I am eleven.

i. My name is Santiago. I am ten. I have a brother and a sister.

j. My sister is called Ana. She is twelve.

THE LANGUAGE GYM

Unit 1. Talking about my age: WRITING

1. Complete the words

a. M__ ll_____ Paco

b. Te_____ cato_____ a_____

c. _____ngo un___ h_____a

d. M__ h_____o se ll_____ Julio

e. Me _____mo Patricio

f. Mi _____rmano s__ _____ma Pablo

g. _____go tr____e años

h. Mi he_____a se ll_____ Ana

2. Write out the numbers in Spanish

a. Nine   N_____

b. Seven   S_____

c. Twelve   D_____

d. Five   C_____

e. Fourteen   C_____

f. Sixteen   D_____

g. Thirteen   T_____

h. Four   C_____

3. Spot and correct the spelling mistakes

a. Me lamo Paco.

b. Tengo trece anos.

c. Mi hermano tene cinco anos.

d. Mi hermano se llama María.

e. Mi llamo Patricio.

f. Mi hermana se llamo Alejandra.

4. Complete with a suitable word

a. Mi hermana se

_____ Laura.

b. _____ hermano tiene quince

años.

c. Me _____ Mario.

d. Tengo un _____ que

se llama Felipe.

e. Tengo una _____

que se llama Arantxa.

f. Mi hermano _____

catorce años.

5. Guided writing: write 4 short paragraphs in the first person singular (I) describing the people below

	Age	Lives in	Nationality	Brother's name and age	Sister's name and age
Samuel	12	Buenos Aires	Argentinian	Gonzalo 9	Anna 8
Rebeca	15	Madrid	Spanish	Jaime 13	Valentina 5
Michael	11	Berlin	German	Thomas 7	Gerda 12
Kyoko	10	Osaka	Japanese	Ken 6	Rena 1

6. Describe this person in the third person (he):

Name: Jorge

Age: 12

Lives in: Barcelona

Brother: Mario, 13 years old

Sister: Soledad, 15 years old

THE LANGUAGE GYM

TERM 1 - BRINGING IT ALL TOGETHER - 1

Juan: ¡Hola! ¿Cómo te llamas?

María: Hola, me llamo María. ¿Y tú?

Juan: Mucho gusto, María. Me llamo Juan. ¿Cómo estás hoy?

María: Estoy bien, gracias. Estoy muy contenta. ¿Y tú, Juan? ¿Cómo estás hoy?

Juan: También estoy bastante bien, pero un poco cansado, gracias por preguntar. ¿De dónde eres, María?

María: Soy de Barcelona, en España. ¿Y tú, Juan?

Juan: Soy de Buenos Aires, en Argentina.

María: Vale. ¿Tienes familia, Juan?

Juan: Sí, tengo una familia pequeña. Tengo una hermana y un hermano. ¿Y tú, María?

María: Tengo una familia grande. Tengo dos hermanos y una hermana. ¿Cuántos años tienen tus hermanos?

Juan: Mi hermana menor tiene cinco años y se llama Ana. Mi hermano mayor se llama Paco y tiene quince años. ¿Y tus hermanos, cómo se llaman?

María: Mi hermano mayor se llama Felipe y tiene diecisiete años, mi hermana mediana se llama Carlota y tiene doce años y mi hermano menor se llama Tomás y tiene ocho años.

Juan: ¡Vaya! ¡Qué interesante! Mucho gusto, María.

María: Igualmente, mucho gusto, Juan. ¡Adiós!

---

1. Juan or María?

a. Is from Latin America

b. Is from Spain

c. Is feeling well and happy

d. Is feeling quite well but a bit tired

e. Has a small family

f. Has a big family

g. Has three siblings

h. Their siblings' ages add up to 20 years

2. Complete with a suitable word

a. Hola, ¿cómo te _____?

b. ¿De dónde _____?

c. ¿Cómo _____ hoy?

d. Tengo una familia _____

e. Tengo un _____

f. ¿Cómo se _____ tu hermano?

g. ¿Cuántos _____ tiene tu hermana?

h. Mi _____ menor se llama Juan.

i. Mi hermano mayor ____ llama Carlos.

j. Mi hermana _____ ocho años.

k. Mucho _____, Juan.

l. Igualmente, _____ gusto.

3. Translate

a. What is your name?

b. Where are you from?

c. How are you today?

d. I have a big family

e. I have a sister

f. What is your brother called?

g. How old is your brother?

h. My sister is ten years old

i. Nice to meet you

j. Me too (*likewise*)

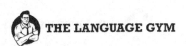

UNIT 2
Saying when my birthday is

In this unit you will learn to say:

- When your birthday is
- Numbers from 15 to 31
- Months
- I am / He is / She is
- Names of Spanish speaking locations
- Where you and another person (e.g. a friend) are from

UNIT 2
Saying when my birthday is

¿Cómo te llamas?			What is your name?		
¿Cuándo es tu cumpleaños?			When is your birthday?		

Me llamo José *My name is José*	**soy de Madrid** *I am from Madrid* ***tengo X años** *I am X years old*	**y** *and* **mi cumpleaños es el** *my birthday is the*	1 - **uno / primero** 2 - **dos** 3 - **tres** 4 - **cuatro** 5 - **cinco** 6 - **seis** 7 - **siete** 8 - **ocho** 9 - **nueve** 10 - **diez** 11 - **once** 12 - **doce** 13 - **trece** 14 - **catorce** 15 - **quince** 16 - **dieciséis** 17 - **diecisiete** 18 - **dieciocho** 19 - **diecinueve** 20 - **veinte** 21 - **veintiuno** 22 - **veintidós** 23 - **veintitrés** 24 - **veinticuatro** 25 - **veinticinco** 26 - **veintiséis** 27 - **veintisiete** 28 - **veintiocho** 29 - **veintinueve** 30 - **treinta** 31 - **treinta y uno**	**de** *of*	**enero** *January* **febrero** **marzo** **abril** **mayo** **junio** **julio** **agosto** **septiembre** **octubre** **noviembre** **diciembre**
Mi amiga se llama Catalina *My friend is called Catalina* **Mi amigo se llama Francisco** *My friend is called Francisco*	**es de Bilbao** *he/she is from Bilbao* ***tiene X años** *he/she is X years old*	**y** *and* **su cumpleaños es el** *his/her birthday is the*			

Author's note: **Don't forget! "Tengo/Tiene" actually means "I have" and "he/she has" in Spanish. You use this verb for telling age. You will see it many times throughout this booklet!* ☺

1. Fill in the blanks

a. Me _ _ _ _ _ Ramón y mi cumpleaños
es _ _ quince de _ _ _ _.

b. _ _ llamo Tomás y _ _ cumpleaños es el _ _ _ _
de _ _ _ _ _ _.

c. Me llamo _ _ _ _ y mi cumpleaños es el
_ _ _ _ _ _ _ _ de _ _ _ _ _ _.

d. _ _ llamo Alfonso y mi _ _ _ _ _ _ _ _ _ _ _ _
es el _ _ _ _ de _ _ _ _ _ _ _ _ _ _ _.

e. _ _ llamo Paloma y mi cumpleaños _ _ el _ _ _ _
_ _ _ de _ _ _ _ _ _ _ _ _.

2. Break the flow: draw lines between each word

a. Micumpleañoseseltrecedeoctubre

b. Micumpleañoselnuevedemayo

c. ¿Cuándoestucumpleaños?

d. Micumpleañoseselunodeagosto

e. Micumpleañoseseldieciséisdemayo

f. ¿Cuándoessucumpleaños?

g. Mihermanotienecatorceaños

h. Sucumpleañoseseldosdeenero

3. Listen and spot the differences

a. Te llamas Jorge.
b. No tengo hermanos.
c. Soy hija única.
d. Soy de Perú.
e. ...pero vivo en Italia.
f. Tengo cinco años.
g. Mi cumpleaños es el catorce de junio.
h. Mi novia Luisa tiene trece años.
i. Su cumpleaños es el dieciocho de octubre.

4. Listen, spot and correct the errors

a. Mi cumpleaños el veinte de junio.

b. Mi amiga se llama Patricia. Es diez años y su
cumpleaños es el quince de mayo.

c. El cumpleaños de mi amiga es en el nueve de
abril.

d. Mi madre tengo treinta y ocho años y su
cumpleano es el treinta de noviembre.

e. Mi amigo se llamo Roberto. Su cumpleaños es
el catorce de octobre.

5. Listen and choose the option that you hear

a. **Andrea:** Edad: 12 / 13 / 14 años
Cumpleaños: 2 / 3 / 4 de junio

b. **Paco:** Edad: 12 / 13 / 15 años
Cumpleaños: 17 de junio/julio/enero

c. **Nina:** Edad: 8 / 9 / 10 años
Cumpleaños: 10/11/12 de noviembre

d. **Dylan:** Edad: 8 / 7 / 19 años
Cumpleaños: 10/11/12 de junio

e. **Miguel:** Edad: 6 / 16 / 60 años
Cumpleaños: 20/21/10 de septiembre

f. **Marta:** Edad: 13 /14 / 4 años
Cumpleaños: 14 / 4 / 12 de diciembre

6. Narrow listening: gap-fill

a. Hola, me llamo Silvia y _____ de Bilbao,
España. Tengo _____ años. Mi cumpleaños es el
_____ de mayo. Tengo dos hermanos, Felipe y
Gonzalo.

b. Felipe _____ catorce años y su cumpleaños es
el veintiuno _____ marzo. Mi hermano Gonzalo
tiene dieciséis años y _____ cumpleaños es el
_____ de junio.

c. En _____ tenemos un hámster también. Se
_____ Guapo y tiene dos años. Mi mejor
_____ se llama Magda. Tiene _____
años. Su cumpleaños es el _____ de enero.

7. Narrow listening: gapped translation

a. __ _____ is Ariella. I am _____ years old. I am from _____, in _____. My birthday is on 16th _____.

b. I have a _____ called _____. He is _____ years old. _____ birthday is on _____ December.

c. My best friend is called _____. She is _____ years old and her birthday is on _____ _____.

d. My _____ is called Andrea. She is _____ years old and her birthday is on _____ _____.

e. At home we have a pet. It is a _____. _____ Maite and it is _____ years old.

8. Listening slalom: follow the speaker from top to bottom and number the boxes accordingly

a. Vero	b. Leo	c. Alejandro	d. Gabriela	e. Carlos
My name is Vero	My brother is called Leo	My name is Alejandro	My name is Gabriela	My name is Carlos
I am from Valencia	**I am from Barbastro**	I am from Barcelona	He is from Santiago	I am from Granada
He is 14	I am 21	**I am 13**	I am 9	I am 16
His birthday is on 15th March	**My birthday is on 16th July**	My birthday is on 21st May	My birthday is on 23rd June	My birthday is on 30th August
I have a friend	I have a hamster	I have a boyfriend	He has a girlfriend	**I have a sister**
His birthday is on 12th	Her birthday is on 7th	**Her birthday is on 1st**	His birthday is on 2nd	Her birthday is on 30th
January.	March.	October.	June.	September.

9. Faulty translation: spot the translation errors and correct them

My name is Marco, I am from Spain. I am 13 years old. My parents are called Adolfo and Marina. They are 38 years old. My mother's birthday is on 21st March. My father's birthday is on 4th August. I have two sisters, Rafa and Antonio. Rafa is 10 years old and Antonio is 12. Rafa's birthday is on 11th July. Antonio's birthday in on 31st April. At home we have a pet, a snake. Its name is Pablo and it is one year old. I have a girlfriend. Her name is Petra. She is 14. Her birthday is on 16th September.

Unit 2. Saying when my birthday is: VOCABULARY BUILDING

1. Complete with the missing word

a. Me _____ Gonzalo   *My name is Gonzalo*

b. Mi _____ se llama María   *My friend is called María*

c. _____ amigo se llama Jaime   *My friend is called Jaime*

d. Mi _____ es el...   *My birthday is on the...*

e. El _____ de mayo   *The fifth of May*

f. El _____ de noviembre   *The 18th November*

g. El cuatro de _____   *The 4th July*

h. _____ cumpleaños es el...   *His/her birthday is on the...*

2. Match

abril	May
noviembre	my birthday
diciembre	my friend (f)
mayo	April
enero	November
febrero	he/she is called
mi cumpleaños	December
mi amigo	I am called
mi amiga	February
me llamo	January
se llama	my friend (m)

3. Translate into English

a. El catorce de enero

b. El ocho de mayo

c. El siete de febrero

d. El veinte de marzo

e. El diecinueve de agosto

f. El veinticinco de julio

g. El veinticuatro de septiembre

h. El quince de abril

4. Add the missing letter

a. cum__leaños   c. ma__zo   e. a__ril   g. e__ero   i. ju__io   k. d__ciembre

b. fe__rero   d. ma__o   f. jun__o   h. a__osto   j. noviem__re   l. se__tiembre

5. Broken words

a. E___ t_____ d__ e_____   *3rd Jan*

b. E___ c_____ d__ j_____   *5th July*

c. E___ n_____ d__ a_____   *9th Aug*

d. E___ d_____ d__ m_____   *12th March*

e. E___ d_____ d__ a_____   *16th April*

f. E___ d_____ d__ d_____   *19th Dec*

g. E___ v_____ d__ o_____   *20th Oct*

h. E___ v_____ d__ m_____   *24th May*

i. E___ t_____ d__ s_____   *30th Sept*

6. Complete with a suitable word

a. Me _____ Dylan

b. Mi _____ es el dos de mayo

c. Tengo nueve _____

d. Mi _____ se llama Gian

e. Gian _____ diez años

f. Su _____ es el tres de junio

g. Mi _____ es el dieciocho de julio

h. Mi amigo _____ llama Ronan

i. _____ cumpleaños es el cuatro de agosto

j. El ocho de n_____

k. _____ llamo Gabriel García

Unit 2. Saying when my birthday is: READING

Me llamo Rodrigo. Tengo doce años y vivo en México. Mi cumpleaños es el doce de septiembre. Mi amiga se llama Gabriela y tiene catorce años. Su cumpleaños es el veintiocho de mayo. En mi tiempo libre siempre toco la guitarra. ¡Gabriela también!

Mi amiga se llama Carlota. Tiene treinta y cinco años y es profesora. Su cumpleaños es el veintiuno de junio. Carlota tiene un hermano mayor. Su cumpleaños es el ocho de enero.

Me llamo Sergio. Tengo veintidós años y vivo en Lepe, en el sur de España. Mi cumpleaños es el diez de septiembre. Mi amiga se llama Ivana y tiene quince años. Su cumpleaños es el veintiocho de mayo. En mi tiempo libre siempre veo la tele.

Me llamo Mercedes. Tengo siete años y vivo en Santiago, la capital de Chile. Mi cumpleaños es el cinco de diciembre. Tengo dos hermanos, Julio y Enrique. Julio tiene once años y es muy bueno. Su cumpleaños es el treinta de septiembre. Enrique es muy muy malo. Tiene trece años y su cumpleaños es el cinco de enero.

Me llamo Antonio. Tengo ocho años y vivo en Málaga, en Andalucía, en el sur de España. Mi cumpleaños es el nueve de agosto. Mi hermana pequeña tiene cuatro años. Es muy simpática. Su cumpleaños es el nueve de agosto. ¡Igual que yo!

Mi amigo se llama Vidal y tiene diecisiete años. Su cumpleaños es el veinticinco de octubre.

1. Find the Spanish for the following items in Rodrigo's text

a. I am called

b. I am 12 years old

c. I live in Mexico

d. My birthday is

e. the twelfth of

f. her birthday is on

g. in my free time

h. my friend

i. is called

j. she is 35

k. the 21st of June

l. has an older brother

m. the eighth of January

3. Answer these questions about Mercedes

a. How old is she?

b. Where is Santiago?

c. When is her birthday?

d. How many brothers does she have?

e. Which brother is good?

f. How old is Enrique?

g. When is his birthday?

2. Complete with the missing words

Me llamo Ana. _____ trece

_____ y _____ en Madrid, __

España. _____ un gato en

casa. Mi _____ es

_____ uno _____ diciembre. Mi

hermano _____ nueve

_____ y su cumpleaños es ___

abril.

4. Find someone who...

a. ...has a birthday in December

b. ...is 22 years old

c. ...shares a birthday with a sibling

d. ...likes to play the guitar with their friend

e. ...has a friend who is 35 years old

f. ...has a birthday in late September

g. ...has a little sister

h. ...has one good and one bad sibling

i. ...is from the south of Spain

 THE LANGUAGE GYM

Unit 2. Saying when my birthday is: WRITING

1. Complete with the missing letters

a. Me lla_ _ Paco

b. So_ d_ Bilbao

c. M_ cumpleañ_ _ es el quin_ _ de jun_ _

d. Ten_ _ cat_ _ ce a _ os

e. Mi ami_ a se llam_ Catalina

f. Catalina e_ de Madrid

g. Mi am _ go Miguel e_ d_ Sevilla

h. Miguel tien_ onc_ a_ _s

2. Spot and correct the spelling mistakes

a. Mi cumpleanos es el cuatro de enero

b. Mi llamo Paco

c. Soy di Bilbao

d. Mi amiga se llamo Catalina

e. Catalina tene once años

f. Yo tengo catorse anos

g. Me cumpleaños es el un de marzo

h. Tengo quinse anos

3. Answer the questions in Spanish

¿Cómo te llamas?

¿Cuántos años tienes?

¿Cuándo es tu cumpleaños?

¿Cuántos años tiene tu hermano/a?

¿Cuándo es su cumpleaños?

4. Write out the dates below in words as shown in the example

e.g. 15.05 *el quince de mayo*

a. 10.06

b. 20.03

c. 19.02

d. 25.12

e. 01.01

f. 22.11

g. 14.10

5. Guided writing: write 4 short paragraphs in the first person singular (I) describing the people below

Name	Town/City	Age	Birthday	Name of brother	Brother's birthday
Samuel	Sevilla	11	25.12	José	19.02
Ale	Bilbao	14	21.07	Felipe	21.04
Andrés	Gerona	12	01.01	Julián	20.06
Carlos	Valencia	16	02.11	Miguel	12.10

6. Describe this person in the third person (he):

Name: César

Age: 12

Lives in: Aguadulce

Birthday: 21.06

Brother: Jesús, 16 years old

Birthday: 01.12

THE LANGUAGE GYM

Unit 2. Saying when my birthday is: TRANSLATION

1. Faulty translation: spot and correct (in the English) any translation mistakes you find

a. Mi cumpleaños es el veintiocho de abril:
His birthday is on the 27th April

b. Me llamo Roberto y soy de España:
Your name is Roberto and you are from Spain

c. Tengo veintitrés años:
I am 22 years old

d. Mi amigo se llama Jordi:
My friend I am called Jordi

e. Tiene veintiséis años:
I have 26 years old

f. Su cumpleaños es el cuatro de abril:
My birthday is the 14th April

g. Vivo en Madrid:
I am from Madrid

3. Phrase-level translation

a. My name is

b. I am ten years old

c. My birthday is the...

d. ...the seventh of May

e. My friend is called Bella

f. She is twelve years old

g. Her birthday is the...

h. the 23rd of August

i. the 29th April

Author's note: go back to e. Did you make Bella a girl? "amiga" Well done if you did! ☺

2. Translate into English

a. el ocho de octubre

b. mi cumpleaños es el...

c. mi amigo se llama...

d. su cumpleaños es el...

e. el once de enero

f. el catorce de febrero

g. el veinticinco de diciembre

h. el ocho de julio

i. el uno de junio

4. Sentence-level translation

a. My name is César. I am 30 years old. I live in Spain. My birthday is on the 11th March.

b. My brother is called Pedro. He is 14 years old. His birthday is on the 18th August.

c. My friend is called Juan. He is 22 years old and his birthday is on the 14th January.

d. My friend is called Ángela. She is 18 years old and her birthday is on the 25th July.

e. My friend is called Anthony. He is 20 years old. His birthday is on the 24th September.

 THE LANGUAGE GYM

TERM 1 - BRINGING IT ALL TOGETHER - 2

Pedro: ¡Hola! ¿Cómo te llamas?

Ana: Hola, me llamo Ana. ¿Y tú, cómo te llamas?

Pedro: Mucho gusto, Ana. Me llamo Pedro. ¿De dónde eres *(where are you from)*, Ana?

Ana: Soy de Madrid. ¿Y tú, Pedro?

Pedro: Yo soy de Barcelona. ¿Cómo estás, Ana?

Ana: Estoy bien, gracias, pero estoy un poco cansada. ¿Y tú, Pedro?

Pedro: También estoy bien, gracias por preguntar. Estoy muy contento. ¿Cuántos años tienes, Ana?

Ana: Tengo catorce años. ¿Y tú, Pedro?

Pedro: Tengo trece años. Por cierto *(by the way)*, ¿tienes hermanos o hermanas, Ana?

Ana: Sí, tengo un hermano mayor y una hermana menor. Mi hermano se llama Luis y mi hermana se llama Marta. ¿Y tú, Pedro?

Pedro: Yo también tengo un hermano mayor y una hermana menor. Se llaman Tomás y Paloma.

Ana: ¡Qué bien! ¿Cuándo es tu cumpleaños Pedro?

Pedro: Mi cumpleaños es el dieciocho de julio, ¿y tú?

Ana: Mi cumpleaños es el dieciocho de julio también, ¡qué coincidencia!

Pedro: Sí, es increíble. ¿Cuándo es el cumpleaños de tu hermano Luis?

Ana: El cumpleaños de Luis es el trece de enero. ¿Y el cumpleaños de tu hermana Paloma?

Pedro: El cumpleaños de Paloma es el veinticuatro de marzo.

Ana: Vale, me tengo que ir *(I've got to go)*, adiós Pedro.

Pedro: Hasta luego Ana, cuídate *(take care)*.

1. Complete with the missing details

a. Ana is from _____, whilst Pedro is from _____

b. Ana is feeling a bit _____

c. Ana is _____ years old, whilst Pedro is _____

d. Ana has an older _____ and a younger _____

e. Ana's birthday is on _____

f. Pedro's birthday is on _____

g. Luis is Ana's _____

h. Paloma's birthday is on _____

i. _____ birthday is on 13th January

2. Find someone...

a. whose birthday is on 13th January

b. who has a sister called Marta

c. who has a brother called Luis

d. who is feeling a bit tired

e. who is from Barcelona

f. who has a younger sister

g. whose birthday is on 24th March

h. who is from Madrid

i. whose birthday is on 18th July

j. who has a sister called Paloma

k. who is thirteen

3. Find the Spanish equivalent in the text and write it in the spaces provided

a. My name is: M

b. I am from: S

c. I am thirteen: T

d. When is your birthday?: ¿C

e. I've got to go: M

f. Luis' birthday: E

g. On 24th March: E

h. Your brother Luis: T

i. By the way: P

j. My birthday is: M

k. Thanks for asking: G

l. They are called: S

THE LANGUAGE GYM

27

Roberto: ¡Hola! ¿Cómo te llamas?

Inés: Hola, me llamo Inés. ¿Y tú, cómo te llamas?

Roberto: Mucho gusto, Inés. Me llamo Roberto. ¿De dónde eres, Inés?

Inés: Soy de Polonia *(Poland)*. ¿Y tú, Roberto?

Roberto: Yo soy de Alicante. ¿Cómo estás, Inés?

Inés: Estoy muy bien, gracias, pero estoy un poco estresada. ¿Y tú?

Roberto: Estoy bastante bien, gracias por preguntar. Estoy muy feliz. ¿Cuántos años tienes, Inés?

Inés: Tengo doce años. ¿Y tú, Roberto?

Roberto: También tengo doce años. Por cierto, ¿tienes hermanos o hermanas, Inés?

Inés: Sí, tengo dos hermanos mayores. Mis hermanos se llaman Alfredo y Alfonso. ¿Y tú, Roberto?

Roberto: Yo tengo un hermano mayor y una hermana menor. Se llaman Leonardo y Ariana.

Inés: ¡Qué bien! ¿Cuándo es tu cumpleaños?

Roberto: Mi cumpleaños es el once de enero, ¿y tú?

Inés: Mi cumpleaños es el once de febrero.

Roberto: ¡Qué gracioso! *(how funny)* ¡El once es mi número favorito!

Inés: También me gusta el número once. ¡Qué coincidencia!

Roberto: Vale, me tengo que ir, adiós Inés.

Inés: Hasta luego Roberto, cuídate.

4. Find in the text Spanish words that look/sound like the English words below

a. Much

b. Poland

c. Stressed

d. Certain

e. Major

f. Minor

g. Leonard

h. Favourite

i. Coincidence

j. Number

5. Translate into English

a. ¿De dónde eres?

b. Soy de Alicante

c. Estoy un poco estresada

d. Tengo doce años

e. Tengo dos hermanos mayores

f. Se llaman Alfredo y Alfonso

g. Tengo un hermano menor y una hermana menor

6. The sentences below have been copied incorrectly. Can you fix them?

a. Tengo doce anos

b. Mis hermanos se llama

c. Tengo dos mayores hermanos

d. ¿Cuándo tu cumpleanos, Roberto?

e. Mi cumpleaños es el once febrero

f. ¡Que gracioso!

g. ¿Cuántos anos tienes?

7. Match questions and answers

¿Cómo te llamas?	Sí, tengo dos
¿De dónde eres?	El once de enero
¿Cómo estás?	Soy de Polonia
¿Tienes hermanos?	El número once
¿Cuándo es tu cumpleaños?	Estoy bien, gracias
¿Cuál es tu número favorito?	Roberto

 THE LANGUAGE GYM

UNIT 3
Saying where I live and am from

In this unit you will learn to talk about:

- Where you live and are from
- If you live in an apartment or a house
- What your accommodation looks like
- Where it is located
- The names of renowned cities and countries in the Hispanic world
- The verb 'I am'

You will also revisit:
- Introducing yourself
- Telling age and birthday

UNIT 3
Saying where I live and am from

¿Cómo te llamas?	*What is your name?*
¿Dónde vives?	*Where do you live?*
¿De dónde eres?	*Where are you from?*

Me llamo David y *My name is David and*	**vivo en** *I live in*	**una casa** *a house*	**bonita** *pretty* **fea** *ugly* **grande** *big* **pequeña** *small*		**en el centro** *in the centre* **en las afueras** *on the outskirts*
		un piso *a flat*	**en un edificio antiguo** *in an old building* **en un edificio moderno** *in a modern building*		**en la costa** *on the coast*
	soy de *I am from*	Barcelona	**en Cataluña (en España)** *northwest region of Spain*		
		Bilbao	**en el País Vasco (en España)** *northern region of Spain*		
		Bogotá	**en Colombia (la capital)** *capital of Colombia*		
		Buenos Aires	**en Argentina (la capital)** *capital of Argentina*		
		Cádiz	**en Andalucía (en España)** *south of Spain*		
		Cartagena	**en Colombia (en la costa)** *coast of Colombia*		
		La Habana	**en Cuba (la capital)** *capital of Cuba*		
		Lima	**en Perú (la capital)** *capital of Peru*		
		Madrid	**en España (la capital)** *capital of Spain*		
		Quito	**en Ecuador (la capital)** *capital of Ecuador*		
		Santiago	**en Chile (la capital)** *capital of Chile*		
		Montevideo	**en Uruguay (la capital)** *capital of Uruguay*		
		Zaragoza	**en Aragón (en España)** *northern region of Spain*		

THE LANGUAGE GYM

1. Fill in the blanks

a. Hola. Me _____ David. Vivo en una _____ muy grande en el centro de la _____.

b. Buenos días. Me llamo Conchi. ____ de Madrid. _____ en un piso pequeño en las _____.

c. ¿Qué tal? ____ llamo Maya. Soy ____ Cádiz. Vivo en un _____ bonito en la costa.

d. Hola. Me llamo _____. Soy de Quito, en _____. Vivo en una casa muy _____ en la montaña.

e. Buenos ____. Me llamo Daniel, vivo en Buenos Aires, en _____. Vivo en un edificio _____ en el centro de Buenos Aires.

f. _____. Me llamo Beatriz. Vivo en ____ casa grande pero un poco ____ en La Habana.

2. Multiple choice quiz: select the correct location

	1	2	3
a. Javier	Bilbao	Valencia	Granada
b. Samuel	Cartagena	Madrid	La Habana
c. Juan Pablo	Lima	Zaragoza	Cádiz
d. Paco	Santiago	Quito	Madrid
e. Selina	Madrid	Barcelona	Bilbao
f. Ariana	Gerona	Zaragoza	Málaga
g. Patricio	Lima	Bogotá	Santiago
h. Manuel	Barcelona	Montevideo	Marbella

3. Spot the intruders: identify the words the speaker is NOT saying

Hola. Me llamo Jaime. Tengo un catorce años y vivo ya en La Habana, el la capital de Cuba. En mi familia somos hay cuatro personas: mis padres, mi hermana, mi hermano y yo. Mi hermano que se llama Benicio. Vivo en una la casa pequeña en el centro de La Habana. Mi casa es muy bonita.

4. Geographical mistakes: listen and correct

a. Me llamo Nina. Soy de Barcelona. Barcelona está en Aragón.

b. Me llamo Pedro. Soy de Santiago. Santiago está en Argentina.

c. Me llamo Consuelo. Soy de Madrid. Madrid está en Cataluña.

d. Me llamo Juan. Soy de Quito. Quito está en Perú.

e. Me llamo Jaime. Soy de La Habana. La Habana está en España.

f. Me llamo Ariana. Soy de Cartagena. Cartagena está en Venezuela.

5. Spelling challenge: which place names are being spelled out? Fill in the grid

1	
2	
3	
4	
5	
6	
7	

6. Faulty translation: spot the translation errors and correct them

My name is Maya. I am from Peru. I am twelve. I live in Catalunya, a region in the south of Spain. I have blond hair and green eyes. My hair is long and curly. I live with my mother, Eugenia and my two brothers, Silvia and Paola, in a small flat in the centre of Barcelona. My flat is in an old building. It is beautiful. My father lives in a small house in the mountains. His house is ugly and modern.

7. Spot the missing words and write them in

a. Vivo Bogotá, la capital Colombia. Bogotá es una ciudad hermosa. Vivo en un piso en un edificio moderno en el centro ciudad.

b. Vivo con mi familia en Málaga, una ciudad turística en el sur España. Vivo en casa moderna en las afueras de ciudad.

c. Vivo en Quito, la capital de Ecuador. Vivo allí con mi familia y perro. Vivo en un piso grande feo en un edificio.

d. Vivo en Valencia, España. Vivo en una casa grande y moderna en la costa.

8. Narrow listening: gapped translation

My name is Julián. I am _____years old and my birthday is on _____ August. I _____in Bilbao, in the Basque Country, in the _____of Spain. I live in an _____house in the _____. I have two _____, Maite and Silvia. Maite is very _____ but a bit silly. Silvia is a bit _____ but very _____ and funny. My friend Rubén _____ in Barcelona but he is from Bilbao like _____. He lives in a modern _____ in the _____. He has a big dog called _____. He lives in a big and _____ flat.

9. Listening slalom: follow the speaker from top to bottom and number the boxes accordingly

e.g.	a	b	c	d
I live in Argentina,	I am from Bolivia and	I am from Peru and	I am from Spain and	I am from Colombia and
I live in Málaga.	I live in Lima.	I live near La Paz.	I live in Bogotá.	**near Buenos Aires.**
I am 12 and	**I am 15 and**	I am 14 and	I am 16 and	I am 13 and
I live in a big house	I live in a small house	I live in a very small house	**I live in a small flat**	I live in a flat
in a modern building.	in an old building.	in the city centre.	near a lake.	on the coast.
I like my house	**My flat is ugly**	My house	My flat is cosy	My house is pretty
and beautiful.	and spacious.	**but very big.**	is modern.	because it is big.

Unit 3. Saying where I live and am from: VOCABULARY BUILDING

1. Complete with the missing word

a. Vivo en _____ casa bonita   *I live in a pretty house*

b. Me gusta mi _____   *I like my flat*

c. Soy ___ Madrid   *I am from Madrid*

d. _____ en un piso pequeño   *I live in a small flat*

e. Un piso en un _____ antiguo   *A flat in an old building*

f. ____ de Santiago, la capital de Chile   *I'm from Santiago...*

g. Vivo en una casa _____   *I live in an ugly house*

h. Vivo en las _____   *I live on the outskirts*

2. Match

el centro	big
bonita	small
grande	old
edificio	pretty
antiguo	the centre
las afueras	the coast
la costa	I am from
España	the outskirts
soy de	ugly
fea	I live in
pequeña	Spain
vivo en	building

3. Translate into English

a. Soy de Argentina

b. Vivo en una casa

c. Mi piso es pequeño

d. Soy de Santiago, en Chile

e. en un edificio moderno

f. Soy de Lima, la capital de Perú

g. Vivo en un piso en la costa de...

h. Soy de Cartagena, en Colombia

4. Add the missing letters

a. Bog_tá   c. Bar_elona   e. Bue_os A_res   g. Car_agena   i. P_ís Vasco

b. Madri_   d. Mon_evideo   f. Z_ragoza   h. Colom_ia   j. C_ba

5. Broken words

a. S_____ d___ l___ H_____, e___C_____
I am from La Habana, in Cuba

b. V___ e___ u___ c_____ a_____ *I live in an old house*

c. S___ d___ M_____, l__ c_____ d___ E_____
I am from Madrid, the capital of Spain

d. V_____ e__ u___ p_____ e__ l__ c_____ d__ Chile
I live in a flat on the coast of Chile

e. V_____ e__ u____ c_____ p_____ pero b_____
I live in a small but pretty house

f. S___ d__ M_____ y v_____ e__ u__ e_____
a_____ *I'm from Montevideo and I live in an old building*

g. S____ d____ Q_____ *I am from Quito*

6. Complete with a suitable word

a. Soy ____ Bilbao

b. Vivo ____ un piso bonito

c. En un _____ antiguo

d. Vivo en una casa en el _____

e. Lima es la capital de _____

f. Vivo en una casa _____

g. Soy de _____

h. Vivo en un piso _____

i. Soy de Santiago, en _____

j. Bogotá es la capital de _____

k. Vivo en una casa en la _____

 **THE LANGUAGE GYM**

Unit 3. "Geography test": Using your own knowledge (and a bit of help from Google/your teacher) match the numbers to the cities

Spain	
Num	**City**
	Barcelona
	Bilbao
	Cádiz
	La Coruña
	Madrid

Latin America	
Num	**City**
	Bogotá (Colombia)
	Buenos Aires (Argentina)
	La Habana (Cuba)
	La Paz (Bolivia)
	Lima (Perú)
	Quito (Ecuador)
	México D.F. (México)
	Montevideo (Uruguay)
	Santiago (Chile)

THE LANGUAGE GYM

Unit 3. Saying where I live and am from: READING

Me llamo Carlos. Tengo veintidós años y mi cumpleaños es el nueve de agosto. Vivo en Bilbao en el País Vasco en el norte de España. Vivo en una casa bonita en el centro de la ciudad. Tengo dos hermanos, Eduardo y Rubén. Me gusta mucho Eduardo pero Rubén es muy tonto. Mi amigo José vive en Barcelona, en el noreste de España. Él vive en un piso en un edificio antiguo, también en el centro.

Me llamo Ramón. Tengo quince años y vivo en la Habana, la capital de Cuba. En mi familia somos cuatro personas: mis padres, mi hermano, Guillermo, y yo. Mi cumpleaños es el once de septiembre y el de Guillermo también. ¡Somos gemelos!

Me llamo Estefanía. Tengo nueve años y vivo en Cartagena, en la costa de Colombia. Vivo en mi casa con mi familia: mis padres, mi hermana mayor, Shakira y yo. Mi cumpleaños es el nueve de mayo y el cumpleaños de Shakira es el treinta de marzo. Ella tiene once años. Mi casa es grande y bonita y está en la costa. ¡Me gusta mucho!

Me llamo Isabela. Tengo veintiún años y vivo en Buenos Aires, la capital de Argentina con mi muy buena amiga, Marina. Vivimos en un piso grande, bonito y moderno en las afueras. Mi cumpleaños es el dos de junio y el cumpleaños de Marina es el doce de julio.

En el piso tengo un perro que se llama Gnarls 'Barkley'. Es muy grande y bueno. Su cumpleaños es el uno de abril. Gnarls 'Barkley' tiene tres años. También tengo una araña, buena pero muy fea, que se llama Luisa. El cumpleaños de mi araña también es el uno de abril. Entonces hago una fiesta para las dos mascotas al mismo tiempo. Es muy práctico.

1. Find the Spanish for the following in Isabela's text

a. My name is

b. I am 21 years old

c. I live in…

d. A big flat

e. On the outskirts

f. The 2nd of june

g. I have a dog

h. He is very big

i. His birthday is on the 1st April

j. He is 3 years old

k. I also have a spider

2. Complete the statements below based on Carlos' text

a. I am _____ years old

b. My birthday is the ____of _____

c. I live in a _____ house

d. My house is in the _____ of town

e. I like Eduardo but Rubén is _____

f. My friend José _____ in Barcelona

g. He lives in an old _____

3. Answer the questions on the four texts above

a. How old is Ramón?

b. Why do Ramón and Guillermo have the same birthday? *(what do you think a 'gemelo' is?)*

c. Who only likes one of his siblings?

d. Who has two pets that share a birthday?

e. Why is it convenient that they share a birthday?

f. Who has a friend that lives in a different city?

g. Who lives with their really good friend?

h. Who does not live in Latin America?

i. Whose birthday is on the twelfth of July?

4. Correct any incorrect statements about Estefanía's text

a. Estefanía vive en Cartagena, en el centro de Colombia

b. En la familia de Estefanía hay *(there are)* cuatro personas

c. Su cumpleaños es en marzo

d. El cumpleaños de Shakira es el tres de marzo

e. Estefanía vive en una casa grande pero fea en la costa

f. Le gusta mucho su casa

 **THE LANGUAGE GYM**

Unit 3. Saying where I live and am from: TRANSLATION/WRITING

1. Translate into English

a. vivo en

b. una casa

c. un piso

d. bonito

e. grande

f. en un edificio

g. antiguo

h. moderno

i. en el centro

j. en las afueras

k. en la costa

l. soy de

m. en España

n. en Perú

2. Gapped sentences

a. Vivo en una _____ fea — *I live in an ugly house*

b. Un piso en un _____ nuevo — *A flat in a new building*

c. Vivo en un _____ pequeño — *I live in a small flat*

d. Una _____ en las _____ — *A house on the outskirts*

e. _____ ___ Madrid — *I am from Madrid*

f. La _____ de España — *The capital of Spain*

3. Complete the sentences with a suitable word

a. Vivo en _____ , la capital de Cuba

b. Soy de Santiago, en _____

c. Vivo en un _____ bonito en las _____

d. Vivo en una casa bonita y _____

e. _____ de Quito, la _____ de Ecuador

f. Vivo en un _____ moderno en el centro

4. Phrase-level translation

a. I live in

b. I am from

c. a house

d. a flat

e. ugly (m)

f. small (m)

g. in an old building

h. in the centre

i. on the outskirts

j. on the coast

k. in Catalunya

5. Sentence-level translation

a. I am from Bilbao, in the Basque Country in Spain. I live in a big and pretty house on the outskirts.

b. I am from Buenos Aires, the capital of Argentina. I live in a small and ugly flat in the centre.

c. I am from Montevideo, the capital of Uruguay. I live in a flat in a new building on the coast. My flat is big but ugly.

d. I am from Cádiz in Andalucía, in Spain. I live in a flat in an old building on the outskirts. I like my flat.

THE LANGUAGE GYM

36

Unit 3. Saying where I live and am from: WRITING

1. Complete with the missing letters

a. Me lla_ _ Paco

b. Vi_ _ en una ca_ _ bon_t_

c. V_v_ en un p_so grand_

d. _ _vo en una _ _sa en el cent_ _

e. So_ de Bogo_ _ en Colom_ _a

f. Yo _oy de Bueno_ Aire_ en Argentin_

g. V_ _ _ en un pis_ peque_o en las afuer_ _

h. _oy de La Haba_ _ en Cu_ _

2. Spot and correct the spelling mistakes

a. Soy de Bogota, en Colombia

b. Vivo en Bilbao en el Pais Basco

c. Vivo en una casa feo

d. Vivo en un piso pequeña

e. Vivo en un moderno edificio

f. Vivo en Andalucia

g. Soy de Barcelona, en Cataluna

h. Soy de Cadiz, en Espana

3. Answer the questions in Spanish

a. ¿Cómo te llamas?

b. ¿Cuántos años tienes?

c. ¿Cuándo es tu cumpleaños?

d. ¿De dónde eres?

e. ¿Dónde vives?

f. ¿Vives en una casa o en un piso?

4. Anagrams: regions of Spain and Latin American countries

a. hiCel

b. luñCataa

c. anlucíadA

d. ubaC

e. rcuaEdo

f. spEaañ

g. erPú

h. loCombia

i. Uguayr

j. nraAgó

5. Guided writing: write 5 short paragraphs in the first person singular (I) describing the people below

Name	Age	Birthday	City	Country or region
Samuel	12	20.06	Buenos Aires	Argentina
Ale	14	14.10	Madrid	Spain
Andrés	11	14.01	Bogotá	Colombia
Carlos	13	17.01	La Habana	Cuba
Nina	15	19.10	Santiago	Chile

6. Describe this person in the third person (he):

Name: Alejandro
Age: 16
Birthday: 15 May
Country of origin: Quito, Ecuador
Country of residence: Madrid, Spain

 THE LANGUAGE GYM

TERM 1 - BRINGING IT ALL TOGETHER – 3

Me llamo Paco. Soy cubano. Tengo once años y vivo en La Habana, la capital de Cuba. Hoy estoy bastante bien. Estoy feliz y muy tranquilo.

Mi cumpleaños es el doce de septiembre. Tengo una hermana que se llama Bárbara y un hermano que se llama Lionel. Bárbara tiene cinco años y Lionel tiene nueve años. Hoy Bárbara no está muy bien, está un poco triste. Sin embargo *(however)*, Lionel está fenomenal. Está muy feliz porque es su cumpleaños.

Mi familia y yo vivimos en un piso grande, bonito y moderno en las afueras de La Habana. Me gusta mi piso porque es grande y bonito.

Mi amiga se llama Sofía y tiene doce años. Su cumpleaños es el veintiocho de marzo. Ella vive en una casa pequeña en la costa. Su casa es muy pequeña y un poco fea pero siempre está muy limpia. En su tiempo libre siempre toca el piano.

Mi mejor amigo *(best friend)* se llama Carlos. Tiene diez años y también vive en La Habana. Su cumpleaños es el siete de febrero. Carlos vive en un piso en un edificio moderno. En su tiempo libre siempre toca el ukelele.

Paco, 11 años, La Habana, Cuba

1. Find the Spanish equivalent in the text

a. I am Cuban

b. Today

c. I am happy

d. I have a sister

e. Who is called

f. (She) has

g. She is a bit sad

h. His birthday

i. In a big flat

j. On the outskirts

k. Big and beautiful

l. A small house on the coast

2. Complete the sentences based on Paco's text

a. My name is Paco. Today I am feeling _____

b. I am _____ and calm

c. My sister is _____ years old

d. Today Bárbara is feeling a bit _____

e. Today Lionel is happy because it is _____

f. Paco lives in a big, _____ and modern flat

g. Sofía lives in a _____ house on the _____

h. Carlos lives in a modern _____

3. Answer the questions below in English

a. Who is feeling happy and calm today?

b. Who is Carlos?

c. Who lives in a small house?

d. Who plays musical instruments? (2)

e. Whose house is always clean?

f. Who lives on the outskirts of Habana?

g. Whose birthday is on 28th March?

4. The second paragraph in Paco's text was copied incorrectly with EIGHT words missing. Can you spot them and add them in?

Mi cumpleaños es el doce septiembre. Tengo una hermana se llama Bárbara y un hermano que llama Lionel. Bárbara tiene cinco y Lionel tiene nueve años. Hoy Bárbara no muy bien, está poco triste. Sin embargo *(however)*, Lionel fenomenal. Está muy feliz porque su cumpleaños.

1. Me llamo Ramón. Soy venezolano. Tengo nueve años y vivo en Caracas, la capital de Venezuela. Hoy estoy muy bien. Estoy feliz y muy relajado. Mi cumpleaños es el tres de agosto.

2. Tengo una hermana que se llama Leona y un primo (cousin) que se llama Félix. Leona tiene ocho años y Félix tiene once años. Hoy Leona no está muy bien, está muy estresada. Sin embargo (however), Félix está fenomenal. Hoy está muy feliz.

3. Mi familia y yo vivimos en una casa grande y moderna, pero un poco fea, en La Guaira, en la costa de Caracas. Me gusta mi casa porque está cerca de la playa (near the beach).

4. Mi amiga se llama Renata y tiene once años. Su cumpleaños es el diecisiete de abril. Ella también vive en una casa en la costa. Su casa es muy pequeña, pero muy moderna y bonita. Normalmente está muy limpia. En su tiempo libre siempre toca el violín.

5. Mi mejor amigo (best friend) se llama Paco. Tiene ocho años y también vive en mi pueblo (my town), cerca de Caracas. Su cumpleaños es el veintidós de enero. Paco vive en un piso en un edificio antiguo. En su tiempo libre siempre juega al fútbol.

Ramón, 9, Venezuela

5. Spot the 9 mistakes in the following translation of Ramón's first 2 paragraphs

My name is Ramón. I am Venezuelan. I am eight years old and live in Caracas, the capital of Venezuela. Today I am quite well. I am happy and very excited. My birthday is on 3rd August. I have a sister who is called Leona and a brother called Félix. Leona is nine and Félix is twelve. Today Leona is not very well. She is very tired. However, Félix is OK. Today he is very calm.

6. Complete the following translation of paragraphs 3 and 4 in Ramón's text

My family and I live in a _____ and modern, but a bit ugly house, in La Guaira, on the _____ of Caracas. I _____ my house because it is _____ the beach.

My friend is called Renata and is _____ years old. Her _____ on _____ April. She _____ lives in a house on the _____. Her house is very _____, but very modern and _____. Normally it is very _____. In her _____ she _____ plays the violin.

7. Tick the words on the list below which are included in the text and translate them into English

a. Hoy	h. Nunca
b. Su	i. A veces
c. Con	j. También
d. De	k. Me encanta
e. Además	l. Toca
f. Desde	m. Juego
g. Siempre	n. Tampoco

8. Answer the following questions in Spanish, as if you were Ramón. Note: you can use whole sections of the text, provided they are relevant

a. ¿Cómo te llamas?

b. ¿De dónde eres?

c. ¿Cómo estás hoy?

d. ¿Cómo se llama tu primo?

e. ¿Cómo está Leona hoy?

f. ¿Quién es Paco?

g. ¿Dónde vive Renata?

h. ¿Cómo es su casa?

i. ¿Cuántos años tiene Paco?

j. ¿Qué hace Paco en su tiempo libre?

 **THE LANGUAGE GYM**

TERM 1 – MIDPOINT – RETRIEVAL PRACTICE

1. Answer the following questions in Spanish

¿Cómo te llamas?	
¿Cómo estás hoy?	
¿Cuántos años tienes?	
¿Cuándo es tu cumpleaños?	
¿Tienes hermanos o hermanas?	
¿Cómo se llama tu hermano/hermana?	
¿Cuántos años tiene?	
¿Cuándo es su cumpleaños?	
¿De dónde eres?	
¿Dónde vives?	
¿Cómo es tu casa?	
¿Dónde está tu casa?	

2. Write a paragraph in the first person singular (I) providing the following details

a. Your name is Fabio

b. You are Italian but live in Cádiz in the south of Spain

c. You are 11 years old and your birthday is on 29th July

d. You have an older brother called Mauro and a younger brother called Silvio

e. Your older brother is 16 and your younger brother is 8

f. Mauro's birthday in on 1st January and Silvio's birthday on 30th June

g. You live in a house on the outskirts

h. You like your house because it is always clean and quite spacious

3. Write a paragraph in the third person singular (he/she) providing the following details about your best friend or a member of your family.

Say:

a. Their name

b. Where they are from and live

c. How old they are and when their birthday is

d. How many siblings they have

e. Say how old they are

f. Say when their birthdays are

g. Where their house/flat is located

h. Why they like or dislike their house

THE LANGUAGE GYM

UNIT 4
Things I like/dislike: school subjects & teachers

In this unit you will learn to talk about:

- Which school subjects you study
- Which subjects you like/dislike
- Which subjects a friend likes/dislikes
- Adjectives for describing activities
- Reasons for liking or disliking a class

You will also revisit
- Adjectival agreements: masculine/feminine/plural

UNIT 4
Things I like/dislike: school subjects & teachers

¿Qué asignaturas estudias?	*What subjects do you study?*
¿Cuál (no) te gusta? ¿Por qué?	*Which one do you (**not**) like? Why?*
¿Te gusta el español? ¿Por qué?	*Do you like Spanish? Why?*

En el colegio estudio *At school I study*	alemán / ciencias / historia / etc.

Me gusta *I like*	el	alemán *German*			**es** *it is*	aburrido *boring*
		arte *art*				agotador *tiring*
No me gusta *I don't like*		español *Spanish*				complicado *complicated*
		francés *French*				divertido *fun*
		inglés *English*				fácil *easy*
						interesante *interesting*
						útil *useful*
A mi amigo/a le gusta *My friend likes*	la	educación física *PE*		**pero** *but*	**no es** *it is not*	aburrida
		geografía *geography*				agotadora
		historia *history*				complicada
A mi amigo/a no le gusta *My friend does not like*		informática *ICT*		**porque** *because*		divertida
		química *chemistry*				fácil
		religión *RE*				interesante
						útil
*Me gustan *I like*	las	ciencias			**son** *are*	aburridas
		lenguas				agotadoras
No me gustan *I don't like*		matemáticas				complicadas
						divertidas
						fáciles
						interesantes
						útiles

Además,	**me encanta** *I love it*	**porque**	aprendo mucho	*I learn a lot*		
			es útil para el futuro	*it is useful for the future*		
			tengo amigos en clase	*I have friends in class*		
	me gusta *I like it*		**el profesor es** *the teacher (m) is*	**bastante** *quite*	antipático/a *mean* bueno/a *good*	
			la profesora es *the teacher (f) is*	**muy** *very* **un poco** *a bit*	gracioso/a *funny* paciente *patient* simpático/a *nice*	

---

*Author's note: If the noun being liked is a singular noun, we use **gusta** (3rd person singular of **gustar**). If the noun being liked is a plural noun, we use **gustan** (3rd person plural of **gustar**).

e.g. • *Me gusta <u>el inglés</u> (singular)* • *Me gustan <u>las ciencias</u> (plural)*

🔊 Unit 4. Things I like/dislike: school subjects & teachers: LISTENING 🔊

1. Underline the word you hear

a. La profe de francés es **aburrida/graciosa/divertida**

b. La geografía es **divertida/interesante/difícil**

c. Las ciencias son muy **duras/complicadas/útiles**

d. La educación física es **divertida/agotadora/aburrida**

e. **Me gusta/me encanta/no me gusta** la música

f. La profe de alemán es **simpática/antipática/estricta**

g. Las matemáticas son **interesantes/difíciles/aburridas**

h. El profe es un poco **simpático/antipático/severo**

2. Break the flow

a. Megustaelalemánperoesdifícil

b. Amiamigolegustaelespañol

c. Nomegustanlasmatemáticas

d. Megustaporqueaprendomucho

e. Esútilparaelfuturo

f. Tengoamigosenclase

g. Laprofesoraesmuybuena

3. Listening for detail: what subjects does Paloma do each day? Tick the correct ones

lunes *Monday*	Spanish German	French Art
martes *Tuesday*	Maths Art	Science Geography
miércoles *Wednesday*	PE Religion	French IT
jueves *Thursday*	Geography Art	History German
viernes *Friday*	Chemistry Spanish	Maths English

4. Complete with the missing words

a. Me encanta ____ español porque es _____

b. A mi amigo ____ gustan las matemáticas

c. No me _____ las ciencias

d. ...porque no ____ muy interesantes

e. Me gusta _____ tengo _____ en clase

f. El arte es un poco _____

g. La _____ es muy _____ para el futuro

h. El profesor ____ muy _____

5. Listen and fill in the grid

	Subject	Love/Like/Dislike	Reason
e.g.	*Spanish*	*Like*	*Teacher is very good*
a.	**Maths**		
b.			**Learn a lot in class**
c.		Dislike	
d.	**Science**		
e.		Like	

THE LANGUAGE GYM

6. Listen and correct the mistakes

a. En la colegio estudio historias

b. Me gusto el español porque es divertida

c. Me gusta porque tengo amigo en clase

d. No mi gustan las ciencias porque son aburrido

e. Mi amigo no le gusta la químicry

f. Las matemáticas es muy útil

g. Me gusta porque la profesor es bueno

h. No mi gusta porque aprendo mucha en clase

7. Spot the difference and correct the text

Me llamo Jaume Llorens. Soy de Barcelona. En el colegio estudio inglés, catalán, alemán y francés. Me gusta un poco el español porque es muy fácil y aprendo mucho en casa. Es muy aburrido y útil para el futuro. Además, tengo muchos perros en clase. Mi amigo estudia francés y español. A mi amigo le gusta mucho el francés porque es bastante interesante.

8. Narrow listening - Gapped translation

My name is Gary. I am _____ years old. I am _____ Bilbao, in the Basque Country. At _____ I study English, Spanish, French and _____. My favourite subject is _____ because the teacher is _____ _____ and because I _____ a lot in _____. My friend doesn't like _____ because he thinks that the _____ is a bit _____ and he doesn't have many _____ in class. However, it is an important subject because it is _____ for the _____. I also like _____, but they are quite _____.

9. Listening slalom: follow the speaker from top to bottom and number the boxes accordingly

a.	b.	c.	d.
At school,	I like art	On Mondays	My favourite
subject	I have	I study	because
IT class and	Spanish,	it is interesting	is German
because	and	I love it	French
and history.	my teacher	I have	because
is very	My favourite	it is useful	many friends
good.	in class.	subject is history.	for the future.

Unit 4. Things I like/dislike: school subjects & teachers: VOCAB BUILDING

1. Match

Me gusta	Because
Las ciencias	Boring
Porque	I like
No me gusta	Interesting
Aburrido	Science
Mi amigo	Fun
Divertido	I don't like
Fácil	My friend
Interesante	Easy

2. Faulty translation: correct the English

a. Me gustan las ciencias — *I like maths*

b. El inglés es aburrido — *English is hard*

c. El francés es divertido — *French is easy*

d. La historia es interesante — *Drama is interesting*

e. A mi amigo le gusta el arte — *My friend hates art*

f. Las matemáticas son fáciles — *Maths is complicated*

g. La informática es aburrida — *ICT is exciting*

h. Aprendo mucho — *I listen a lot*

i. Es útil para el futuro — *It is useless for the future*

3. Spot the hidden word in each sequence of letters

a. *Fun*   aburridofácilmuchogustadivertidodifícilamigociencias

b. *Easy*   cienciasfácilmuchomatemáticasdivertidodifícilamigo

c. *Boring*   megustaescuchoaprendoaburridomeencantainglés

d. *Because*   artecomplicadogustaamigoporqueaprendo

e. *It is*   amigoalemáncomplicadobuenoesporquedivertidomuy

f. *Science*   megustanmucholascienciasporque

g. *Friend (fem.)* amiamiganolegustanlasciencias

4. Translate into English

a. Interesante

b. Complicado

c. Aburrido

d. Divertido

e. Útil

f. Bueno

g. Fácil

5. Complete the table

Español	English
Aburrido	
	Useful
	Fun
Bueno	
	Interesting
Porque	
	Easy
	Complicated
Tengo amigos	
	I have friends
Es útil	

6. Insert 'gusta' or 'gustan' as appropriate

a. Me _____ el arte

b. No me _____ las ciencias

c. Me _____ las matemáticas

d. Me _____ la química

e. Me _____ el inglés

f. Me _____ los idiomas

g. No me _____ el francés

h. Me _____ el español

i. No me _____ la historia

j. Me _____ la música

k. Me _____ los profesores

l. Me _____ la educación física

7. Complete the words

a. P_ _que

b. Cien_ _ _s

c. Le gu_ta el ar_ _

d. El ing_ _s

e. No m_ gus_ _

f. E_ divert_ _a

g. La m_sic_

h. Los idiom_ _

i. El fran_ _ _

j. La histo_ _ _

k. El espa_ _ _

l. Bu_ _o

Unit 4. Things I like/dislike: school subjects & teachers: READING

Me llamo Enrique. Tengo trece años. Vivo en Cádiz. Tengo dos hermanos y una hermana. Voy al instituto La Caleta, una escuela de secundaria bastante grande en las afueras de la ciudad. Me gusta mucho mi escuela porque los profesores son muy trabajadores y simpáticos. Siempre me ayudan. Mi profesor favorito es el profe de español porque es muy bueno y siempre me ayuda. Aprendo mucho en sus *(his)* clases y me encanta el español. Me gustan también las ciencias y las matemáticas porque son divertidas. Me gusta la educación física también, pero es muy agotadora. No me gustan nada la historia y la geografía porque son aburridas.

Me llamo Ignacio. Tengo quince años y mi cumpleaños es el ocho de junio. Vivo en Granada. Soy hijo único. Voy al instituto La Pineda, una escuela de secundaria bastante grande en las afueras de la ciudad, cerca *(near)* del estadio. Me gusta mi escuela porque los profesores son muy buenos, trabajadores y no son estrictos. Mi asignatura favorita es la informática porque es muy interesante y útil y el profesor es divertido y paciente. Aprendo muchísimo en sus clases. Me gustan también los idiomas extranjeros, sobre todo *(above all)* el alemán, porque los profesores son muy buenos y divertidos. No me gustan nada *(at all)* las matemáticas porque son complicadas, aburridas y agotadoras.

Me llamo Roberta. Tengo catorce años y mi cumpleaños es el veinte de diciembre. Vivo en Alicante. Soy hija única. Voy al colegio Jorge Juan. Es una escuela de secundaria bastante pequeña en el centro de la ciudad, cerca del puerto. No me gusta mi colegio porque, aunque los profesores son buenos y trabajadores, también son demasiado estrictos. Mi asignatura favorita es la historia porque es muy fácil para mí y el profesor es muy simpático. Aprendo mucho en sus clases. Me gusta también el inglés, porque es un idioma muy útil y la profesora es muy buena y divertida. No me gustan nada *(at all)* las ciencias, sobre todo la física, porque son complicadas y aburridas. Tampoco me gustan las matemáticas porque el profe es muy estricto y no comprendo nada en las clases.

1. Find the Spanish for the following in Enrique's text

a. I live: V____

b. School: E_____

c. Outskirts: A_____

d. Hard–working: T_____

e. They help me: M_ a____

f. Good (sing.): B_____

g. I learn: A_____

h. Also: T_____

i. Tiring: A_____

2. Complete based on Enrique's text

a. He is _____

b. He has __ siblings

c. His Spanish teacher is ____ and _____

d. He loves _____

e. Science is _____

f. He ____ likes PE

g. PE is _____

h. History is _____

3. Spot and correct the 11 mistakes in the following translation of Ignacio's text

My name is Ignacio. I am sixteen years old and my birthday in on 8th June. I live in Granada. I am unique. I go to the instituto La Pineda, a quite large secondary school in the centre of the city, near the stadium. I like my school because the teachers are very good, friendly and are not strict. My favourite teacher is ICT because it is interesting and fascinating and the teacher is friendly and patient. I listen very much in his lessons. I also like foreign languages, especially French, because the teachers are very interesting and fun. I don't like at all maths because they are complicated, boring and tiring.

4. Find the Spanish for the following in Roberta's text

a. Only child

b. School

c. Port

d. Good

e. Hard-working

f. I learn

g. Friendly

h. English

5. Find someone who

a. ...doesn't like maths

b. ...likes German

c. ...has strict teachers

d. ...likes IT

e. ...likes PE

f. ...doesn't like science

g. ...finds history easy

6. Answer these questions about Roberta

a. Where is her school?

b. What are her teachers like?

c. Why does she like history?

d. What does she think about science?

 **THE LANGUAGE GYM**

Unit 4. Things I like/dislike: school subjects & teachers: TRANSLATION

1. Translate into English

a. Me gusta el inglés

b. El profesor es bueno

c. Aprendo mucho

d. No me gusta nada

e. Es complicado

f. Es aburrido

g. Me gusta mucho la historia

h. Me encantan las ciencias

i. Tengo amigos en clase

j. Es agotador

k. Me gustan mucho los idiomas

2. Gapped translation

a. Me gusta _____ el inglés   *I like English a lot*

b. _____ mucho   *I learn a lot*

c. Me encantan las _____   *I love science*

d. Tengo _____ en clase   *I have friends in lessons*

e. Es _____ para el futuro   *It is useful for the future*

f. Es profesor es _____   *The teacher is good*

3. Tangled translation: into Spanish

a. Me gusta el **English** porque tengo **friends in** clase

b. No me gustan **nothing** las **science because** son **boring**

c. **I don't like** las **maths** porque la profesora es **mean**

d. No me gusta la **education** física **because** es **tiring**

e. **I love** el español porque **the** profesora **is funny** y **friendly**

f. **I like** la informática **because** es **useful** para el **future**

g. No me gusta el **French** porque **it is** complicado

4. Phrase level translation: English to Spanish

a. I like sciences

b. I learn a lot

c. I have friends

d. It is complicated (f)

e. They are boring (f)

f. They are useful

g. I love French

h. In class

i. It is tiring

j. I like maths

k. For the future

l. I like history a lot

m. The teacher is good

n. The teacher is bad

5. Sentence level translation: English to Spanish

a. I like French because I have friends in lessons

b. I don't like the sciences because the teacher is boring

c. I love Spanish because it is useful for the future

d. I don't like maths because they are complicated

e. I don't like history because the teacher is mean

f. I don't like PE because it is tiring

g. I like ICT because the teacher is good and fun

Unit 4. Things I like/dislike: school subjects & teachers: WRITING

1. Anagrams

e.g. eM stagu al grafíageo: Me gusta la geografía

a. asL cicienas nos iburradas

b. lE glésin se dotidiver

c. repAndo chomu ne sal clesas

d. oN em sutang sla catemátimas

e. eM sguta sbanteta le fréasnc

f. sE litú rapa le rotufu

g. aL fepro se anebu

h. goTen imagos ne acles

2. Broken words

a. Apre_ _ _ mu_ _ _ en las cla_ _ _

b. Mi profe_ _ _ _ es simp_ _ _ _ _

c. N_ me gu_ _ _ _ las cien_ _ _ _

d. E_ út_ _ para el fut_ _ _

e. El profes_ _ de art_ es agot_ _ _ _

f. Ten_ _ ami_ _ _ en clase

g. Mi profesor es divert_ _ _

h. No m_ gusta el fra_ _ _ _

i. Las mate_ _ _ _ _ _ son aburri_ _ _

3. Complete with the missing words

a. No me _ _ _ _ _ _ las ciencias

b. Me _ _ _ _ _ mucho el francés

c. No _ _ gustan _ _ _ matemáticas

d. Me gusta _ _ inglés porque el _ _ _ _ _ _ _ es bueno

e. A mi amigo _ _ gusta el arte _ _ _ _ _ _ es divertido

f. Me encanta _ _ español porque _ _ apasionante

g. Me gusta la informática porque es _ _ _ _ para el futuro

h. Tengo muchos _ _ _ _ _ _ en clase

4. Complete with *gusta* or *gustan* as appropriate

a. No me _____ las matemáticas

b. Me _____ mucho el francés

c. A mi amigo le _____ las ciencias

d. A Marina le _____ el arte

e. A mi amiga le _____ el español

f. ¿No te _____ los idiomas?

g. Me _____ mucho mis profesores

h. A mi hermano no le _____ la música

5. Guided writing: write 5 short paragraphs in the 1st person singular (I) describing the people below

Name	Subject they like	Reason	Subject they dislike	Reason
Samuel	French	Fun	Science	Boring
Ale	ICT	Useful	Maths	Teacher is not good
Andrés	English	Interesting	Art	Not fun
Carlos	Science	Fascinating	PE	Tiring
Nina	Spanish	Fun and interesting	History	Teacher is mean and no friends in class

6. Describe this person in the third person (he):

Name: Manuel

Age: 13

From: Mexico

Lives in: Spain

Subjects he likes:

-French, because it is fun and useful for the future

- Maths, because it is exciting and the teacher is very good and funny

Subject he dislikes:

Geography because it is boring and the teacher is mean

Me llamo Miguel y tengo doce años. Soy de Perú pero vivo en Bogotá, la capital de Colombia. Hoy estoy fenomenal. Estoy muy feliz porque estoy de vacaciones *(on holiday)*. Además, ¡hoy es mi cumpleaños!

Tengo un hermano mayor que se llama Ramón. Ramón tiene quince años y es muy simpático *(nice)*. Hoy Ramón está regular porque está muy cansado.

Mi familia y yo vivimos en una casa grande y moderna en el centro de Bogotá. Me gusta mi casa porque es muy grande y hay muchas tiendas *(shops)* cerca. En mi tiempo libre siempre toco la guitarra.

Mi mejor amiga se llama Antonia y tiene doce años, igual que yo *(same as me)*. Su cumpleaños es el treinta de abril. Ella vive en un piso en un edificio antiguo en las afueras de Bogotá. Le gusta su piso porque es bonito y hay muchos restaurantes cerca.

Voy al Colegio Bilingüe Nueva Alejandría, un colegio bastante grande cerca del centro de la ciudad. Me gusta mi colegio porque los profesores son muy buenos, trabajadores y no son estrictos. Es un colegio bilingüe, así que *(therefore)* estudio algunas clases en inglés y otras en español. Me encanta el inglés.

Mi asignatura favorita es la historia porque es muy interesante y útil y el profesor es divertido y siempre me ayuda. Siempre aprendo muchísimo en sus clases. Me gustan también las lenguas, sobre todo *(above all)* el inglés, porque las clases son muy divertidas, aprendo mucho y tengo muchos amigos en clase.

Sin embargo, no me gustan nada *(at all)* las ciencias porque son complicadas, aburridas y agotadoras. Además, el profe es un poco aburrido y no tengo amigos en clase.

Miguel, 12, Perú

1. Find the Spanish equivalent in the text

a. I am 12

b. Today I am feeling great

c. I have an older brother

d. We live

e. I like my house

f. There are many shops nearby

g. In my free time

h. My best friend

i. On the outskirts of

j. I go

k. A quite big school

l. I like my school

m. The teachers are very good

n. Hard–working

o. It is a bilingual school

p. I love English

2. Arrange the information below in the same order as it occurs in the text

His name is Miguel	
He likes his school	
Antonia lives in Bogota	
Miguel is feeling great today	
He likes his house	
Miguel loves English	
There are many restaurants near Antonia's house	
Miguel is on holidays	
Antonia's birthday is on 30th April	

THE LANGUAGE GYM

1. Me llamo Lionel y tengo catorce años. Soy de Argentina y vivo en Buenos Aires, la capital. Hoy estoy regular. Estoy un poco estresado porque tengo muchos deberes.

2. Tengo un hermano menor que se llama Geraldo. Geraldo tiene trece años y normalmente es muy amable. Hoy Geraldo está muy feliz porque es su cumpleaños.

3. Vivo con mi familia en una casa bastante grande y un poco antigua en las afueras de Buenos Aires. Me gusta mi casa aunque es *(although it is)* un poco pequeña. Hay muchos restaurantes cerca. En mi tiempo libre siempre toco la flauta.

4. Mi mejor amigo se llama Antonio y tiene quince años, casi igual que yo *(nearly the same as me)*. Su cumpleaños es el trece de febrero. Él vive en un piso enorme en un edificio moderno en el centro de Buenos Aires. Le gusta su piso porque es muy grande y bonito y hay un polideportivo *(sports centre)* cerca.

5. Voy al Colegio Mariano Moreno, un colegio muy bueno cerca del centro de la ciudad. El colegio es histórico: se creó *(it was made)* en 1898. Me gusta mi colegio porque los profesores son muy inteligentes y son muy pacientes. Estudio muchas clases diferentes, como la historia, la geografía y la música. Me encanta el español.

6. Mi asignatura favorita es el español porque es muy interesante y útil *(useful)* para el futuro. La profesora se llama Paloma y es muy inteligente y graciosa. Siempre me ayuda y nunca me chilla, es muy paciente. Me gusta también la música porque las clases son muy buenas y tengo a mi mejor amigo en clase.

7. Sin embargo, odio *(I hate)* las matemáticas porque son duras *(hard)*, y aburridas. Sé *(I know)* que son importantes, ¡pero me da igual! Además, el profe es muy impaciente. A veces nos chilla.

Lionel, 14, Argentina

3. Faulty translation: correct the 10 mistakes found in the translation below of paragraphs 1, 2 and 3 of Lionel's text

1. My name is Lionel and I am fifteen years old. I am from Argentina and live in Buenos Aires, the capital. Today I am unwell. I am a bit agitated because I have a lot of homework.

2. I have an older brother whose name is Geraldo. Geraldo is thirteen and usually is very mean. Today Geraldo is very sad because it is his birthday.

3. I live with my family in a quite small and old house in the center of Buenos Aires. I like my house even though it is a bit ugly. There are many restaurants nearby. In my free time I occasionally play the drums.

4. Complete the translation of paragraph 4

My _____ friend is called Antonio and is ___ years old, nearly the _____ as me. His birthday is on ___ February. He lives in a a huge _____ in the centre of Buenos Aires. He _____ his flat because it is very _____ and _____and there is a sports centre _____.

5. Complete the sentences below based on paragraphs 5 to 7

a. Lionel' school is located_____

b. He likes his school because the teachers are (1) _____ and (2) _____

c. His favourite subject is _____ because it is (1) _____ and (2) _____ _____

d. His Spanish teacher is very (1) _____ and (2) _____

e. She always _____ him and never _____ him off

f. He also enjoys music because the lessons are _____ and he has _____

g. He hates maths because they are _____ and _____. Also, the teacher is very _____

UNIT 5
Things I like/dislike: free time

In this unit you will learn to talk about:

- What sports and activities you do in your free time
- The "me gusta + infinitive" structure with "jugar", "hacer" & "ir"
- Different places you can go to – using the verb "ir"
- Who you do the activities with
- Reasons for liking/disliking an activity

You will also revisit
- Previously seen adjectives, applied to a different context

UNIT 5
Things I like/dislike: free time

¿Qué te gusta hacer en tu tiempo libre?			*What do you like to do in your free time?*	
Cuando tengo tiempo *When I have free time* **En mi tiempo libre** *In my free time*	**me encanta** *I love*	**jugar** *to play*	**a la Play** **a videojuegos** **al ajedrez** **a las cartas** **al baloncesto** **al fútbol** **al tenis** **en el ordenador**	*Playstation* *videogames* *chess* *cards* *basketball* *football* *tennis* *on the computer*
	me gusta *I like*	**hacer** *to do*	**ciclismo** **deporte** **equitación** **footing** **natación** **senderismo**	*cycling* *sport* *horse riding* *jogging* *swimming* *hiking*
	no me gusta *I don't like*	**ir** *to go*	**a casa de mi amigo** **al centro comercial** **al gimnasio** **al parque** **al polideportivo** **a la piscina** **de paseo** **de pesca**	*to my friend's house* *to the shopping mall* *to the gym* *to the park* *to the sports centre* *to the pool* *for a walk* *fishing*

con *with*	**mi amiga Ana** **mi amigo Pedro** ***mis amigos/as**	*my friend Ana* *my friend Pedro* *my friends*	**mi hermana** **mi hermano** **mis hermanos**	*my sister* *my brother* *my siblings*

me gusta *I like it* **no me gusta** *I don't like it*	**porque** *because*	**es** *it is* **no es** *it is not*	**aburrido** **agotador** **divertido** **emocionante** **interesante** **saludable**	*boring* *tiring* *fun* *exciting* *interesting* *healthy*

***Author's note:** Use **"mis amigos"** for a group of friends that are either **all boys, or a mix of boys & girls**. Use **"mis amigas"** for a group of friends that are made up of **girls only**.

THE LANGUAGE GYM

1. Select the correct answer

a. Me gusta jugar al tenis/baloncesto/fútbol

b. Me gusta hacer deporte/deberes/equitación

c. Me gusta jugar al ajedrez/a las cartas/al golf

d. Me gusta hacer footing/natación/senderismo

e. Me gusta ir al parque/al gimnasio/al cine

f. Me gusta ir de paseo/de marcha/de pesca

g. Me gusta porque es divertido/aburrido/agotador

h. No me gusta porque es aburrido/tonto/divertido

2. Break the flow: draw a line between each word

a. Enmitiempolibremegustajugar

b. Megustajugaralbaloncesto

c. Nomegustahacerequitación

d. Megustairalaplayaconmiamigo

e. Megustaporqueesinteresante

f. Nomegustaporqueesagotador

g. Megustairdepaseoenbici

3. Listening for detail: what activities does Paloma do each day? Tick the correct ones

lunes *Monday*	Cycling Sport	Jogging Horse riding
martes *Tuesday*	Chess Cards	Go for walk Football
miércoles *Wednesday*	Swimming Cycling	Hiking Sport
jueves *Thursday*	Pool Fishing	Videogames Park
viernes *Friday*	Tennis Golf	Chess Shopping mall

4. Complete with the missing words

a. Me gusta jugar al _____

b. No me gusta ir al _____

c. No me gusta hacer _____

d. Me gusta mucho ir de _____

e. No me gusta hacer _____

f. Me gusta jugar al _____

g. Me gusta porque es _____

h. Me gusta ir al _____

5. Listen and fill in the grid

	Opinion	Activity	Reason
e.g.	*Dislikes*	*Jogging*	*Not fun*
a.			
b.			
c.			
d.			
e.			

 THE LANGUAGE GYM

6. Listen and correct the mistakes

a. Me gusta ir paseo

b. Me gusta jugar natación

c. Me gusta porque divertido

d. Me gusta mucho ir de parque

e. No me gusto hacer deporte

f. Me gusta bastante ir a marcha

g. Me gusta porque emocionante

h. No me gusta jugar ciclismo

7. Spot the differences between the sentences you hear and those written down and make changes to the latter. Don't make any changes if identical.

a. No me gusta jugar a las cartas

b. Me gusta mucho ir de pesca

c. Me gusta jugar al tenis

d. Me gusta ir a la piscina

e. No me gusta hacer nada

f. Me gusta mucho porque es divertido

g. No me gusta hacer equitación

h. Me gusta mucho ir de compras

i. No me gusta hacer deporte

8. Narrow listening: gapped translation

Hola, __ _____ Ana y soy de Madrid. Tengo _____ años. En my familia hay _____ personas: mi madre, mi padre, mi hermano _____, Roberto y mi hermano _____, Paco. Mi cumpleaños es el _____ de julio. No me gusta _____ estudiar. En el _____ estudio muchas asignaturas, pero solo me gustan el _____ y la educación física. ¡Odio hacer ___ _____! En mi tiempo libre me gusta hacer _____. Me gusta mucho jugar al _____, ir en _____ y hacer _____. Me encanta jugar al baloncesto porque es _____. No me gusta hacer _____ porque es aburrido y _____.

9. Listening slalom: follow the speaker from top to bottom and number the boxes accordingly

a	b	c	d
En mi tiempo	Cuando tengo	No me gusta	Me gusta
mucho	ir	libre	tiempo
en bici	me gusta ir	me gusta jugar	jugar
a los	al ajedrez	porque es	de pesca
y	videojuegos	porque	aburrido
con	hacer	y	es
muy interesante.	mi padre.	natación.	agotador.

THE LANGUAGE GYM

Unit 5. Things I like/dislike: free time – VOCABULARY BUILDING

1. Match

Ir de pesca	To go for a walk
Hacer natación	To go fishing
Jugar al ajedrez	To play basketball
Ir de paseo	To go to my friend's house
Jugar al baloncesto	To go swimming
Hacer deporte	To go hiking
Ir al polideportivo	To go cycling
Hacer footing	To play chess
Ir en bici	To go to the sports centre
Hacer senderismo	To go jogging
Ir a casa de mi amigo	To do sport

2. Faulty translation

a. Hacer equitacion: *to go horse riding*

b. Hacer deporte: *to go jogging*

c. Ir al polideportivo: *to go to the cinema*

d. Hacer footing: *to go cycling*

e. Ir en bici: *to go climbing*

f. Hacer senderismo: *to go swimming*

g. Ir de pesca: *to go for a walk*

h. Jugar al ajedrez: *to play basketball*

i. Ir de paseo: *to go for a walk*

j. Jugar al baloncesto: *to play basketball*

k. Hacer natacion: *to go horse riding*

3. Sentence puzzle: rewrite the jumbled up Spanish

a. tiempo En me encanta mi libre ir en bici   *In my free time I love to go cycling*

b. Me divertido porque es muy encanta   *I love it because it is a lot of fun*

c. mis amigos Me gusta hacer footing con mucho   *I like a lot to go jogging with my friends*

d. porque Me gusta relajante muy es   *I like it because it is very relaxing*

e. No al ajedrez jugar me gusta   *I don't like to play chess*

f. me es aburrido No gusta porque   *I don't like it because it is boring*

4 Translate into English

a. Paseo

b. Equitación

c. Ajedrez

d. Footing

e. Bici

f. Ir

g. Me gusta

h. Me encanta

i. Jugar

j. Piscina

k. Amigos

l. Casa

m. Relajante

n. Agotador

5. Tick all the adjectives

a. Relajante

b. Casa

c. Agotador

d. Equitación

e. Emocionante

f. Paseo

g. Divertido

h. Fenomenal

Unit 5. Things I like/dislike: free time – VOCABULARY BUILDING

6. Complete with the correct option

a. Me gusta ir de _____ con mis amigas

b. No me _____ jugar al fútbol

c. Me encanta _____ footing

d. Me gusta mucho hacer _____

e. Me encanta porque es _____

f. _____ gusta jugar al ajedrez

g. Me gusta _____ es divertido

h. Me gusta jugar _____ baloncesto

gusta	divertido	paseo	natación
al	me	hacer	porque

7. Complete the table

English	Español
Friends	
	Ajedrez
	Baloncesto
I love	
Because	
	Paseo
	Pesca
To do	
To play	

8. Gapped translation

a. En mi tiempo libre me gusta hacer senderismo: _____ I like to go _____

b. Me encanta porque es muy relajante: I love it because it is _____ _____

c. Me gusta mucho hacer footing con mis amigos: I like _____ to go _____ with my friends

d. Me encanta porque es muy relajante: I _____ it because it is very _____

e. No me gusta jugar al ajedrez. Es aburrido: I don't like to play _____. It is _____

f. No me gusta porque es agotador: I _____ it because it is _____

g. Me encanta ir de pesca porque es divertido: I love to go _____ because it is _____

9. Find the Spanish for the words/phrases below

p	e	b	d	r	a	m	p	o	r	q	u	e	r
s	a	p	a	s	e	o	l	n	p	e	m	a	l
r	i	r	j	l	n	r	d	o	i	s	s	e	m
h	a	m	e	d	o	e	l	r	e	m	u	a	j
a	r	y	d	s	e	n	d	e	r	i	s	m	o
g	o	a	r	o	a	l	c	ü	g	l	o	o	l
o	d	i	e	r	n	m	i	e	h	n	s	l	i
t	a	y	z	r	i	o	n	r	s	g	i	a	n
a	t	s	l	h	a	c	e	r	m	t	s	p	d
p	o	v	u	l	o	s	o	p	o	r	o	q	a
o	g	b	e	a	b	u	r	r	i	d	o	u	p
r	a	p	a	s	i	o	n	a	n	t	e	e	a
f	r	i	o	l	e	r	n	i	t	r	a	m	r

a. Walk

b. Chess

c. To do

d. Basketball

e. Hiking

f. Exciting

g. Tiring

h. Because

i. Boring

Unit 5. Things I like/dislike: free time: READING

- ¿Cómo te llamas?
- Me llamo Carlos.
- ¿Qué te gusta hacer en tu tiempo libre?
- En mi tiempo libre me gusta hacer deporte. Me gusta jugar al baloncesto con mis amigos, ir a la piscina y al gimnasio con mi hermano y hacer ciclismo. También me gusta hacer senderismo con mi padre el fin de semana. Es emocionante.
- ¿Qué no te gusta hacer en tu tiempo libre?
- No me gusta nada jugar al fútbol porque es aburrrido.

- ¿Cómo te llamas?
- Me llamo Isabel.
- ¿Qué te gusta hacer en tu tiempo libre?
- En mi tiempo libre me gusta ir de tiendas y de paseo con mis amigas. También me gusta jugar al ajedrez con mi hermana mayor e ir a la piscina con mi familia. Me gusta porque es relajante.
- ¿Qué no te gusta hacer en tu tiempo libre?
- No me gusta nada hacer deporte porque es muy agotador y aburrido.

- ¿Cómo te llamas?
- Me llamo Estefanía.
- ¿Qué te gusta hacer en tu tiempo libre?
- En mi tiempo libre me gusta jugar a videojuegos en mi ordenador o en el móvil. También me gusta mucho hacer natación con mis amigos. Es divertido.
- ¿Qué no te gusta hacer en tu tiempo libre?
- No me gusta ir de pesca con mi padre el fin de semana.

1. Find the Spanish for the following in Isabel's text

a. In my free time

b. To go shopping

c. Also

d. To play chess

e. Older

f. To go to the pool

g. Relaxing

h. In your free time

i. I don't like at all

j. To do sport

k. Tiring

2. Complete the statements below based on Carlos' text

a. In my free time I like to do _____.

b. I like to play _____ with my friends.

c. I like to go to the _____ and to the _____ with my brother and to go _____.

d. At the weekend I enjoy to go _____ with my father because it is _____.

e. I don't like at all to _____ _____ because it is _____.

3. Tick or cross? Tick the 9 words on the list below which are included in Estefanía's text and cross the remaining ones out

a. Free
b. Video games
c. Female friends
d. Bike
e. Shopping centre
f. Fun
g. Weekend
h. Computer
i. Swimming
j. Jogging
k. I don't like
l. Because
m. Fishing
n. Time
o. Saturday
p. Walk

4. Find someone who...

a. ...likes to play videogames

b. ...doesn't like football

c. ...likes to play chess

d. ...thinks sport is tiring

e. ...likes to go cycling

f. ...doesn't like to fish with their father

g. ...likes to go hiking with their father

h. ...has an older sister

i. ...likes to play on their mobile phone

 THE LANGUAGE GYM

Unit 5. Things I like/dislike: free time: WRITING

1. Transl-Anagrams: unjumble the words and translate them into English

a. sE vertidido

b. eM tagus chomu

c. sE doaribur

d. gaJur la drajeza

e. ceraH derisemnos

f. graJu a sol deviojugeos

g. recaH canatión

2. Broken words

a. Pas_ _   *Walk*

b. Pes_ _   *Fishing*

c. Me enc_ _ _ _   *I love*

d. I_ a l_ p_ _ _ _   *To go to the beach*

e. Sender_ _ _ _   *Hiking*

f. Equi_ _ _ _ _ _   *Horse riding*

g. Dep_ _ _ _   *Sport*

h. Balonc_ _ _ _   *Basketball*

3. Complete the sentences with HACER, IR or JUGAR as appropriate

a. Me gusta _____ al tenis

b. Me gusta _____ senderismo

c. Me gusta _____ de paseo

d. Me gusta _____ en bici

e. Me gusta _____ natación y equitación

f. Me encanta _____ al fútbol

g. Me gusta mucho _____ footing

h. Me gusta _____ al baloncesto

i. Me gusta _____ de pesca

j. Me encanta _____ a videojuegos

4. Translate into Spanish

a. Videogames

b. Horse riding

c. Swimming

d. Fishing

e. Hiking

f. Tiring

5. Translate into Spanish

a. I like to go hiking

b. I don't like to go swimming

c. I love to play videogames

d. It is tiring

e. I like to go fishing

f. It is exciting

6. Translate into Spanish

a. I love to play basketball with my friends. I love it because it is fun.

b. I don't like to go hiking with my family. I don't like it because it is boring.

c. I like to go to the swimming pool with my friends. It is fantastic!

d. I don't like to go cycling with my father and brother. It is tiring.

e. I love to go for a walk with my best (female) friend. It is very relaxing.

f. I like a lot to go shopping with my friends. It is exciting!

g. I don't like to go fishing with my family. It is very boring.

Me llamo Marta y tengo diez años. Mi cumpleaños es el ocho de septiembre. Soy de Argentina pero vivo en Santiago, la capital de Chile. Hoy estoy fenomenal. Estoy muy feliz porque después voy a jugar al fútbol con mis amigas.

Tengo una hermana mayor que se llama Carolina. Carolina tiene dieciséis años y es muy amable *(kind)*. Hoy ella está regular porque está un poco enferma *(sick)*.

Mi familia y yo vivimos en un piso acogedor *(cosy)* en el centro de Santiago. Me gusta mucho mi piso porque es cómodo y hay muchos parques cerca. Mi perro se llama Merlín y es muy cariñoso *(affectionate)*.

Mi mejor amigo se llama Andrés y tiene diez años, igual que yo. Su cumpleaños es el veinte de junio. Él vive en una casa en las afueras de Santiago. Le gusta su casa porque es tranquila y hay muchos árboles *(trees)* alrededor *(all around)*.

Voy al Colegio Manuel Bulnes De Santiago, una escuela pequeña en el centro de la ciudad de Santiago. Me gusta mi escuela porque los profesores son muy buenos y amables. No son severos. Me encanta la educación física, pero es un poco agotadora. Mi asignatura favorita es la literatura porque es muy interesante y me ayuda *(helps me)* a desarrollar *(develop)* mi imaginación. Además, el profesor es divertido y siempre me ayuda.

En mi tiempo libre me gusta ir de tiendas y de paseo con mis amigas. También me gusta jugar a videojuegos con mi hermana mayor e ir a la piscina con mi mejor amiga. Me gusta porque es relajante. No me gusta mucho jugar al ajedrez porque es un poco aburrido. Sin embargo, a mi mejor amiga le encanta el ajedrez. Ella piensa *(thinks)* que es muy interesante y emocionante.

Marta, 10, Argentina

1. Complete the sentences, based on Marta's text

a. Marta is _____ years old.

b. Today she is feeling _____.

c. Carolina is her _____.

d. Carolina is a bit _____ today.

e. Near her flat there are many _____.

f. Her dog is very _____.

g. Andrés is her _____.

h. Marta attends a _____ school in the centre of Santiago.

i. She likes her school because her teachers are _____ and _____.

j. She likes PE but it is a bit _____.

k. Her literature teacher is _____.

l. In her free time she enjoys going shopping and _____ with her friends.

m. She also plays videogames with her _____ sister and goes to the _____ with her _____ friend.

2. Find and correct the 8 mistakes in the below translation of the second last paragraph

I go to *Colegio Manuel Bulnes De Santiago*, a large school in the centre of the city of Santiago. I like my school because the teachers are very hard-working and kind. They aren't silly. I love physics, but it is a bit boring. My favourite subject is literature because it is very fascinating and helps me develop my imagination. Also, the teacher is competent and always listens to me.

3. Find the Spanish equivalent in the last paragraph

a. Free time

b. Shops

c. Older sister

d. Best friend

e. Relaxing

f. Chess

g. Boring

h. Exciting

1. Me llamo Santiago y tengo dieciséis años. Mi cumpleaños es el ocho de septiembre. Soy de España y vivo en Galicia, en el norte de España. Hoy estoy fatal porque estoy muy cansado y estresado. ¡Mi caballo *(horse)* está enfermo *(sick)*!

2. Tengo una hermana menor que se llama Lucía. Lucía tiene dieciocho años y es muy divertida. Hoy ella está fenomenal. Está muy feliz porque es el cumpleaños de su mejor amiga, Marta.

3. Mi familia y yo vivimos en un piso bonito en Pontevedra. Es un pueblo muy bonito en la costa. Me gusta mucho mi piso porque es bastante grande y hay muchas playas cerca. En mi tiempo libre, me gusta nadar *(swim)* en la playa. Mi caballo se llama Paco y es muy grande y fuerte. También me gusta ir de pesca *(go fishing)*.

4. Mi mejor amigo se llama Rafael y tiene quince años, un año menos que yo. Su cumpleaños es el veintisiete de julio. Él vive en una casa en la montaña. Le gusta su casa porque es tranquila y hay un lago *(lake)* bonito cerca de donde vive.

5. Voy al Colexio Público Froebel, un colegio plurilingüe *(multilingual)* en el centro de Pontevedra, cerca del río. En mi colegio aprendemos *(we learn)* en español, en gallego, la lengua de Galicia, y en inglés también. Me encantan las lenguas *(languages)* porque son muy útiles.

6. Me gusta mi colegio porque los profesores son muy interesantes y simpáticos. Me encantan las ciencias, pero a veces son un poco complicadas. Mi asignatura favorita es la geografía porque es muy interesante y me ayuda *(helps me)* a entender *(understand)* mejor el mundo natural.

7. En mi tiempo libre me gusta ir al cine y al centro comercial con mis amigas. También me gusta jugar a las canicas *(marbles)* con mi hermana menor e ir a la playa con mi mejor amigo, Rafael. Me gusta porque es muy divertido. Siempre nos reímos *(we laugh)* mucho. Me gusta mucho leer libros porque es muy interesante. Sin embargo, a mi mejor amiga le encanta tocar la guitarra. Ella piensa *(thinks)* que es muy bonito y divertido.

Santiago, 16, Pontevedra, España

4. Answer the following questions on Santiago's text (paragraphs 1 to 4)

a. How old is Santiago?

b. Where in Spain is Galicia?

c. Why is he not feeling good today?

d. What is wrong with his horse?

e. Why is his younger sister happy?

f. Why does Santiago like his flat? (2)

g. What is his horse like? (2)

h. Where is Rafael's house located?

i. Why does he like his house? (2)

5. Complete the following translation of paragraph 5

I attend Colegio Publico Froebel, a _____ school in the _____ of Pontevedra, near the _____. In my school we learn in _____, in Gallego, the _____ of Galicia and in _____ too. I _____ languages because they are very _____.

6. Find the Spanish equivalent in paragraphs 6

a. I like my school

b. Friendly

c. Sometimes

d. Subject

e. Helps me understand

f. Better

g. The natural world

7. Translate into English the following phrases from paragraph 7

a. En mi tiempo libre

b. Con mis amigas

c. Me gusta jugar

d. Es muy divertido

e. Leer libros

f. Le encanta tocar la guitarra

TERM 1 - BRINGING IT ALL TOGETHER – QUESTION SKILLS

1. Fill in the missing words 🔊

a. ¿Cómo te l_____?

b. ¿C___ e____ hoy?

c. ¿C_____ años tienes?

d. ¿C_____ es tu cumpleaños?

e. ¿T_____ hermanos o hermanas?

f. ¿C___ se l____ tu hermano?

g. ¿C_____ es su cumpleaños?

h. ¿C_____ años t___?

i. ¿D_ d____ eres?

j. ¿D____ vives?

k. ¿Q__ asignaturas estudias?

l. ¿C___ te g____?

m. ¿P__ q__?

n. ¿Q__ te g____ hacer en tu tiempo libre?

2. Listen and choose the option that you hear 🔊

a. Me llamo **Ramona / Paloma / Carlota**

b. Hoy estoy **genial / fatal / regular**

c. Tengo **veintiséis / seis/ dieciséis** años

d. Mi cumpleaños es el **treinta / trece / tres** de septiembre

e. Sí, tengo **un hermano/ una hermana / un primo** menor

f. Mi **hermano / padre / tío** se llama José

g. Tiene **ocho / nueve / diez** años

h. Su cumpleaños es el veinticinco de **enero / febrero / mayo**

i. **Eres / Somos / Soy** de España

j. Vivo en Cádiz, en el **este /sur / norte** de España

k. Estudio **inglés / matemáticas / ciencias**

l. No me gustan las **matemáticas / ciencias / lenguas**

m. En mi tiempo libre me gusta hacer **deporte / natación / equitación**

3. Listen and write in the missing information 🔊

a. ¿ _____ te llamas? *Me _____ Paloma*

b. ¿ _____ estás hoy? *Hoy _____ genial*

c. ¿ _____ años tienes? *Tengo _____ años*

d. ¿ _____ es tu cumpleaños? *Mi cumpleaños es el _____ de _____*

e. ¿ _____ hermanos o hermanas? *Sí, tengo _ _____ menor*

f. ¿ _____ se llama tu hermano? *Mi _____ se _____ José*

g. ¿ _____ años tiene? *Tiene _____ años.*

h. ¿ _____ es su cumpleaños? *Su _____ es el veinticinco de _____*

i. ¿ _ _____ eres? *Soy de _____*

j. ¿ _____ vives? *_____ en Cádiz, en el _____ de España*

k. ¿ _____ asignaturas _____? *_____ ciencias, _____, geografía, y educación _____*

l. ¿ _____ no te gusta? ¿Por qué? *No me _____ las ciencias _____ son demasiado _____*

m. ¿ _ _____ el español? ¿Por qué? *Me encanta el _____ porque es _____ y muy _____ para el _____*

n. ¿ _____ te gusta hacer en tu tiempo libre? *En mi _____ libre me gusta _____ deporte y _____ con mis _____*

TERM 1 - BRINGING IT ALL TOGETHER – QUESTION SKILLS

4. Fill in the grid with your personal information

Question	
1. ¿Cómo te llamas?	
2. ¿Cómo estás hoy?	
3. ¿Cuántos años tienes?	
4. ¿Cuándo es tu cumpleaños?	
5. ¿Tienes hermanos o hermanas?	
6. ¿Cuándo es su cumpleaños?	
7. ¿De dónde eres?	
8. ¿Dónde vives?	
9. ¿Qué asignatura estudias?	
10. ¿Cuál (no) te gusta?	
11. ¿Te gusta _____?	
12. ¿Qué te gusta hacer en tu tiempo libre?	

5. Survey two of your classmates using the same questions as above– write down the main information you hear in Spanish

Q.	Person 1	Person 2
1.		
2.		
3.		
4.		
5.		
6.		
7.		
8.		
9.		
10.		
11.		
12.		

No Snakes No Ladders

TERM 1

7 Nice to meet you	6 I am a bit stressed and angry	5 I am bad because I am tired	4 Today I am great	3 I am well thanks	2 How are you today?	1 Good morning
8 My name is Diego	9 I am ten years old	10 My brother is called Roberto	11 He/she is twelve years old	12 He/she is thirteen years old	13 He/she is fourteen years old	14 He/she is fifteen years old
23 I am from London, the capital of England	22 I am from Cádiz, in Andalucía	21 I live in an ugly flat in the centre	20 I live in a pretty house on the coast	19 His/her birthday is the 20th of October	18 His/her birthday is the 18th of August	17 His/her birthday is the 10th of January
24 At school I study history	25 I like Spanish because it is fun	26 I don't like ICT because it is boring	27 I like it because the teacher (f) is good	28 I like it because I have friends in class	29 I like it because it is useful for the future	30 I like it because I learn a lot

START

15 I am from Madrid, the capital of Spain

16 My friend is called Luisa

FINISH

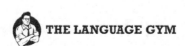 THE LANGUAGE GYM

63

No Snakes No Ladders

TERM 1

7 Mucho gusto	6 Estoy un poco estresado y enfadado	5 Estoy mal porque estoy cansado	4 Hoy estoy fenomenal	3 Estoy bien, gracias	2 ¿Cómo estás hoy?	1 Buenos días
8 Me llamo Diego	9 Tengo diez años	10 Mi hermano se llama Roberto	11 Tiene doce años	12 Tiene trece años	13 Tiene catorce años	14 Tiene quince años
23 Soy de Londres, la capital de Inglaterra	22 Soy de Cádiz, en Andalucía	21 Vivo en un piso feo en el centro	20 Vivo en una casa bonita en la costa	19 Su cumpleaños es el veinte de octubre	18 Su cumpleaños es el dieciocho de agosto	17 Su cumpleaños es el diez de enero
24 En el colegio estudio historia	25 Me gusta el español porque es divertido	26 No me gusta la informática porque es aburrida	27 Me gusta porque la profesora es buena	28 Me gusta porque tengo amigos en clase	29 Me gusta porque es útil para el futuro	30 Me gusta porque aprendo mucho

		15 Soy de Madrid, la capital de España
		SALIDA
		16 Mi amiga se llama Luisa
		LLEGADA

THE LANGUAGE GYM

64

PYRAMID TRANSLATION

Unit 5 Recap – Free Time

Translate each part of the pyramid out loud with your partner, then write it into the spaces provided below.

a. In my free time...

b. In my free time I love to play videogames...

c. In my free time I love to play videogames with my friends...

d. In my free time I love to play videogames with my friends and to do jogging in the park with my brother.

e. In my free time I love to play videogames with my friends and to do jogging in the park with my brother. I also like to go to the shopping centre with my sister.

f. In my free time I love to play videogames with my friends and to do jogging in the park with my brother. I also like to go to the shopping centre with my sister. However, I don't like to go fishing. It is too boring.

Write your translation here:

THE LANGUAGE GYM

One pen One dice

Play in pairs. You only have 1 pen and 1 dice.

One person has the pen and starts translating the sentence into **English.** The other person rolls the dice until they roll a 6, they swap the pen and translate. The winner is the person who finishes translating all the sentences first.

1. Buenas tardes, ¿cómo estás hoy?	
2. Hoy estoy regular porque estoy cansado/a.	
3. Mucho gusto.	
4. Mi hermano se llama Paco.	
5. Su cumpleaños es el 19 de julio.	
6. Soy de Barcelona, en España.	
7. Me gusta la historia porque es interestante.	
8. Me gusta porque tengo amigos/as en clase.	
9. En mi tiempo libre juego al fútbol con mis amigos/as.	
10. También me gusta hacer equitación.	

One pen One dice

Play in pairs. You only have 1 pen and 1 dice.

One person has the pen and starts translating the sentence into **Spanish.** The other person rolls the dice until they roll a 6, they swap the pen and translate. The winner is the person who finishes translating all the sentences first.

1. Good afternoon, how are you today?	
2. Today I am so-so because I am tired.	
3. Nice to meet you.	
4. My brother is called Paco.	
5. His birthday is the 19th July.	
6. I am from Barcelona, in Spain.	
7. I like history because it is interesting.	
8. I like it because I have friends in class.	
9. In my free time I play football with my friends.	
10. I also like to do horseriding.	

THE LANGUAGE GYM

TERM 2 – OVERVIEW

This term you will learn:

Unit 6 - How to talk about your family
• Who is in your family
• How old they are
• How you get on with them

Unit 7 -Describing my hair and eyes (OPTIONAL)
• What colour your hair and eyes are
• What your hair style is like

Unit 8 -Describing myself and another family member
• How to say what your immediate family members are like
• How to describe physical and personality traits
• All the persons of the verb 'Ser' in the present indicative

Unit 9 -Comparing people's appearance & personality
• How to use comparatives: more/less than
• New adjectives to describe people

Unit 10 -Describing my teachers
• How to talk about teachers using adjectives
• Review school subjects
• How to describe positive/negative behaviours

Unit 11 - Saying what I and others do in our free time
• What activities you do and when
• The verbs 'jugar', 'hacer' and 'ir'
• Other free time activities

KEY QUESTIONS

- ¿Cuántas personas hay en tu familia?	*How many people are there in your family?*
- ¿Con quién te llevas bien en tu familia?	*Who do you get on well with in your family?*
- ¿Te llevas mal con alguien?	*Do you get on badly with anyone?*
- ¿Por qué te llevas bien/mal con tu padre?	*Why do you get on well/badly with your dad?*
- ¿Cuántos años tiene tu hermano/a?	*How old is your brother/sister?*
- ¿Cómo es tu hermano/hermana?	*What is your brother/sister like?*
- ¿Cómo tienes el pelo?	*What is your hair like?*
- ¿De qué color son tus ojos?	*What colour are your eyes?*
- ¿Cuántos años tiene?	*How old is he/she?*
- ¿Cuándo es su cumpleaños?	*When is his/her birthday?*
- ¿Te gusta tu profe de inglés?	*Do you like your English teacher?*
- ¿Cuál es tu profesor/a favorito/a?	*Which is your favourite teacher?*
- ¿Hay algún profesor/a que no te gusta? ¿Cuál?	*Is there any teacher you do not like? Which one?*
- ¿Qué profesor siempre te ayuda?	*Which teacher always helps you?*
- ¿Cuál es tu asignatura favorita?	*Which is your favourite subject*
- ¿Qué haces en tu tiempo libre?	*What do you do in your free time?*
- ¿Qué deportes haces?	*What sports do you do?*
- ¿Qué haces cuando hace buen/mal tiempo?	*What do you do when the weather is good/bad?*

UNIT 6
Talking about my family members, saying their age and how well I get on with them. Counting to 100.

**In this unit you will learn
to talk about:**
- How many people there are in your family and who they are
- If you get on well with them
- Words for family members
- What their age is
- Numbers from 31 to 100

You will also revisit
- Numbers from 1 to 31
- Hair and eyes description

UNIT 6
Talking about my family members, saying their age and how well I get on with them. Counting to 100.

¿Cuántas personas hay en tu familia?		*How many people are there in your family?*		
¿Con quién te llevas bien en tu familia?		*Who do you get on well with in your family?*		
¿Te llevas mal con alguien?		*Do you get on badly with anyone?*		
¿Por qué te llevas bien/mal con tu padre?		*Why do you get on well/badly with your dad?*		

			un*		año
	mi abuelo Jaime *my grandfather Jaime*				
	mi padre Juan *my father Juan*		dos		
			tres		
Hay cuatro personas en mi familia *There are four people in my family*	**mi tío Iván** *my uncle Iván*	**Él tiene** *he has*	cuatro		
			cinco		
			seis		
			siete		
	mi hermano mayor *my older brother*		ocho		
			nueve		
			diez		
	mi hermano menor *my younger brother*		once	11	
			doce	12	
En mi familia somos cinco *There are five of us in my family*	**mi primo Ian** *my cousin Ian*		trece	13	
			catorce	14	
			quince	15	
			dieciséis	16	
	mi abuela Adela *my grandmother Adela*		diecisiete	17	años
			dieciocho	18	
			diecinueve	19	
Me llevo bien con *I get on well with*	**mi madre Ángela** *my mother Ángela*		veinte	20	
			veintiún	21	
	mi tía Gina *my aunt Gina*		veintidós	22	
			treinta	30	
		Ella tiene *she has*	treinta y un	31	
Me llevo mal con *I get on badly with*	**mi hermana mayor** *my older sister*		treinta y dos	32	
			cuarenta	40	
			cincuenta	50	
	mi hermana menor *my younger sister*		sesenta	60	
			setenta	70	
			ochenta	80	
	mi prima Clara *my cousin (f) Clara*		noventa	90	
			cien	100	

Author's note:
The number one, "uno", becomes shortened to "un" before a masculine noun. Watch out for it!

1. Fill in the blanks

a. En mi _ _ _ _ _ _ _ hay _ _ _ _ _ personas

b. Mi abuelo tiene _ _ _ _ _ _ años

c. En _ _ familia _ _ _ seis _ _ _ _ _ _ _ _

d. Mi _ _ _ _ _ se llama _ _ _ _ _

e. Me _ _ _ _ _ bien con _ _ hermano _ _ _ _ _

f. Me _ _ _ _ _ _ _ _ con mi _ _ _ _ _

g. Me llevo _ _ _ bien _ _ _ mi _ _ _ _ _

2. Break the flow

a. Haycuatropersonasenmifamilia

b. Mellevobienconmispadres

c. Miabuelotieneochentaaños

d. Mitíotienecuarentaaños

e. Mihermanomayorsellamajuan

f. Enmifamiliahaycincopersonas

g. Mipadretienecuarentaydosaños

3. Multiple choice quiz: select the correct age

	1	2	3
a. Jaime	40	50	60
b. Silvia	90	80	70
c. Juan	30	40	60
d. Pedro	60	70	100
e. Marina	36	46	56
f. Consuelo	65	85	95
g. Enrique	33	63	73
h. Pablo	71	21	41
i. Manuela	57	67	47

4. Spot the intruders: identify the word(s) in each sentence the speaker is NOT saying

a. En mi familia hay cinco mil personas

b. Mi tío Pedro tiene cuarenta y un años

c. Me llevo muy bien con mis padres

d. Mi primo Ian tiene como cincuenta años

e. Mis abuelos maternos tienen ochenta años

f. Yo me llevo fatal con mi primo José

5. Faulty translation: spot the translation errors and correct them

a. My name is Juan Francisco. I am 16 years old.

b. I have blond and long hair.

c. I have green eyes.

d. In my family there are 4 people: my father, my mother, my cousin, my brother and I.

e. My father is 54, my mother is 34.

f. My sister is 9 and my brother is 7.

g. My grandparents are called Roberta and Rafa.

h. My aunt is 51 years old and my uncle is 70.

i. My maternal grandparents are 80 years old.

j. My paternal grandfather is 76.

6. Spot and write in the missing words

a. Hola llamo Dylan.

b. Soy España.

c. Tengo hermano.

d. Mi cumpleaños el veinte de marzo.

e. En mi familia cinco personas.

f. Está mi padre, mi madre, mis hermanos y yo.

g. Yo tengo treinta siete años. Mi madre tiene sesenta y dos años y mi padre sesenta un años.

h. Mi hermano tiene cuarenta años y mi hermano tiene treinta y cinco años.

i. Me llevo bien mis padres.

THE LANGUAGE GYM

7. Narrow listening: gapped translation

My name is Paco. I am from _____. I am _____ years old. My birthday is on _____

_____. I have _____, long and _____ hair. I have _____ eyes. In my family there are

_____ people: my stepfather, my _____ and my two sisters. My older sister is _____ years

old. My younger sister is _____ years old. I _____ with my parents. My maternal _____

lives with us. He is _____ years old. I get on well with him.

8. Listening slalom: follow the speaker from top to bottom and number the boxes accordingly

a. Elena	b. Felipe	c. Maite	d. Javier	e. Juan
My name is Elena	My name is Felipe	My name is Maite	My name is Javier	My name is Juan
I am 17	I am 16	I am 20	I am 11	I am 30
My birthday is on 25th October	My birthday is on 20th June	My birthday is on 31st December	My birthday is on 15th March	My birthday is on 7th January
My mother is 50	My mother is 48	My mother is 44	My mother is 39	My mother is 62
My father is 49	My father is 43	My father is 53	My father is 64	My father is 52
My grandad is 81	My grandad is 75	My grandad is 76	My grandad is 73	My grandad is 90
My grandma is 68	My grandma is 80	My grandma is 81	My grandma is 72	My grandma is 79

9. Narrow listening: listen and fill in the missing details on the grid

Name	Age	Birthday	Family size	Older sibling's age	Mother's age	Father's age
a. Andrea		20th June		16		41
b. Felipe	14		4			44
c. Sofía		15th Sept			43	
d. Eugenio	13		5		39	
e. Myriam	28			31		55

Unit 6. Talking about my family + Counting to 100: VOCAB BUILDING

1. Complete with the missing word

a. En mi f_____ hay...   *In my family there is...*

b. Hay_____ personas   *There are five people*

c. Mi _____ , Jaime   *My grandfather, Jaime*

d. Mi abuelo _____ ochenta años *My grandfather is 80*

e. Mi _____ Ángela   *My mother Ángela*

f. Ella _____ cincuenta años   *She is 50 years old*

g. Me _____ bien con mi hermano   *I get on well with my brother*

2. Match

Dieciséis	12
Doce	48
Veintiún	13
Diez	16
Treinta y tres	10
Trece	21
Cuarenta y ocho	15
Cincuenta y dos	5
Cinco	33
Quince	52

3. Translate into English

a. Me llevo mal con...

b. Mi abuela, Adela

c. Mi tío

d. Hay cuatro personas...

e. En mi familia...

f. Me llevo bien con...

g. Mi padre

h. Tiene veinte años

4. Add the missing letter

a. fa_ilia   c. p _rsonas   e. he _mano   g. ma_re   i. me ll_vo   k. qu__nce

b. te_go   d. a_uelo   f. ma_or   h. p__imo   j. b_en   l. die_

5. Broken words

a. H____ s_____ p_____ e__ m__ f_____

There are 6 people in my family

b. M_ h_____ t____ d_____ a_____

My sister is 12 years old

c. E__ m_ fam_ ten_____...   *In my family I have...*

d. M_ p_____ s___ l_____   *My male cousin is called*

e. M_ p_____ t_____ c_____ y c_____ a_____.

My father is 55 years old

f. M_ l_____ m_____ c__ m_ h_____ m_____

I get on badly with my older brother...

g. M_ l_____ b_____ c__ m_...   *I get on well with my...*

6. Complete with a suitable word

a. En mi _____

b. _____ tres personas

c. Mi hermana _____

d. Tiene catorce _____

e. Mi _____, Gina tiene treinta y cinco años

f. Me llevo _____ con mi padre

g. Hay cuatro _____ en mi familia

h. Me _____ bien con mi abuela

i. No _____ llevo bien con mi tío

j. Mi primo tiene quince _____

k. Me llevo bien _____ mi abuelo

THE LANGUAGE GYM

73

Unit 6. Talking about my family + Counting to 100: VOCABULARY DRILLS

1. Match

En mi	There are
Familia	In my
Hay	With
Siete	Family
Me llevo bien	I get on well
Con	Seven

2. Complete with the missing word

a. _____ cinco personas — *There are five people*

b. Mi _____ Juan tiene sesenta años — *My father, John, is 60*

c. Me _____ bien con mi tío — *I get on well with my uncle*

d. Me llevo _____ con mi... — *I get on badly with my...*

e. Mi tía Gina _____ cuarenta años — *My aunt, Gina, is 40*

f. Él tiene _____ años — *He is 18*

g. _____ tiene veintiséis años — *She is 26*

h. Mi _____ Adela tiene ochenta años — *My gran, Adela is 80*

3. Translate into English

a. Él tiene nueve años

b. Ella tiene cuarenta años

c. Mi padre tiene cuarenta y cuatro años

d. Me llevo mal con mi abuelo

e. Me llevo bien con mi hermano

f. Mi hermana menor tiene cinco años

g. Hay ocho personas en mi familia

h. En mi familia tengo seis personas

4. Complete with the missing letters

a. Mi hermano m_ _or *My older brother*

b. En mi fa_ _lia h_ _ tres personas
In my family there are 3 people

c. Mi primo t_ _ ne dieci_ _ _o años
My cousin is 18

d. Me _ _evo muy m_ _ con mi hermano
I get on very badly with my brother

e. Mi t_ _ tiene cuarenta _ñ_s
My uncle is 40 years old

f. _ _ llevo muy bi_ _ con mi prima
I get on very well with my cousin

g. Mi pr_ _a t_ _ne q_ _nce años
My cousin is 15 years old

h. Me llevo regular con _ _ _ _
I get on so so with her

i. ¿Cómo e_ _ _ tú? *What are you like?*

5. Translate into Spanish

a. In my family

b. There are

c. My father...

d. is 40 years old

e. I get on well...

f. ...with

6. Spot and correct the errors

a. En mi familia hoy tres personas

b. Mi abela Adela

c. Mi hermano tene nueve años

d. Me lavo mal con mi primo

e. Mi primo tiene ocho anos

f. Mi hermano major, Darren

Unit 6. Talking about my family + Counting to 100: TRANSLATION

1. Match

Veinte	30
Treinta	70
Cuarenta	100
Cincuenta	50
Sesenta	20
Ochenta	80
Noventa	40
Cien	60
Setenta	90

3. Write in the missing number

a. Tengo _____ y un años   *I am 31*

b. Mi padre tiene _____ y siete años   *My dad is 57*

c. Mi madre tiene _____ y ocho años   *My mum is 48*

d. Mi abuelo _____ años   *My grandad is 100*

e. Mi tío tiene _____ y dos años   *My uncle is 62*

f. Tienen _____ años   *They are 90*

g. Mis primos tienen _____ y cuatro años   *My cousins are 44*

h. ¿Tiene _____ años?   *Is he/she 70?*

2. Write out in Spanish

a. 35 treinta y cinco

b. 63 s

c. 89 o

d. 74 s

e. 98 n

f. 100 c

g. 82 o

h. 24 v

i. 17 d

4. Correct the translation errors

a. *My father is forty*   mi padre tiene catorce años

b. *My mother is fifty-two*   mi madre tiene cincuenta años

c. *We are forty-two*   tenemos cuarenta dos años

d. *I am forty-one*   tengo treinta y un años

e. *They are thirty-four*   tienen treinta y dos años

5. Translate into Spanish (please write out the numbers in letters)

a. In my family there are 6 people:

b. My mother is called Susana and is 43:

c. My father is called Pedro and is 48:

d. My older sister is called Juanita and is 31:

e. My younger sister is called Amparo and is 18:

f. I am called Arantxa and am 27:

g. My grandfather is called Antonio and is 87:

Unit 6. Talking about my family + Counting to 100: WRITING

1. Spot and correct the spelling mistakes

a. quarenta   *cuarenta*

b. treintaiuno

c. ocenta y dos

d. veinte y uno

e. nuevanta

f. sien

g. septenta

h. dieciseis

3. Rearrange the sentence below in the correct word order

a. mi En cuatro familia personas hay
In my family there are four people

b. bien con llevo mi No hermano me
I don't get on well with my brother

c. padre Mi se llama dos Miguel y cincuenta tiene y años
My father is called Miguel and is fifty-two

d. padre y mi yo En familia mi mi madre, hay personas: tres
In my family there are three people: my mother, my father and I

e. se Mi primo y años Paco siete llama y treinta tiene
My cousin is called Paco and is thirty-seven

f. abuelo, y años Fernando y Mi siete ochenta tiene se llama
My grandfather is called Fernando and is eighty-seven

2. Complete with the missing letters

a. Mi m__dre ti__ne cuar__nta año_

b. Mi pad__e tie__e cin__enta y un a___os

c. Mis abu___los tienen oc__enta añ___s

d. M__ her__ana meno__ t__ene ve__nte añ_ _

e. __i ab__ela t_ _ n __ no__enta a _ _ _ _

f. Mi h_ __m__ __o ma__or t__ne treint__ __ñ__ __

4. Complete

a. In my family: E__ m__ f_____

b. There are: H_____

c. Who is called: Q_____ s___ l_____

d. My mother: M__ m_____

e. My father: M__ p_____

f. He is fifty: T_____ c_____ a_____

g. I am sixty: T_____ s_____ a_____

h. He is forty: T_____ c_____ a_____

5. Write a relationship sentence for each person as shown in the example

e.g. Mi mejor amigo, que se llama Paco, tiene quince años

Name	Relationship to me	Age	How I get on with them
e.g. Paco	*Best friend*	*15*	*Very well*
Steve (Smith)	Father	57	Well
Ana	Mother	45	Very badly
Arantxa	Aunt	60	Quite well
Andrés	Uncle	67	Not well
Miquel	Grandfather	75	Very well

TERM 2 - BRINGING IT ALL TOGETHER – 6

1. Me llamo Laura y tengo ocho años. Mi cumpleaños es el tres de abril. Soy de Palencia, en España, pero vivo en París, la capital de Francia. Hoy me siento bastante bien. Estoy muy contenta porque después voy a ir a casa de mis abuelos. Me gusta mucho mi abuela porque es muy simpática y siempre me da *(gives me)* caramelos *(sweets)*.

2. En mi familia hay cinco personas: mi hermano mayor Julio, mi hermana menor Julia, mi padre Juan, mi madre Ángela, y yo. También tengo un perro blanco que se llama Lily. Mi abuelo se llama Jaime y tiene ochenta años y mi abuela se llama Elena y tiene setenta y nueve años. Mis abuelos son muy pacientes y amables.

3. Mi hermano mayor se llama Julio. A Julio le encanta cantar y tocar la guitarra. Tiene trece años y es muy gracioso. Su cumpleaños es el tres de julio. Creo que se llama Julio porque nació en julio.

4. Mi familia y yo vivimos en una casa bonita en las afueras de París. No me gusta mi casa porque no es muy moderna y no hay tiendas ni restaurantes cerca. Es muy aburrido. Sin embargo, tengo un jardín con muchas flores, es mi espacio favorito de mi casa. En mi tiempo libre, me gusta patinar en el parque. Mi mejor amiga se llama Luisa y también le gusta patinar conmigo en el parque. Es muy divertido.

5. Voy a un colegio muy grande en mi barrio *(neighbourhood)*. Me gusta mi colegio porque los profesores son amables y divertidos. Sin embargo, no me llevo bien con mi profesora de música porque es un poco impaciente. Mi asignatura favorita es matemáticas porque me gusta resolver problemas y tengo amigos en clase.

Laura, 8, Palencia, España

1. Find the Spanish equivalent in paragraph 1

a. I am from: S

b. But: P

c. I live: V

d. Today: H

e. I feel: M

f. Happy: C

g. Afterwards: D

h. I am going: V

i. Friendly: S

j. Gives me: M

2. Complete the statements below about Laura's family based on paragraphs 2 and 3

a. In Laura's family there are _____ people

b. Her younger sister is called _____

c. Lily is their _____ and she is _____ (colour)

d. Her grandparents are very patient and _____

e. Julio loves to _____ and _____

f. He is _____ years old and is very _____

g. She thinks he is called Julio because _____ _____ _____ ___ _____

3. Answer the following questions (in English) about paragraph 4

a. Where in Paris do they live?

b. Why does she not like her house? (3)

c. What is there in her garden?

d. What part of her house does she like the most?

e. What sport does she enjoy doing in the park?

f. What does she have in common with Luisa?

4. Answer the following questions on paragraph 5 (in Spanish) as if you were Laura

a. ¿Cómo es tu colegio?

b. ¿Dónde está tu colegio?

c. ¿Por qué te gusta tu colegio?

d. ¿Por qué no te llevas bien con tu profesora de música?

e. ¿Cuál es tu asignatura favorita? ¿Por qué?

 **THE LANGUAGE GYM**

Me llamo Luna y tengo diez años. Mi cumpleaños es el tres de abril. Soy de Córdoba, en España, pero vivo en Berlín, la capital de Alemania. Hoy me siento regular. Estoy más o menos *(more or less)* contenta pero estoy muy cansada. Después voy a ir a un restaurante con mis padres. Me llevo bien con mi madre porque es muy simpática y siempre me escucha *(listens to me)*.

En mi familia hay cinco personas: mi hermano mayor, Carlos, mi hermana menor, Andrea, mi padre, Alejandro, mi madre, Marta, y yo. También tenemos un perro blanco que se llama Nieve. Mi abuelo se llama Rafael y tiene ochenta y cinco años, mientras que mi abuela se llama Carmen y tiene setenta y seis años. Mis abuelos son muy amables y cariñosos.

Mi hermano mayor se llama Ángel. A Ángel le apasiona la pintura y tocar el piano. Tiene catorce años y es muy inteligente. Su cumpleaños es el veintidós de agosto. Mi hermano siempre es muy bueno y siempre me ayuda, ¡es un ángel de verdad!

Mi familia y yo vivimos en una casa grande en las afueras de Berlín. No me gusta mi casa porque es demasiado grande. No hay muchas tiendas ni restaurantes en mi barrio, es una pena *(a shame)*. Sin embargo, tengo un parque con muchos árboles cerca de mi casa. Es mi lugar *(place)* favorito para leer libros. En mi tiempo libre, me gusta patinar en el parque. Mi mejor amiga se llama Marisa y también le gusta leer libros conmigo en el parque.

Voy a un colegio pequeño en mi barrio. Me gusta mi colegio porque los profesores son muy graciosos y tengo muchos amigos. Sin embargo, no me llevo bien con mi profesora de inglés. ¡Siempre me chilla! Mi asignatura favorita es el arte porque soy una persona bastante creativa. Me gusta pintar y dibujar animales.

Luna, 10, Córdoba, España

5. Arrange the following information in the same order as it occurs in the text

Luna's birthday is on 3rd April	
Her grandparents are very kind	
Her name is Luna and she is 16	**1**
Her brother always helps her	
There aren't many restaurants in her area	
Luna lives in Germany	
There is a park near her house	
Her school is small	
Luna gets on well with her mother	
In her free time she goes skating	
They live in a big house	
They have a white dog	
Her older brother loves painting	

6. Identify the false statements about her school (last paragraph) and correct them

a. Luna's school is big

b. Luna doesn't like her teachers

c. Luna has friends in the school

d. Luna doesn't get on well with her French teacher

e. Her English teacher always mocks her

f. Luna likes art

g. Luna is quite a creative person

h. She loves to take photos of animals

7. Circle and translate into English the 5 words on the list below which are found in Luna's text

a. demasiado   d. para   g. delante

b. cerca   e. por   h. nunca

c. lejos   f. mientras   i. siempre

8. The following phrases have been copied incorrectly from Luna's text. Can you fix them?

a. En mi tiempo libro   e. Con muchos arboles

b. No mi gusta mi casa   f. Tengo muchos amigo

c. Mi mejora amiga   g. Mi hermano major

d. Mi favorita asignatura   h. Es muy simpatica

UNIT 7
Describing hair and eyes

In this unit you will learn:

- To describe what a person's hair and eyes are like
- To describe details about their faces (e.g. beard and glasses)
- Colours
- I wear
- He/she wears

You will also revisit:
- Common Spanish names
- The verb "Tener" in the first and third person singular
- Numbers from 1 to 16

UNIT 7
Describing hair and eyes

¿Cómo te llamas?	*What is your name?*	¿Cuántos años tienes?	*How old are you?*
¿Cómo tienes el pelo?	*What is your hair like?*	¿De qué color son tus ojos?	*What colour are your eyes?*

¿Cómo se llama?	*What is his/her name?*	¿Cuántos años tiene?	*How old is he/she?*
¿Cómo tiene el pelo?	*What is his/her hair like?*	¿De qué color son sus ojos?	*What colour are his/her eyes?*

Me llamo *My name is* **Mi hermano se llama** *My brother's name is* **Mi hermana se llama** *My sister's name is*	**Antonio** **Carlos** **Diego** **Emilia** **Isabel** **Jaume** **José** **Julián** **María** **Paloma** **Verónica**	**y** *and*	**tengo** *I have* **tiene** *he/she has*	**seis años** — *6 years* **siete años** — *7 years* **ocho años** — *8 years* **nueve años** — *9 years* **diez años** — *10 years* **once años** — *11 years* **doce años** — *12 years* **trece años** — *13 years* **catorce años** — *14 years* **quince años** — *15 years* **dieciséis años** — *16 years*

Tengo el pelo *I have ... hair* **Tiene el pelo** *He/She has ... hair*	**blanco** — *white* **castaño** — *brown* **gris** — *grey* **moreno** — *dark brown* **negro** — *black* **rubio** — *blond*	**y**	**a media melena** — *medium length* **corto** — *short* **en punta** — *spiky* **largo** — *long* **liso** — *straight* **rapado** — *very short / crew-cut* **rizado** — *curly* **ondulado** — *wavy*

Soy *I am* **Es** *He/she is*	**moreno/a** — *(a) brunette* **pelirrojo/a** — *(a) redhead* **rubio/a** — *(a) blond/blonde*

Tengo los ojos *I have ... eyes* **Tiene los ojos** *He/She has ... eyes*	**azules** — *blue* **grises** — *grey* **marrones** — *brown* **negros** — *black* **verdes** — *green*	**y**	**(no) llevo** *I don't wear* **(no) lleva** *he/she doesn't wear*	**gafas** *glasses* **bigote** *a moustache* **barba** *a beard*

1. Fill in the blanks

a. Soy p_ _ _ _ _ _ _ _ .

b. Mi hermano _ _ _ _ _ el pelo _ _ _ _ _ _ .

c. Tengo _ _ _ ojos _ _ _ _ _ _ .

d. Antonio _ _ _ _ _ el _ _ _ _ rubio y los ojos
_ _ _ _ _ _ .

e. _ _ hermana _ _ _ _ _ gafas.

f. Tengo _ _ _ _ _ _ corto y en _ _ _ _ _ .

g. Tengo los _ _ _ _ marrones y _ _ _ _ _ barba.

2. Break the flow

a. Tengoelpelomorenoyliso

b. Tienelosojosazulesygrandes

c. Tieneelpelomorenoyamediamelena

d. Tieneelpelocastaño,largoyrizado

e. Notienepelo

f. Tienelosojosnegrosyllevagafas

g. Tienelosojosmarronesyllevabigote

3. Arrange in the correct order

My name is Fran	1
I am twelve years old	
My birthday is on 30th March	
I have dark brown, straight, short, hair	
I am from Valladolid, in Spain	
He is blond and has green eyes	
He is fifteen years old	
His birthday is on 14th March	
I have a brother	

4. Spot the intruders: identify the word in each sentence the speaker is NOT saying

a. Tengo el pelo muy largo.

b. Tengo el pelo a la media melena.

c. Mi padre tiene el pelo bastante corto.

d. Mi madre no tiene el pelo largo.

e. Mi hermano menor tiene el pelo rubio.

f. Mi hermana tiene el pelo moreno en punta.

5. Listen, spot and correct the errors

a. Te llamo Silvia

b. Tengo dieciséis años

c. Soy de Argentina

d. …pero vivo en Escocia

e. Tengo el pelo rubio y los ojos marrones

f. Tengo el pelo largo y ondulado

g. Mi mejor amiga, Kat, tiene catorce años

h. Es guapa. Tiene el pelo rubio, muy largo y liso

i. Tiene los ojos grises y lleva gafas

6. Fill in the blanks

a. Tengo el pelo en pun_____

b. Tengo el pelo casta_____

c. Tengo los ojos ne_____

d. Tengo el pelo lar_____

e. Tengo los ojos azu_____

f. No llevo ga_____

g. No llevo bigo_____

h. Llevo bar_____

i. Mi padre lle_____ bigote

j. Mi hermano tiene los ojos gri_____

7. Narrow listening: gapped translation

My name is Verónica, I am _____ years old. My birthday is on the_____ of

_____. In my family there are _____ people: my father, my mother, my two

_____ and me. My mother has _____, _____ and curly hair. She has

_____ eyes. My father has grey, _____ and straight hair. He has _____ eyes.

My two sisters have _____, long and straight hair. They both have _____ eyes. I have

brown, _____ hair. However, before, I used to have it _____.

8. Fill in the grid in English

Name	Age	Birthday	Siblings	Hair (3 details)	Eyes
a. Mario	12		one brother one sister		brown
b. Andrea		20th June		dark brown, long, wavy	
c. Andrés	16		two brothers		blue
d. Eugenio		8th March		dark brown, short, spiky	
e. Alfonso		19th May			

9. Translate the ten sentences you hear into English

a.   f.

b.   g.

c.   h.

d.   i.

e.   j.

Unit 7. Describing hair and eyes: VOCABULARY BUILDING

1. Complete with the missing word

a. Tengo el pelo c_____   *I have brown hair*

b. Soy r_____   *I am a blonde lady*

c. Llevo _____   *I wear* a beard*

d. Tengo los ojos a_____   *I have blue eyes*

e. No llevo g_____   *I don't wear glasses*

f. Tengo el pelo a med___ mel_____   *I have mid-length hair*

g. Tengo los ojos n_____   *I have black/dark eyes*

h. Soy p_____   *I am a redhead (m)*

2. Match

El pelo castaño	Brown hair
El pelo moreno	Grey eyes
El pelo rubio	Moustache
Los ojos grises	Green eyes
Las gafas	Dark brown hair
El bigote	Short hair
Los ojos azules	Long hair
Los ojos verdes	Red hair
El pelo corto	Blond hair
El pelo largo	Glasses
Pelirrojo	Blue eyes

3. Translate into English

a. El pelo rizado

b. Los ojos azules

c. Llevo gafas

d. El pelo rubio

e. Los ojos verdes

f. Vero es pelirroja

g. Los ojos grises

h. El pelo moreno

4. Add the missing letter

a. La_go   c. _elo   e. Azu_   g. Riza_o   i. More_o   k. O_os

b. Ga_as   d. Bigo_e   f. V_rdes   h. _iso   j. A media me_ena   l. Lle_o

5. Broken words

a. T_____ e__ p_____ r_____   *I have curly hair*

b. L_____ g_____   *I wear glasses*

c. _e_____ _l _____o c_____   *I have short hair*

d. N_ l_____ b_____   *I don't have a moustache*

e. _____o ____s o_____ marrones   *I have brown eyes*

f. ____v__ b_____   *I have a beard*

g. T_____ o_____ a____   *I am eight years old*

h. M__ l_____ M_____   *My name is María*

i. ____n__ n_____ a____   *I am nine years old*

6. Complete with a suitable word

a. Tengo diez _____

b. _____ barba

c. Me _____ Antonio Ruiz

d. Llevo _____

e. Tengo el _____ liso y corto

f. _____ llevo gafas

g. Tengo ____ ojos marrones

h. Tengo ____ pelo negro

i. No _____ bigote

j. _____ rubia

k. ____ llamo Pedro Ximénez

l. Tengo _____ años

Unit 7. Describing hair and eyes: READING

Me llamo Marta. Tengo doce años y vivo en Buenos Aires, la capital de Argentina. Tengo el pelo negro, liso y corto y los ojos azules. Llevo gafas. Mi cumpleaños es el diez de septiembre. Mi hermana tiene el pelo liso. Ella tiene diez años.

Me llamo Inma. Tengo quince años y vivo en La Paz, la capital de Bolivia. Soy pelirroja y tengo el pelo ondulado y largo y los ojos azules. No llevo gafas. Mi cumpleaños es el quince de diciembre.

Me llamo Alejandro. Tengo nueve años y vivo en Santiago, la capital de Chile. Tengo el pelo castaño, ondulado y a media melena y los ojos marrones. No llevo gafas. Mi cumpleaños es el cinco de diciembre. Mi hermano se llama Travis. Tiene quince años. Es pelirrojo y tiene el pelo largo y liso y los ojos azules. Lleva gafas. Su cumpleaños es el trece de noviembre. Es muy musculoso.

Me llamo Alina. Tengo ocho años y vivo en Quito, la capital de Ecuador. Tengo el pelo castaño, largo y rizado y los ojos verdes. Llevo gafas. Mi cumpleaños es el nueve de mayo. En mi casa tengo tres animales: un caballo, un perro y un gato. Mi hermano se llama Sergio. Tiene catorce años. Tiene el pelo rubio, largo y liso y los ojos verdes, como yo. También lleva gafas, como mi padre. Su cumpleaños es el dos de junio. Es muy inteligente.

Me llamo Pablo. Tengo diez años y vivo en Madrid, la capital de España. Tengo el pelo rubio, liso y corto y los ojos verdes. Llevo gafas. Mi cumpleaños es el ocho de abril.

1. Find the Spanish for the following items in Marta's text

a. I am called:

b. In:

c. I wear glasses:

d. My birthday is:

e. The tenth of:

f. I have:

g. Straight:

h. Black:

i. The eyes:

2. Answer the following questions about Inma's text

a. How old is she?

b. Where is La paz?

c. What colour is her hair?

d. Is her hair wavy, straight or curly?

e. What length is her hair?

f. What colour are her eyes?

g. When is her birthday?

3. Complete with the missing words

Me llamo Pedro. _____ diez años y vivo _____ Caracas, la _____ de Venezuela. Tengo el _____ rubio, liso y corto y los _____ verdes. _____ gafas. Mi cumpleaños ___ el ocho _____ abril.

4. Answer the questions below about all five texts

a. Who has a brother called Sergio?

b. Who is eight years old?

c. Who celebrates their birthday on 9 May?

d. How many people wear glasses?

e. Who has red hair and blue-coloured eyes?

f. Who has a very intelligent brother?

g. Whose birthday is in April?

h. Who has brown, wavy hair and brown eyes?

Unit 7. Describing hair and eyes: TRANSLATION

1. Faulty translation: spot and correct (in the English) any translation mistakes you find

a. Tengo el pelo gris: *I have grey eyes*

b. Tiene los ojos azules: *He/she has brown eyes*

c. Llevo barba: *He has a beard*

d. Se llama Pedro: *I am called Pedro*

e. Tiene el pelo rapado: *I have long hair*

f. Tengo los ojos verdes: *I have green eyes*

g. Vivo en Madrid: *I am from Madrid*

2. From Spanish to English

a. Tengo el pelo rubio

b. Tengo los ojos grises

c. Tiene el pelo liso

d. Lleva gafas y barba

e. Llevo bigote

f. Llevo gafas de sol

g. No llevo barba

h. Tengo el pelo rizado

i. Tengo el pelo largo

3. Phrase-level translation

a. 'The' blond hair

b. I am called

c. I have

d. 'The' blue eyes

e. 'The' straight hair

f. He/she has

g. Ten years

h. I have black eyes

i. I have nine years

j. 'The' brown eyes

k. 'The' dark brown hair

4. Sentence-level translation

a. My name is Mark. I am ten years old. I have dark brown and curly hair and blue eyes.

b. I am twelve years old. I have green eyes and blond, straight hair.

c. I am called Ana. I live in Madrid. I have long blond hair and brown eyes.

d. My name is Pedro. I live in Argentina. I have dark brown, very short and wavy hair.

e. I am fifteen years old. I have dark brown, curly long hair and green eyes.

f. I am thirteen years old. I am a redhead (f) and I have straight long hair and brown eyes.

 **THE LANGUAGE GYM**

Unit 7. Describing hair and eyes: WRITING

1. Split sentences

Tengo el pelo	ojos verdes
Llevo	barba
Tengo los	rubio
Tengo el	y rizado
Tengo el pelo rubio	pelo negro
Me llamo	años
Tengo diez	Marta

2. Rewrite the sentences in the correct order

a. pelo el tengo rizado

b. llevo no barba

c. llamo me Ricardo

d. pelo soy pelirrojo largo y tengo el

e. se hermano llama Pablo mi

3. Spot and correct the grammar and spelling errors

a. Tengo los ojo negros

b. Mi hermano me llaman Antonio

c. Tiene pelo rizado

d. Se llamo Marta

e. Tengo catorce anos

f. Tengo el liso pelo

g. Tengo el ojos verdes

h. Llevo barbas

i. Llevo gafa

j. Llebo no bigote

4. Anagrams

a. lope pelo

b. rbaba

c. joso

d. soña

e. zulase

f. bioru

g. grosne

h. zadori

5. Guided writing: write 3 short paragraphs in the first person singular (I) describing the people below

Name	Age	Hair	Eyes	Glasses	Beard	Moustache
Luis	12	Brown Curly Long	Green	Wears	Does not have	Has
Ana	11	Blond Straight Short	Blue	Doesn't wear	Does not have	Does not have
Alejo	10	Redhead Wavy Medium-length	Black	Wears	Has	Does not have

6. Describe this person in the third person:

Name: Jorge

Age: 15

Hair: Black, curly, very short

Eyes: Brown

Glasses: No

Beard: Yes

TERM 2 - BRINGING IT ALL TOGETHER – 7

1. Me llamo Ángela y tengo dieciocho años. Mi cumpleaños es el veinticinco de julio. Soy de Gibraltar. Vivo aquí con mi familia y mi gato, el Señor Bigotes. Hoy estoy muy feliz porque es el cumpleaños de mi gato. Más tarde voy a ir a la playa con mis padres y mi hermano Carlos. Me encanta nadar en el mar con él.

2. En mi familia somos cinco personas: mi hermano mayor, Carlos, mi hermana menor, Rosa, mi padre, Luca, mi madre, Isabela, y yo. También tenemos un gato que se llama Señor Bigotes. Mi padre es rubio y tiene el pelo largo y liso. No lleva barba. Mi madre es pelirroja y tiene el pelo a media melena. Es muy guapa y simpática.

3. Mi gato, el Señor Bigotes, es pequeño y blanco. Es muy divertido pero a veces es un poco malo. Tiene ocho años y es muy tranquilo. Su cumpleaños es el once de octubre. Su comida favorita es el pollo *(chicken)* y el pescado *(fish)*. Es inteligente pero muy tímido.

4. Mi hermana menor Rosa es muy mona y bastante inteligente. Tiene los ojos verdes y el pelo corto y ondulado. Es muy graciosa y siempre me hace reír *(makes me laugh)*. En el colegio su asignatura favorita es la química porque se lleva muy bien con el profe. Los dos tienen buena... química. No le gusta el arte porque piensa que no es muy útil.

5. Vivo con mi familia y el Señor Bigotes (realmente el gato es parte de la familia) en un piso pequeño en un edificio bastante moderno en el centro de Gibraltar. Me encanta mi piso porque es bonito y tengo muchos libros en mi dormitorio. Hay muchas playas bonitas en Gibraltar. Siempre voy a la playa en autobús con mi mejor amiga, Simona. Mi playa favorita se llama la Caleta.

6. En mi tiempo libre, me gusta descansar y ver series en Netflix. Cuando hace buen tiempo *(nice weather)* me gusta salir *(go out)* con mis amigos al centro de la ciudad y comprar ropa *(clothes)* en el centro comercial. También me gusta hacer actividades al aire libre como hacer footing en el parque y jugar al tenis. Me encanta la comida italiana, y mi plato favorito es la pizza margarita.

Ángela, 18, Gibraltar

1. Complete the following translation of the first paragraph

My name is Ángela and I am _____ years old. My birthday is on the _____ July. I am _____ Gibraltar. I live here with my _____ and my _____, Mr. Whiskers. Today I am very _____ because it is my _____ _____. Later I am going to go to _____ with my _____ and my _____ Carlos. I love _____ in the _____ with him.

2. Answer (in English) the questions below on paragraphs 2, 3 and 4

a. Who is Isabela?

b. What is her cat's name?

c. Who has long straight blond hair?

d. Who likes chicken and is sometimes a bit bad?

e. Who makes Ángela laugh?

f. Who does Rosa have good chemistry with?

g. What does Rosa think about art?

3. Find the 9 mistakes in the following translation of paragraph 5

I live with my family and Mrs. Whiskers (the dog is really part of the family) in a small flat in a quite old building in the outskirts of Gibraltar. I love my flat because it's clean and I have a lot of freedom in my bedroom. There are many beautiful trees in Gibraltar. I never go to the beach by bus with my best friend, Simona. My favourite mountain is called *la Caleta*.

4. Find the Spanish equivalent for the items below in paragraphs 5 & 6

a. A small flat

b. I have many books

c. There are many...

d. Beautiful beaches

e. My favourite beach

f. I like to rest

g. I like to go out

h. To the city centre

i. I love Italian food

j. My favourite dish

THE LANGUAGE GYM

UNIT 8
Describing myself and another family member: physical and personality

In this unit you will learn:

- What your immediate family members are like
- Useful adjectives to describe them
- The third person of the verb 'Ser'(to be): 'es' (he is)
- All the persons of the verb 'Tener' in the present indicative

You will also revisit
- Numbers from 1 to 31
- Hair and eyes description

UNIT 8
Describing myself and another family member

¿Cuántas personas hay en tu familia?	*How many people are there in your family?*
¿Cómo es tu padre/madre?	*What is your father/mother like?*
¿Te llevas bien con tu hermano/a?	*Do you get on well with your brother/sister?*

En mi familia hay cuatro personas	*In my family there are four people*
Hay cinco personas en mi familia	*There are five people in my family*

Me gusta *I like* **No me gusta** *I don't like*	**mi abuelo Jaime** *my grandfather Jaime* **mi hermano mayor** *my older brother* **mi hermano menor** *my younger brother* **mi padre Juan** *my father Juan* **mi perro/gato** *my dog/cat* **mi primo Ian** *my cousin Ian* **mi tío Iván** *my uncle Iván*	**porque** *because*	**es** *he/she is* **es bastante** *he/she is quite*	**alto** *tall* **amable** *kind* **bajo** *short* **bueno** *good* **delgado** *slim* **fuerte** *strong* **gordo** *fat* **guapo** *handsome* **antipático** *mean* **divertido** *fun* **generoso** *generous* **inteligente** *clever* **simpático** *nice* **terco** *stubborn* **tranquilo** *calm*
Me llevo bien con *I get on well with* **Me llevo mal con** *I get on badly with*	**mi abuela Adela** *my grandmother Adela* **mi hermana menor** *my younger sister* **mi hermana mayor** *my older sister* **mi madre Ángela** *my mother Ángela* **mi prima Clara** *my cousin Clara* **mi tía Gina** *my aunt Gina* **mi tortuga** *my turtle*		**es muy** *he/she is very* **es un poco** *he/she is a bit*	**alta** **amable** **baja** **buena** **delgada** **fuerte** **gorda** **guapa** **antipática** **divertida** **generosa** **inteligente** **simpática** **terca** **tranquila**

THE LANGUAGE GYM

1. Multiple choice quiz: select which adjective you hear

		a	b	c
a.	My father is...	generous	mean	patient
b.	My older sister is...	silly	fun	muscular
c.	My mother is...	fat	intelligent	thin
d.	My younger sister is...	tall	short	pretty
e.	My cousin Pablo is...	big	strong	small
f.	My brother is not...	ugly	mean	friendly
g.	My cousin Marta is...	lazy	bad	boring
h.	My grandad is a bit...	mean	stubborn	annoying
i.	My grandma is...	generous	good	fun
j.	My boyfriend is...	patient	fat	muscular

2. Split sentences: listen and match

a. Jaime	1. Fun
b. Silvia	2. Boring
c. Juan	3. Short
d. Pedro	4. Tall
e. Marina	5. Good-looking
f. Consuelo	6. Bad
g. Enrique	7. Muscular
h. Pablo	8. Ugly
i. Paola	9. Stubborn
j. Manolo	10. Strong

3. Spot the intruders: identify the word in each sentence the speaker is NOT saying

a. Mi hermano es muy guapo.

b. Mi tío Pedro tiene cuarenta y un años. Es bastante divertido.

c. Me llevo muy bien con mi padre porque es paciente y generoso.

d. Mi primo Ian no es muy alto.

e. Mi padre es de la estatura media.

f. Mi novia es demasiado habladora.

g. Yo soy alto, musculoso y fuerte.

4. Spot the differences and correct the text

a. Mi abuela es muy paciente.

b. Mi madre es muy inteligente.

c. En mi familia hay cinco personas: mi madre, mi padre, mis dos hermanos y yo.

d. ¿Cómo estás?

e. Mi tío tiene sesenta años pero es muy aburrido.

f. Me llevo mal con mis padres, especialmente con mi madre porque es muy antipática.

g. En mi familia somos todos bajos.

5. Categories: listen to the words below and classify them in positive and negative

ADJETIVOS POSITIVOS	ADJETIVOS NEGATIVOS

6. Faulty translation: spot and correct the translation errors

a. My name is Ana del Casar. I am 16 years old. I have dark brown hair and green eyes. I am tall, muscular and quite good-looking. I am nice, talkative and quite generous.

b. My mother is called Paola. She is 55 years old. She is short, slim and very funny. She is generous but a bit mean.

c. My father is called Roberto. He is 63 years old. He is neither tall nor short. He is very generous, mean and impatient.

d. My sister is called Carmen. She is 17. She is quite tall and slim, but sometimes a bit mean and boring. She is also quite funny and lazy.

e. I also have a cat. It is very beautiful, but it is funny.

7. Listen and complete with the correct masculine/feminine ending

a. Es muy simpátic_ .

b. Son muy terc_ _ .

c. Mi madre y mi padre son muy alt_ _ .

d. Soy baj_ y pacient_ .

e. ¡Qué gracios_ eres!

f. ¡Qué mal_ _ son!

g. Mis herman_ _ son muy trabajador_ _ .

h. ¡Qué divertid_ eres!

8. Listening slalom: follow the speaker from top to bottom and number the boxes accordingly

a. Nina	b. Manuela	c. Juan Carlos	d. Ana
My name is Nina	My name is Manuela	My name is Juan Carlos	My name is Ana
I am 15 years old	I am 17 years old and	I am 13 years old	I am 12 years old
I am tall and slim	I am neither tall nor short	I am not very tall	I am short and slim
My older sister is short and slim	My older sister is short and very pretty	My younger brother is short and slim	My younger brother is tall and strong
I love her	I get on very well with him	I get on well with him	I like her a lot
because he is nice and positive	because she is generous	because she is fun	because he is patient and helpful. Also,
and kind.	Also, he is very funny.	he is very generous and kind.	and funny.

9. Narrow listening: fill in the grid

Name	Name of older sibling	Age of older sibling	Birthday of older sibling	Character of older sibling	Appearance of older sibling
a. Felipe					
b. Andrea					
c. Eugenio					
d. Melania					

Unit 8. Describing my family: VOCABULARY BUILDING

1. Match

Soy simpático	I am fun
Soy antipático	I am slim
Soy terco	I am generous
Soy guapo	I am mean
Soy divertido	I am nice
Soy generoso	I am short
Soy fuerte	I am strong
Soy malo	I am good-looking
Soy bajo	I am bad
Soy alto	I am tall
Soy delgado	I am stubborn

2. Complete

a. Mi hermano menor es d_____
My younger brother is slim

b. Mi padre es a_____
My father is mean

c. Mi hermana mayor es t_____
My older sister is stubborn

d. Soy m_____ *I am muscular*

e. Mi hermano mayor es d_____
My older brother is fun

f. Mi amigo Paco es f_____
My friend Paco is strong

3. Categories: sort the adjectives below in the categories provided

a. fuerte; b. musculoso; c. simpático; d. terco; e. guapo;
f. inteligente; g. paciente; h. malo; i. generoso; j. aburrido;
k. gordo; l. feo; m. divertido

El físico	La personalidad

4. Complete the words

a. Soy aburr_ _ _ (m)

b. Soy f_ _ (m)

c. Soy muscu_ _ _ _ (f)

d. Soy te _ _ _ (m)

e. Soy ma_ _ (f)

f. Soy gua_ _ (m)

g. Soy sim_ _ _ _ _ _ (f)

h. Soy go_ _ _ (m)

5. Translate into English

a. Mi hermana mayor es generosa

b. Mi hermano menor es gordo

c. Mi hermano mayor es aburrido

d. Mi madre es divertida

e. No soy feo

f. Soy un poco terco

g. Soy muy guapo

h. Mi amigo Valentino es fuerte

8. Translate into Spanish

a. I am strong and funny (f)

b. My mother is very stubborn

c. My sister is short and slim

d. My brother is intelligent

e. I am kind and fun (f)

f. My father is tall and fat

g. Gargamel is ugly and mean

6. Spot and correct the translation mistakes

a. Soy fuerte: *He is strong*

b. Es gordo: *He is slim*

c. Soy muy guapa: *I am very ugly*

d. Mi madre es alta: *My mother is short*

e. Mi rata es fea: *My rat is small*

f. Mi hermana es terca: *My sister is three*

g. Mi padre es bueno: *My father is bad*

7. Complete

a. M_ m_ _ _ _ _

b. M_ her_ _ _ _ _

c. M_ p_ _ _ _ _

d. S_ _ fue_ _ _

e. E_ t_ _ _ _ _

f. S_ _ m_ _ _

g. S_ _ am_ _ _ _ _

Unit 8. Describing my family: VOCABULARY BUILDING

1. Complete with the missing word

a. En mi familia t_____   *In my family I have...*

b. Tengo_____ personas   *I have four people...*

c. Mi _____ , Ángela   *My mother, Ángela*

d. Me llevo _____ con   *I get on well with*

e. Me llevo _____ con   *I get on badly with*

f. Mi tío ____ muy alto   *My uncle is very tall*

g. Mi _____ es muy simpática   *My aunt is very nice*

h. Mi prima Clara es _____   *My cousin Clara is fun*

2. Match

Mi tía	My cousin (f)
Mi abuelo	My granddad
Mi madre	My mum
Mi padre	My dad
Mi abuela	My aunt
Mi primo	My brother
Mi hermana mayor	My uncle
Mi tío	My grandma
Mi hermano	My big sister
Mi prima	My cousin (m)

3. Translate into English

a. Me gusta mi tío   e. No me gusta mi...

b. Mi prima es generosa   f. Me llevo mal con...

c. Tiene el pelo rubio   g. Es terco

d. Me llevo bien con...   h. Es tranquila

4. Add the missing letter

a. Te_co   c. _impático   e. _rimo   g. Ma_or   i. Tambié_   k. Me gus_a

b. Me ll_vo   d. _buelo   f. _enor   h. M_dre   j. _ío   l. Por_ue

5. Broken words

a. E__ m__ fam__ ten_____...
In my family I have...

b. C_____ p_____
Four people

c. M__ m_____ e__ m ____ s_____
My mother is very nice

d. M__ l_____ b_____ c____ m__...
I get on well with my...

e. M__ t_____ e__ m_____ g_____
My uncle is very generous

f. M__ l_____ m_____c___ m__...
I get on badly with my...

g. M__ h_____ t_____ e__ p_____ l_____
My sister has long hair

h. M__ p_____ e__ b_____ i_____
My father is quite clever

6. Complete with a suitable word

a. Tengo cuatro_____

b. _____ simpática

c. Me _____ bien

d. Es muy _____

e. Tiene el _____ rubio

f. ____ gusta mi madre

g. Me llevo _____ con mi tío

h. Tiene el pelo negro y _____

i. Tiene los _____ azules

j. Mi primo es _____ divertido

k. Mi _____ es muy inteligente

l. Mi abuela tiene ochenta _____

 **THE LANGUAGE GYM**

Unit 8. Describing my family: READING

Soy Carlos. Tengo diez años y vivo en Kuala Lumpur, la capital de Malasia. En mi familia tengo cinco personas, mi padre Juan, mi madre Ángela y mis dos hermanos, Darren y Pedro. Me llevo muy bien con Darren porque es simpático y generoso. Sin embargo, me llevo mal con Pedro porque es muy malo.

Me llamo Verónica. Tengo catorce años y vivo en Marbella, en el sur de España. Me gusta mucho mi abuelo porque es muy divertido. Es inteligente pero muy tímido.
Mi padre es muy gordo y muy terco. Tiene los ojos marrones y el pelo rapado.

Me llamo Manolo. Tengo quince años y vivo en Galicia, en el noroeste de España. Tengo el pelo rubio y rapado. En mi familia tengo seis personas. No me llevo bien con mi hermana porque es tonta y terca. Me llevo muy bien con mis primos porque son muy simpáticos.
Mi primo favorito se llama Ian y es alto, grande y fuerte. Es muy divertido y simpático. Tiene el pelo moreno y corto y lleva gafas.

Soy Pedro. Tengo diez años y vivo en Madrid, la capital de España. Soy muy muy guapo. En mi familia tengo muchas personas, ocho en total. Me llevo bien con mi tío pero no me gusta mi tía. Me llevo muy bien con mi tío Enrique porque es divertido y simpático. Sin embargo, mi tía es antipática y horrible.
Mi tía María tiene el pelo rubio, largo y rizado y los ojos azules como yo. Su cumpleaños es el cinco de mayo.

Me llamo Juanjo. Tengo nueve años y vivo en Toledo, en España. En mi familia tengo cuatro personas. Me llevo mal con mi padre porque es muy terco y antipático. Me gusta mucho mi abuela porque es muy buena.

1. Find the Spanish for the following items in Verónica's text

a. I am called:

b. in the south:

c. my grandfather:

d. but:

e. very:

f. my father:

g. brown eyes:

h. very short hair:

2. Answer the following questions about Pedro

a. How old is he?

b. Where is he from?

c. How many people are there in his family?

d. Who does he get on well with?

e. Why does he like Enrique?

f. Who does he not like?

g. When is her birthday?

3. Complete with the missing words

Me llamo Alejandra. _____ diez años y vivo _____ Barcelona. En mi familia tengo cuatro _____.

Me _____ bien con mi abuelo porque _____ muy simpático y bueno. Mi padre tiene el _____ corto y los _____ verdes.

4. Find someone who...

a. ...has a granny who is very good

b. ...is fifteen years old

c. ...celebrates their birthday on 5th May

d. ...has a favourite cousin

e. ...is from the south of Spain

f. ...only gets on well with one of his brothers

g. ...has a shaved head and very short hair

h. ...is a bit arrogant

i. ...has green eyes

 THE LANGUAGE GYM

Unit 8. Describing my family: TRANSLATION

1. Faulty translation: spot and correct any translation mistakes (in the English)

a. En mi familia hay cuatro personas: *In my family there are fourteen people*

b. Mi madre, Ángela y mi hermano Darren: *My mother Ángela and my cousin Darren*

c. Me llevo muy mal con mi padre: *I get on very well with my father*

d. Mi tío se llama Iván: *My father is called Ivan*

e. Iván es muy simpático y divertido: *Ivan is very mean and fun*

f. Iván tiene el pelo rapado: *Ivan has long hair*

3. Phrase-level translation

a. He is nice

b. She is generous

c. I get on well with…

d. I get on badly with…

e. My uncle is fun

f. My little brother

g. I like my cousin Mary

h. She has short and black hair

i. He has blue eyes

j. I don't like my granddad

k. He is very stubborn

2. Translate into English

a. Me gusta mi abuelo

b. Mi abuela es muy buena

c. Mi primo tiene el pelo rapado

d. Me llevo bien con mi hermano mayor

e. Me llevo muy mal con mi prima

f. Me gusta mi abuelo porque es generoso

g. Mi padre es simpático y divertido

h. No me gusta mi hermano menor

i. Me llevo mal con mi primo Ernesto porque es un poco tonto

4. Sentence-level translation

a. My name is Joaquín. I am nine years old. In my family I have four people.

b. My name is Carla. I have blue eyes. I get on well with my brother.

c. I get on badly with my brother because he is stubborn.

d. My name is Frank. I live in Spain. I do not like my uncle David because he is mean.

e. I like my cousin a lot because she is very good.

f. In my family I have five people. I like my father but I do not like my mother.

 THE LANGUAGE GYM

Unit 8. Describing my family: WRITING

1. Split sentences

Mi padre es	pelo negro
Mi madre es	bien con
Tiene los	mi tío
Tiene el	simpático
No me gusta	ojos negros
Me gusta mucho mi	generosa
Me llevo	tía

2. Rewrite the sentences in the correct order

a. en mi seis tengo familia personas

b. me con mi llevo bien hermano

c. no mi me gusta tío

d. mi los ojos madre tiene azules

e. mi y simpática tía es divertida

f. ojos los tengo negros

3. Spot and correct the grammar and spelling errors

a. En mi familia tengos

b. Me lleva bien con...

c. No me gusto mi tía...

d. Mi hermana es divertido

e. Me llevo malo con...

f. Mi padre es generosa

g. Tiene los ojo azul

h. Mi hermana es muy malo

i. Tiene el pelo rapados

j. Mi gusta mucho mi abuela

4. Anagrams

a. fimalia

b. deadlga

c. groda

d. pagua

e. inligteente

f. mispática

g. treco

h. verditida

5. Guided writing: write 3 short paragraphs in the first person singular (I) describing the people below:

Name	Age	Family	Likes	Likes	Dislikes
Paco	12	4 people	Mother because very nice. Has long blond hair.	Older brother because fun and very good.	Cousin Gemma because very mean and bad.
Leo	11	5 people	Father because very fun. Has short black hair.	Grandmother because very nice and generous.	Uncle Eduardo because stubborn and ugly.
Miguel	10	3 people	Grandfather because very funny. Has very short hair.	Younger sister because very good and calm.	Aunt Carolina because very strong but stubborn.

6. Describe this person in the third person (he):

Name: Uncle Antonio
Hair: Blond, crew-cut
Eyes: Blue
Opinion: Like him a lot
Physical: Tall and strong
Personality: Nice, fun, generous.

 **THE LANGUAGE GYM**

TERM 2 - BRINGING IT ALL TOGETHER – 8

1. Me llamo Lily y tengo quince años. Mi cumpleaños es el dieciocho de marzo. Soy de Berlín, la capital de Alemania. Vivo aquí con mi familia. Hoy estoy muy feliz. Estoy emocionada *(excited)* porque más tarde voy a ir al parque con mi mejor amigo Dylan. Mi amigo Dylan es muy alto y gracioso. Me encanta hacer footing con él.

2. En mi familia somos cinco personas: mi hermano mayor, Marco, mi hermana menor, Sofía, mi padre, Luis, mi madre, Ana, y yo. También tenemos un ratón gris que se llama Splinter. Mis abuelos se llaman Hans y Petra. Hans tiene setenta y cinco años y Petra tiene setenta y dos. Son muy cariñosos y amables.

3. Mi hermano mayor se llama Marco. A Marco le gusta pintar y jugar al baloncesto. Tiene once años y es muy creativo. Su cumpleaños es el veinte de noviembre. Marco tiene los ojos marrones y el pelo rapado. Es inteligente pero muy tímido.

4. Mi hermana menor es simpática y generosa. Tiene los ojos azules y el pelo largo y liso. Es muy guapa y elegante. En el colegio su asignatura favorita es el español porque tiene amigos en clase y el profe es muy bueno. No le gustan las ciencias porque son un poco aburridas.

5. Mi familia y yo vivimos en un piso en un edificio moderno en las afueras de Berlín. Me encanta mi piso porque es luminoso y tranquilo. Hay un parque cerca donde me gusta montar en bicicleta. Mi mejor amiga se llama Lisa y también le gusta montar en bicicleta conmigo *(with me)*. Nos divertimos *(we have fun)* mucho juntas.

6. Voy a una escuela pequeña en mi barrio. No me gusta mucho mi escuela porque los profesores son bastante estrictos. Sin embargo, me gusta mucho la clase de geografía porque aprendo mucho y tengo muchos amigos en clase. Mi asignatura favorita es inglés porque me encanta leer y escribir historias.

7. En mi tiempo libre, me gusta explorar nuevos lugares *(places)* e ir al centro comercial con mi familia. También me gusta hacer actividades al aire libre como ir de paseo por el parque y jugar al fútbol. No me gusta mucho la comida picante *(spicy food)*, pero me encanta el helado de fresa

Lily, 13, Berlín, Alemania

1. Complete the following translation of the first paragraph

My name is Lily and I am _____ years old. My birthday is on _____ March. I am from Berlin, the _____ of Germany. I live here with my family. Today I am very _____. I am _____ because later I am _____ with my _____ _____, Dylan. My friend Dylan is very tall and _____. I love going _____ with him.

2. Answer (in English) the questions below on paragraphs 2, 3 and 4

a. How many people are there in Lily's family?
b. What is her younger sister's name?
c. How old is her grandfather?
d. What two hobbies does her older brother do?
e. Who has a shaved head?
f. Who has long and straight hair?
g. What subject does her younger sister dislike? Why?

3. Find the 8 mistakes in the following translation of paragraph 5

My family and I live in a flat in a modern building in the centre of Berlin. I like my flat because it is spacious and beautiful. There is parking lot nearby where I like to go jogging. My best friend is called Lisa and she, too, likes to go jogging with me. We have a lot of fun at her house.

4. Find the Spanish equivalent for the items below in paragraphs 6 and 7

a. A small school
b. Quite strict
c. I learn a lot
d. I have many friends
e. I love reading
f. In my free time
g. New places
h. Outdoors
i. I love ice cream
j. Strawberry

 **THE LANGUAGE GYM**

1. Me llamo Sofía y tengo catorce años. Mi cumpleaños es el veintitrés de junio. Soy de Roma, la capital de Italia. Vivo aquí con mi familia. Hoy estoy muy contenta. Estoy feliz porque después voy a ir al museo con mi mejor amiga, Laura. Mi amiga Laura es muy extrovertida y divertida. Me encanta hacer deporte con ella.

2. En mi familia somos cinco personas: mi hermano mayor, Alejandro, mi hermana menor, Valentina, mi padre, Andrés, mi madre, Elena, y yo. También tenemos un gato negro que se llama Araña. Se llama así porque es un gato, y a veces araña. Mis abuelos se llaman Juan y Marta. Juan tiene ochenta años y Marta tiene setenta y ocho. Son muy cariñosos y tranquilos.

3. Mi hermano mayor se llama Felipe. A Felipe le gusta tocar la guitarra y jugar al fútbol. Tiene doce años. Su cumpleaños es el diez de abril. Felipe tiene los ojos azules y el pelo corto. Es muy fuerte, gracioso y sociable.

4. Mi prima Alba es muy deportista. Tiene los ojos verdes y el pelo largo y rizado. Es muy inteligente y trabajadora. En el colegio su asignatura favorita es la geografía porque dice que *(she says that)* la profe es muy buena y aprende mucho en clase. No le gusta el arte porque dice que no es muy útil.

5. Mi familia y yo vivimos en un piso pequeño en el centro de Roma. Me gusta mucho mi piso porque es muy antiguo y bonito. Hay un parque cerca donde me gusta hacer footing *(jogging)* todos los fines de semana. Normalmente me gusta hacer footing con mi mejor amiga, Carla.

6. Voy a un colegio pequeño cerca de mi barrio. Me gusta mucho mi colegio porque los profesores son muy inteligentes y siempre me ayudan. Me gusta mucho la clase de historia porque aprendo mucho y el profe de historia es mi profe favorito. También me gusta la biología porque me encanta aprender sobre los animales y el cuerpo *(body)* humano .

7. En mi tiempo libre, me gusta ir a la piscina con mi familia y nadar. También me gusta ir al cine para ver películas con mis amigos. Me gusta mucho la comida italiana. Me encanta la pizza y el helado italiano. En italiano se llama 'gelato'.

Sofía, 14, Roma, Italia

5. Spot and circle the 8 differences between the text below and the text in paragraph 1

Me llamo Sofía y tengo trece años. Mi cumpleaños es el veintitrés de julio. Soy de Roma, la capital de Alemania. Vivo aquí con mi abuela. Hoy estoy muy enfadada. Estoy feliz porque después voy a ir al centro con mi mejor amiga, Laura. Mi amiga Laura es muy extrovertida y graciosa. Me encanta salir con ella.

6. Answer the following questions about paragraphs 1, 2 and 3

a. How is Sofía feeling today? Why?

b. What does she enjoy doing with Laura?

c. Who is Araña?

d. Who is 78 years old?

e. What two hobbies does Felipe enjoy?

f. What five details does Sofía provide about Felipe's personality and appearance?

7. Complete the following translation of paragraph 4

My _____ Alba is very _____. She has _____ eyes and long _____ hair. She is very intelligent and _____. In school, her favourite _____ is geography because she says that the teacher is _____ _____ and that she _____ a lot in lessons. She ____ _____ art because she says it ___ ____ _____.

8. Identify and correct any inaccurate statement: paragraphs 5 to 7)

a. They live in a big flat outside Rome

b. Her flat is very old

c. She goes jogging every day of the week

d. Her teachers are nice but not very helpful

d. She learns a lot in her history lessons

e. She enjoys going to the swimming pool with her friends

UNIT 9
Comparing people's appearance and personality

In this unit will learn how to say in Spanish:

- More/less ... than
- As ... as
- New adjectives to describe people

You will revisit the following:

- Family members
- Pets
- Describing animals' appearance and character

UNIT 9
Comparing people

¿Cómo es tu mejor amigo/a? *What is your best friend like?*				
Él Ella Mi abuela Mi abuelo Mi amiga <u>Ana</u> Mi amigo <u>Paco</u> Mi gato Mi hermana Mi hermano Mi hijo Mi hija Mi madre Mi mejor amiga Mi mejor amigo Mi novio *(bf)* Mi novia *(gf)* Mi padre Mi pato Mi perro Mi prima Mi primo Mi tortuga Mi tía Mi tío	es is	más more menos less	aburrido/a *boring* alto/a *tall* amable *kind* antipático/a *mean* bajo/a *short* cariñoso/a *affectionate* débil *weak* delgado/a *slim* deportista *sporty* divertido/a *fun* feo/a *ugly* fuerte *strong* gordo/a *fat* guapo/a *good-looking* *hablador/a *talkative* inteligente *intelligent* joven *young* perezoso/a *lazy* ruidoso/a *noisy* trabajador/a *hard-working*	que than como as	él ella mi abuela mi abuelo mi amiga Ana mi amigo Paco mi gato mi hermano/a mi hija mi hijo mi madre mi mejor amiga mi mejor amigo mi novio/a mi padre mi pato mi perro mi prima mi primo mi tortuga mi tía mi tío yo
Mis abuelos Mis hermanas Mis hermanos Mis padres Mis primas Mis primos Mis tíos	son are	tan as	serios/as *serious* simpáticos/as *nice* tontos/as *silly* *trabajadores/as *hard-working* tranquilos/as *calm* viejos/as *old*		mis abuelos mis hermanas mis hermanos mis padres mis primas mis primos mis tíos nosotros *(us)*

Author's note: Add an 'S' at the end of your adjectives for plurals (when describing more than one person).
E.g. Mis padres son más TRANQUILOS que mis tíos.
*Add an ES/AS on adjectives ending in 'R' – like "trabajador" (trabajadores) or "hablador" (habladoras).

1. Multiple choice quiz: select the correct adjective

	1	2	3
a. Alex	boring	tall	friendly
b. Rosa	short	mean	young
c. Pablo	hard-working	noisy	calm
d. Paco	fat	slim	good-looking
e. Ada	strong	lazy	silly
f. Pepe	short	mean	young
g. Marta	strong	fat	silly
h. Samuel	slim	lazy	friendly
i. Teo	strong	sporty	serious
j. Lea	hard-working	noisy	lazy

2. Listening for detail: masculine or feminine?

	MASCULINE	FEMININE
a.	aburrido	aburrida
b.	hablador	habladora
c.	perezoso	perezosa
d.	ruidoso	ruidosa
e.	tranquilo	tranquila
f.	alto	alta
g.	simpático	simpática
h.	serio	seria
i.	trabajador	trabajadora

3. Complete with 'más…que', 'menos…que' or 'tan…como' as shown in the example

*e.g. Mi madre es **más** alta **que** mi padre.*

a. Mi hermano es _____ deportista _____ yo.

b. Mi gato es _____ tranquilo _____ mi perro.

c. Yo soy _____ fuerte _____ mi primo.

d. Mi abuelo es _____ viejo _____ mi abuela.

e. Mi mejor amigo es _____ bajo _____ yo.

f. Mi tío es _____ gordo _____ mi padre.

g. Mi primo Ian es _____ guapo _____ mi primo Ronnie.

4. Listen and fill in the middle column with the missing information in English.
e.g. Arantxa is taller than Felipe.

a. Silvia		**Alfonso**
b. Juan		**Diego**
c. Paco		**Jaime**
d. Maite		**Gonzalo**
e. Consuelo		**Pilar**
f. Julio		**Yolanda**
g. Felipe		**Jordi**
h. Dylan		**Samuel**
i. Verónica		**Sergio**

5. Spot the differences and correct the text

a. Yo soy más alto que mi madre.

b. Mi primo es tan perezoso como yo.

c. Mi mejor amigo es más trabajador que yo.

d. Mi hermana es menos guapa que mi madre.

e. Mi perro es más ruidoso que mi pato.

f. Mi abuela es menos vieja que mi abuelo.

g. Mi madre es tan deportista como mi hermano y yo.

6. Listen, spot and correct the errors

a. Mi madre es más alto como yo.

b. Mi hermano mayor soy más fuerte que mi hermano menor.

c. Mi padre es más trabajador que mi.

d. Mi abuelo es más vieja que mi abuela.

e. Mis tíos son muy más viejos que mis padres.

f. Mis abuelos maternos son tan viejo como mis paternos abuelos.

g. Yo soy más delgado de mis padres.

h. Mis primos es más ricos que nuestros.

7. Listen and complete the translation

Person	Description
a. My father is	
b. My mother is	
c. My older brother is	
d. My younger brother is	
e. My sister is	
f. My uncle is	
g. My grandma is	
h. My best friend is	
i. My girlfriend is	
j. My dog is	

8. Answer the questions below about Enrique

a. How old is he?

b. Where does he live?

c. How many people are there in the family?

d. Pablo is_____ and _____ than Julio.

e. Julio is _____ and _____than Pablo.

f. Why does he prefer his father?

g. He is as _____ as his mother.

h. Which of his pets is the most talkative?

9. Listening slalom: follow the speaker from top to bottom and number the boxes accordingly

a	b	c	d
My father is more (a)	My aunt is as	My mother is as	My friend is
affectionate as my father,	**talkative than my mother, (a)**	less hard–working than my brother,	hard–working as my uncle,
as sporty as	as lazy as	**as tall as (a)**	less generous than
my sister	me	my older sister	**my younger brother (a)**
and a bit more	and more	**and nicer (a)**	and as
boring	**than (a)**	funny	intelligent than
as my cousin.	her sister.	than my goldfish.	**my older brother. (a)**

Unit 9. Comparing people : VOCABULARY BUILDING

1. Complete with the missing word

a. Mi padre es más alto _____ mi hermano mayor — *My father is taller than my older brother*

b. Mi madre es _____ habladora que mi _____ — *My mother is less talkative than my aunt*

c. Mi _____ es más bajo que _____ padre — *My grandfather is shorter than my dad*

d. Mis primos son _____ perezosos que _____ — *My cousins are lazier than us*

e. Mi perro _____ más _____ que mi _____ — *My dog is more noisy than my cat*

f. Mi tía es _____ guapa que _____ madre — *My aunt is less pretty than my mother*

g. Mi _____ es más _____ que yo — *My brother is more hard-working than me*

h. Mis padres _____ más _____ que mis tíos — *My parents are more kind than my uncles*

i. Mi hermano menor es _____ alto _____ yo — *My younger brother is as tall as me*

2. Translate into English

a. mis primos

b. más

c. mi tío

d. mis abuelos

e. mi hermana

f. mi mejor amigo

g. trabajador

h. mi amiga

i. alto

j. viejo

k. terco

l. perezoso

3. Match Spanish and English

trabajador	strong
guapo	silly
amable	sporty
fuerte	good-looking
deportista	old
viejo	hard-working
tonto	kind

4. Spot and correct any English translation mistakes

a. Es más alto que yo — *He is taller than you*

b. Es tan guapo como yo — *He is as funny as me*

c. Es más tranquila que yo — *She is stronger than me*

d. Soy menos gordo que él — *I am more fat than him*

e. Son menos amables que nosotros — *They are shorter than us*

f. Soy tan viejo como él — *She is as old as him*

g. Es más deportista que yo — *You are sportier than me*

5. Complete with a suitable word

a. Mi madre es _____ alta _____ yo

b. ____ padre _____ más joven que mi tío

c. Mis padres son _____ altos como _____ abuelos

d. _____ hermanos _____ más deportistas que mis primos

e. Mi _____ es menos ruidoso _____ mi pato·

f. Mis abuelos _____ tan cariñosos _____ mis padres

g. Mi novia es _____ guapa que _____ tortuga

h. Mi tío no _____ tan fuerte _____ mi padre

6. Match the opposites

guapo	bajo
trabajador	aburrido
joven	feo
alto	gordo
divertido	menos
débil	perezoso
más	viejo
delgado	fuerte

 THE LANGUAGE GYM

Unit 9. Comparing people : READING

Me llamo Jorge. Tengo veinte años y vivo en Buenos Aires. En mi familia somos cinco personas: mis padres y mis dos hermanos, Felipe y Ale. Felipe es más alto, guapo y fuerte que Ale, pero Ale es más amable, inteligente y trabajador que Felipe.

Mis padres se llaman Antonio y Nina. Ambos son muy amables, pero mi padre es más estricto que mi madre. Además, mi madre es más paciente y menos terca que mi padre. ¡Yo soy tan terco como mi padre!

En casa tenemos dos mascotas: una tortuga y un pato. Ambos son muy simpáticos, pero mi pato es más ruidoso. Tan ruidoso como yo...

Me llamo José. Tengo quince años y vivo en Ceuta. En mi familia somos cinco personas: mis padres y mis dos hermanos, Rubén y Pedro. Rubén es más delgado y deportista que Pedro, pero Pedro es más alto y fuerte.

Mis padres se llaman Carmen y Antonio. Prefiero a mi padre porque es menos estricto que mi madre. Además, mi madre es más terca que mi padre. ¡Yo soy tan terco como ella! En casa tenemos dos mascotas: un loro y una cobaya. Ambos son muy simpáticos, pero mi loro es mucho más hablador. Tan hablador como yo...

Me llamo Victoria. Tengo veinte años y vivo en Toledo con mis padres y mis dos hermanas, Marina y Verónica. Marina es más guapa que Verónica, pero Verónica es más simpática.

Mis padres son muy cariñosos y amables, pero mi padre es más divertido que mi madre. Además, mi padre es más gracioso que mi madre. ¡Yo soy tan gracioso como mi padre!

En casa tenemos dos mascotas: un perro y un conejo. Ambos son muy gordos, pero mi perro es más perezoso. Tan perezoso como yo...

1. Find the Spanish for the following in Jorge's text

a. I live in:

b. My parents:

c. Good-looking:

d. Hard-working:

e. Less stubborn:

f. More patient:

g. But:

h. My duck:

i. Two pets:

j. Very kind:

k. As stubborn as:

2. Complete the statements below based on Victoria's text

a. I am _____ years old

b. Marina is more _____ than Verónica

c. Verónica is more _____

d. My parents are very _____ and _____

e. I am as _____ as my father

f. We have _____ pets: a _____ and a _____

3. Correct any of the statements below (about José's text) which are incorrect

a. José tiene tres mascotas

b. Rubén es menos gordo que Pedro

c. Rubén es más débil que Pedro

d. José es tan hablador como su cobaya

e. José prefiere a su madre

f. José es más terco que su madre

4. Answer the questions on the three texts above

a. Where does José live?

b. Who is stricter, his mother or his father?

c. Who is as talkative as their parrot?

d. Who is as chatty as their duck?

e. Who has a stubborn father?

f. Who has a rabbit?

g. Who has a guinea pig?

h. Which one of José's brothers is sportier?

i. What are the differences between Jorge's brothers?

Unit 9. Comparing people: TRANSLATION/WRITING

1. Translate into English

a. Alto

b. Delgado

c. Bajo

d. Gordo

e. Inteligente

f. Terco

g. Tonto

h. Guapo

i. Feo

j. Más...que

k. Menos...que

l. Fuerte

m. Débil

n. Tan...como...

2. Gapped sentences

a. Mi _____ es _____ alta _____ mi tía

My mother is taller than my aunt

b. _____ padre _____ más _____ que mi hermano mayor

My father is stronger than my older brother

c. Mis _____ son menos _____ que nosotros

My cousins are less sporty than us

d. _____ hermano es _____ tonto que _____

My brother is more silly than me

e. Mi madre _____ _____ amable _____ mi padre

My mother is as kind as my father

f. Mi _____ es _____ trabajadora que _____

My sister is more hard-working than us

g. Mi _____ es menos _____ _____ yo

My girlfriend is less serious than me

h. Mi _____ es _____ terco _____ mi abuela

My grandfather is more stubborn than my grandmother

3. Phrase-level translation English to Spanish

a. My mother is

b. Taller than

c. As slim as

d. Less stubborn than

e. I am shorter than

f. My parents are

g. My cousins are

h. As fat as

i. They are as strong as

j. My grandparents are

k. I am as lazy as

4. Sentence-level translation English to Spanish

a. My older sister is taller than my younger sister.

b. My father is as stubborn as my mother.

c. My girlfriend is more hard-working than me.

d. I am less intelligent than my brother.

e. My best friend is stronger and sportier than me.

f. My boyfriend is better-looking than me.

g. My cousins are uglier than us.

h. My duck is noisier than my dog.

i. My cat is more fun than my turtle.

j. My rabbit is less fat than my guinea pig.

TERM 2 - BRINGING IT ALL TOGETHER – 9

1. Me llamo Nora y tengo quince años. Mi cumpleaños es el veinticinco de agosto. Soy de un pueblo pequeño de México que se llama Chihuahua pero ahora vivo en Ámsterdam, la capital de los Países Bajos, con mi familia. Hoy estoy feliz porque después voy a ir a la piscina para nadar *(swim)* con mi mejor amigo Lucas. Lucas es muy divertido y siempre tiene muy buenas ideas. Me encanta jugar al tenis con él.

2. En mi familia somos cinco personas: mi hermano mayor Daniel, mi hermana menor Sofía, mi padre Andrés, mi madre María, y yo. Prefiero a mi padre porque es menos estricto que mi madre. Mi madre es mucho más paciente que mi padre. Mis abuelos se llaman Carlos y Ana. Carlos tiene ochenta años y Ana tiene setenta y nueve. Son muy cariñosos y siempre juegan *(play)* con nosotros *(with us)*. Mi madre es tan cariñosa como mi abuela pero mi abuelo es más paciente que mi padre.

3. Mi hermano mayor se llama Daniel. A Daniel le gusta tocar la guitarra y jugar al baloncesto. Tiene diecisiete años y es muy talentoso. Su cumpleaños es el siete de noviembre. Daniel tiene el pelo rizado y los ojos verdes. Daniel es más alto que yo, pero yo soy un poco más graciosa que él.

4. Mi hermana menor, Sofía, es más creativa que mi hermano. Tiene los ojos azules y el pelo liso. Le gusta dibujar y bailar ballet. En el colegio, su asignatura favorita es la historia porque le gusta aprender sobre el pasado *(about the past)*. No le gustan las matemáticas porque son un poco complicadas.

5. Mi familia y yo vivimos en un piso acogedor en las afueras de Ámsterdam. Me encanta nuestro piso porque es luminoso y moderno. Siempre está limpio. Hay un polideportivo cerca de mi casa donde me gusta hacer deportes como jugar al fútbol. Mi mejor amiga se llama Emma y también le gusta montar en bicicleta conmigo. Nos divertimos mucho juntas.

6. Voy a un colegio de arte en mi barrio. Me gusta mi colegio porque los profesores son creativos y trabajadores y siempre nos ayudan a expresarnos *(express ourselves)*. También, me encanta la clase de danza contemporánea porque puedo bailar libremente con mis amigas. Mi asignatura favorita es la pintura al óleo *(oil painting)* porque me encanta mezclar *(mix)* colores y crear obras de arte *(works of art)* impresionantes.

Nora, 15, Chihuahua, México

1. Complete the translation of paragraph 1

My name is Nora and I am _____ years old. My birthday is on ___ _____. I am from a _____ village in Mexico which is called Chihuahua, but now I live in Amsterdam, the capital of _____, with my family. Today I am _____ because later I am going to go to the _____ to _____ with my _____ _____, Lucas. Lucas is very _____ and always has _____ _____. I _____ playing tennis with him.

2. Answer the following questions about paragraphs 2 to 4

a. Why does Nora prefer her father?

b. Who is very affectionate?

c. What hobbies does Daniel like?

d. What is Daniel's hair like?

e. Who is taller between Nora and Daniel?

f. Who is Sofía?

g. Why does Sofía dislike maths?

3. Find the Spanish equivalent for the following in paragraphs 4 and 5

a. My younger sister

b. Straight hair

c. Her favourite subject

d. We live in

e. Our flat

f. It is always clean

g. She likes to ride the bike

4. Find the ten mistakes in the following translation of paragraph 6

I go to a science school in my town. I like my school because the teachers are creative and kind and always tell us to express ourselves. Also, I like the classic dance class because I can chat freely with my male friends. My favourite hobby is oil painting because I love to choose colours and create beautiful works of art.

Me llamo Luz y tengo doce años. Mi cumpleaños es el tres de diciembre. Soy de Montevideo, la capital de Uruguay, pero ahora vivo en Londres, la capital de Inglaterra, con mi familia. Hoy estoy feliz porque después voy a ir de tiendas para comprar un regalo para mi hermano Luca. Voy a ir con mi madre. ¡El domingo es su cumpleaños! Luca es muy divertido y siempre tiene muy buenas ideas. Me encanta jugar al baloncesto con él.

En mi familia somos seis personas: mi hermano mayor, Luca, mi hermana mayor, Lola, mi padre, León, mi madre, Alicia, mi abuela, Gloria, y yo. Prefiero a mi abuela porque es más simpática que mi padre. Mi padre es muy fuerte. Creo que se llama León porque es fuerte como un león. Mi abuela es muy buena con nosotros y siempre nos escucha *(listens to us)*. Mi madre es tan graciosa como mi abuela y es mucho más paciente que mi padre.

Mi hermano mayor se llama Luca. A Luca le gusta tocar el saxofón y jugar al ajedrez. Tiene catorce años y es muy inteligente. Su cumpleaños es el dieciséis de junio. Luca tiene el pelo negro muy largo y liso y los ojos marrones. Luca es más alto que yo, pero yo soy más guapa.

Mi hermana mayor Lola es más deportista que yo. Tiene los ojos marrones y el pelo rizado. Le gusta hacer pesas y jugar al baloncesto . En el colegio, su asignatura favorita es la educación física porque así puede hacer más deporte todavía *(even more sport)*. No le gusta el arte porque no es muy artística.

Mi familia y yo vivimos en una casa vieja pero acogedora en Barking, en el este de Londres. Me gusta bastante nuestra casa porque es muy cómoda. A veces no está limpia porque tengo un perro grande. Se llama Rufus. Hay un parque y un lago cerca de mi casa donde me gusta hacer footing y nadar. Mi mejor amiga se llama Juana y también le gusta nadar en el lago. Nos reímos *(we laugh)* mucho juntas.

Voy a un colegio pequeño en mi barrio. Me gusta mi colegio porque los profesores son muy buenos y pacientes. Me encanta la clase de historia porque el profe explica las cosas *(explains things)* muy bien y tengo a mis amigas en la clase. Mi asignatura favorita es el francés porque me encanta hablar en francés y siempre cantamos canciones *(we sing songs)* en clase.

Luz, 12, Montevideo, Uruguay

5. Find someone who...

a. ...is happy today

b. ...always has good ideas

c. ...is as strong as a lion

d. ...always listens to Luz

e. ...plays chess

f. ...has brown hair and curly hair

g. ...enjoys swimming in the lake

h. ...likes French

6. Complete the sentences below

a. Today Luz is going to go _____

b. She and her mum are going to buy _____

c. Her mum is as _____ as her grandmother

d. Luca is _____ than Luz.

e. Lola enjoys doing weights and _____

f. Luz's house is old but _____

g. Luz's house is not too clean at times because _____

h. Juana also enjoys_____

i. Luz enjoy her history lessons because her teacher _____

j. Luz enjoys speaking _____

7. Answer the following questions as if you were Luz

a. ¿De dónde eres?

b. ¿Cómo estás hoy?

c. ¿Cuántas personas hay en tu familia?

d. ¿Cómo son tus padres?

e. ¿Qué hace Luca en su tiempo libre?

f. ¿Qué deportes le gustan a Lola?

g. ¿Cuál es su asignatura favorita?

h. ¿Cómo es tu casa?

i. ¿Quién es Rufus?

j. ¿Cómo es tu colegio?

k. ¿Cómo son los profesores?

l. ¿Qué opinas de tu clase de historia?

m. ¿Por qué te gusta el francés?

 **THE LANGUAGE GYM**

TERM 2 – MIDPOINT – RETRIEVAL PRACTICE

1. Answer the following questions in Spanish

¿Cómo te llamas?	
¿Cómo estás hoy?	
¿Cuántas personas hay en tu familia?	
¿Con quién te llevas bien en tu familia? ¿Por qué?	
¿Con quién te llevas mal en tu familia? ¿Por qué?	
¿Cuántos años tiene tu hermano/a?	
¿Cómo es tu hermano/hermana?	
¿Cuántos años tiene?	
¿Cuándo es su cumpleaños?	
¿Cuál es tu profesor/a favorito/a? ¿Por qué?	
¿Hay algún profesor/a que no te gusta? ¿Cuál? ¿Por qué?	

2. Write a paragraph in the first person singular (I) providing the following details

a. Your name is Sandra. You are 11 and are from England

b. Today you are feeling good

c. In your family there are four people: your father, mother and your younger sister

d. You get on well with your mother but not with your father because he is very strict

e. Your father is 40. He is quite tall and blond. He is intelligent and friendly

f. Your mother is 38. She is short and dark-haired. She is very kind and hard–working

g. Your sister is called Deborah. She is 9. Her birthday is on 20th May. She is more hard-working and sporty than you but you are funnier

h. Your school is big and you like it a lot because the teachers are kind and always listen to you.

i. You love Spanish because the teacher is good, fun and always helps you. Also, you have friends in the class

3. Write a paragraph in the third person singular (he/she) providing the following details about a friend

a. Name, age, birthday and where he/she lives

b. How many people there are in their family and who they are

c. Describe him/her in detail both in terms of appearance and personality

d. Compare him/her with you in terms of height and personality

e. Say if he/she gets on with their siblings or parents and why/why not

f. Say how he/she feels about school

g. Say which subjects they like/dislike and why

h. Say who his/her favourite teacher is and why

UNIT 10 – Describing my teachers and saying why I like them

In this unit will learn:
- How to say which teachers you like/dislike
- To give reasons for liking a teacher
- The good/bad qualities of a teacher
- More adjectives for describing people

You will revisit the following:
- School subjects
- Adjectival agreements – masculine/feminine

Unit 10
Describing my teachers and saying why I like them

¿Qué profesor/a (no) te gusta? ¿Por qué?	*Which teacher do you (not) like? Why?*
¿Te gusta tu profesor/a de español? ¿Por qué?	*Do you like your Spanish teacher? Why?*

Me encanta *I love*	**mi profesor**	**de**	alemán arte ciencias educación física español francés historia informática inglés matemáticas música teatro tecnología	**porque (no) es** *because he/she is (not)*	**aburrido** *boring*
					antipático *mean*
					estricto *strict*
					gracioso *funny*
					simpático *nice*
					trabajador *hard-working*
Me gusta *I like*					**amable** *kind*
					impaciente *impatient*
					inteligente *intelligent*
					interesante *interesting*
					paciente *patient*
No me gusta *I don't like*	**mi profesora**				**aburrida**
					antipática
					estricta
					graciosa
					simpática
					trabajadora

Además, *Furthermore*	**me gusta** *I like him/her*	**porque**	**nunca** *never*	**está de buen humor** *is in a good mood*
				está de mal humor *is in a bad mood*
				me ayuda *helps me*
				me chilla/grita *shouts at me*
	no me gusta *I don't like him/her*		**siempre** *always*	**me comprende** *understands me*
				me escucha *listens to me*
				me regaña *tells me off*
				nos da pocos deberes *gives us little homework*
				nos da muchos deberes *gives us lots of homework*
				se enfada *gets angry*

1. Tick or cross? Tick the words you hear in each sentence and cross the ones you don't

a. Arte

b. Ciencias

c. Historia

d. Teatro

e. Matemáticas

f. Geografía

g. Español

h. Alemán

2. Fill in the gaps

a. Me gusta el profe de _____

b. Me _____ la profe de matemáticas

c. No me gusta ___ profe de tecnología

d. No me gusta el profe de _____

e. Me gusta la profe de _____

f. Me gusta mucho la profe de _____

g. Me gusta el profe de _____

h. Me gusta _____ la profe de español

3. Spot the intruder

a. Me gusta mucho el la profe de geografía porque es paciente

b. Me gusta bastante la profe de inglés porque es simpática

c. No me gusta el profe de alemán porque es paciente

d. Me gusta mucho el profe de arte porque es muy trabajador

e. Me gusta la profe de francés porque nunca siempre se enfada

f. No me gusta la profe de ciencias porque nos da muchos pocos deberes

4. Faulty translation: correct the wrong translations

a. I like the French teacher a lot

b. He never gets angry

c. She gives us a lot of homework

d. He never listens to me

e. The art teacher helps me a lot

f. She always tells me off

5. Listen and write the Spanish translation next to each sentence

a. I like my German teacher

b. She never gets angry

c. He understands me

d. He helps me

e. I like my science teacher

f. He is nice

g. He is mean

h. She is hardworking

6. Subjects & teachers: listen and tick the appropriate box

	Masculine	Feminine
a.		
b.		
c.		
d.		
e.		
f.		
g.		
h.		

7. Gapped translation

I like my school _____. My favourite subject is _____ because the teacher is very _____ and always gives us _____ homework. Furthermore, he is very _____ and _____ a lot. I also like my _____ teacher because she is very kind and _____ and _____ me. She never _____ _____ and never _____ at me. However, I don't like my _____ teacher because he is very strict and _____. He always _____ ___ ___ and gives us _____ of homework.

8. Complete with the missing letters

a. La prof_ de histor_a es trabajador_

b. El profe d_ geogr_fía es antipátic_

c. Me gust_ la profe de ci ncias porque es simpátic_

d. No me gus_a la profe de _rte porque es estrict_

e. M_ profe de inglés e_ muy trabajado_ y pacient_

f. Mi pr_fe de educació_ fís_ca es muy aburrid_

g. Me enca_ta la profe de f_ancés porque es gracios_

h. _o me gusta el _rofe de alemán po_que es arrogant_

9. Guess the next word, then listen to the track to see if you guessed right

a. La profe de ciencias es...

b. El profe de historia es...

c. El profe de inglés es...

d. La profe de arte siempre me...

e. Le profe de geografía es...

f. El profe de tecnología es...

g. La profe de música es...

10. Listen and fill in the grid

	Which subject?	Opinion	Why? (2 details)
e.g.	*French*	*Y*	*Teacher is funny and helps me a lot*
a.			
b.			
c.			
d.			
e.			
f.			
g.			

11. Listening slalom: follow the speaker from top to bottom and number the boxes accordingly

a	b	c	d
Me gusta	No me gusta	Me encanta	Me gusta mucho
el profe de inglés	**la profe de historia**	la profe de ciencias	la profe de español
porque es graciosa	porque es antipática	**porque es simpática**	porque es muy gracioso
e interesante.	y trabajador.	y perezosa	**y paciente.**
Es muy paciente	Nunca nos da	**Ella me comprende**	y nunca
muchos deberes.	y nunca me chilla.	me ayuda.	**y siempre me ayuda.**

 **THE LANGUAGE GYM**

Unit 10. Describing my teachers: VOCAB BUILDING

1. Match

Es interesante	He is nice
Es paciente	He is mean
Es inteligente	He is interesting
Es trabajador	He is intelligent
Es simpático	He is patient
Es antipático	He is hard–working
Es gracioso	He is funny
Es divertido	He is boring
Es aburrido	He is fun

2. Translate into English

a. Me gusta:

b. La profe de historia:

c. Me encanta:

d. Es antipática:

e. Es simpático:

f. Me chilla:

g. Nos da muchos deberes:

h. Es graciosa:

i. Me ayuda:

j. Siempre:

3. Break the flow

a. Megustalaprofedecienciasporqueesmuytrabajadora

b. Nomegustalaprofedeinglésporqueesmuyestricta

c. Nomegustaelprofedematemáticasporquesiemprenosdamuchosdeberes

d. Meencantalaprofedemúsicaporquenuncaseenfada

e. Megustaelprofedeeducaciónfísicaporquesiempreestádebuenhumor

f. Nomegustaelprofedefrancésporqueesaburrido

g. Meencantalaprofedetecnologíaporqueesgraciosa

h. Megustamuchoelprofedeespañolporqueesdivertido

4. Faulty translation

a. El profe de alemán: *The science teacher*

b. Me gusta mucho: *I like him/her a bit*

c. Me encanta: *I hate him*

d. El profe de arte: *The history teacher*

e. Nos da muchos deberes: *He gives us little homework*

f. Siempre me ayuda: *She always tells me off*

g. No me comprende: *He understands me*

h. Nunca se enfada: *He always gets angry*

i. Es aburrida: *She is angry*

j. Es graciosa: *He is funny*

5. Complete the table

Español	English
Aburrido	
Divertido	
	Funny
Interesante	
Simpático	
	Mean
Paciente	
	Hard–working

 **THE LANGUAGE GYM**

Unit 10. Describing my teachers: VOCAB BUILDING

6. Gapped Spanish to English translation

a. Me gusta la profe de ciencias: *I like the _____ teacher*

b. Es muy estricta: *She is very _____*

c. Siempre nos da muchos deberes: *He always gives us _____ homework*

d. Me encanta la profe de música: *I _____ the music teacher*

e. Nunca está de buen humor: *He is _____ in a good mood*

f. No me gusta el profe porque es aburrido: *I don't like the teacher because he is _____*

g. Me encanta la profe porque es graciosa: *I love the teacher because she is _____*

h. Me gusta mucho porque es divertido: *I like him a lot because he is _____*

7. Complete with the correct option

a. Me gusta la profe de _____ porque es muy trabajadora.

b. No me gusta la profe de inglés porque es muy _____.

c. No me gusta el profe de matemáticas porque nos _____ muchos deberes.

d. Me _____ la profe de música porque nunca se enfada.

e. Me gusta el _____ de educación física porque está siempre de buen humor.

f. No me gusta el profe de francés porque es _____.

g. Me gusta mucho el profe de español _____ es divertido.

estricta
profe
da
encanta
aburrido
porque
ciencias

8. Sentence puzzle

a. profe La simpática es   *The teacher is nice*

b. es El antipático profe   *The teacher is mean*

c. Me profe la gusta   *I like the teacher*

d. de inglés El profe   *The English teacher*

e. profe La francés de   *The French teacher*

f. La graciosa profe es   *The teacher is funny*

g. es profe El divertido   *The teacher is fun*

9. Anagrams

e.g. coimSpáti: Simpático

a. rPfoe

b. páticotiAn

c. verDidoti

d. eM hillca

e. eD uenb morhu

f. schoMu bedesre

10. Choose the correct word

a. La profe de *ciencias/sciencias*

b. El profe es *aburrida/aburrido*

c. Siempre se *enfada/enfadas*

d. Está de buen *humour/humor*

e. El profe es *muy/mucho* divertido

f. Me gusta la profe porque es *simpático/simpática*

g. No me gusta la profe porque es *paciente/pacienta*

h. Me gusta *mucho/muy* el profe de español

Unit 10. Describing my teachers: READING

Me llamo Marta. Tengo once años y vivo en Buenos Aires. Mi instituto se llama Instituto Alberdi y es muy bueno. Estudio muchas asignaturas. Mi asignatura favorita es el francés, porque el profe es muy gracioso, amable y paciente y no nos da muchos deberes. También me gusta la profe de inglés porque es muy divertida e interesante y me ayuda cuando tengo problemas. En cambio, no me gusta la profe de arte, porque es muy aburrida y antipática. ¡Siempre me chilla! Tampoco me gusta la profe de ciencias porque nos da muchos deberes y siempre se enfada. Además, nunca me ayuda cuando tengo problemas.

Me llamo José. Tengo quince años y vivo en Zaragoza. Mi instituto se llama Instituto Goya. Estudio muchas asignaturas, pero solo me gustan la historia y la geografía porque los profes son simpáticos y muy buenos. El profe de historia siempre me ayuda cuando no comprendo algo y el profe de geografía siempre está de buen humor. No me gustan la ciencias porque la profe es aburrida y siempre nos chilla. Tampoco me gustan las matemáticas porque la profe es muy estricta y se enfada fácilmente. Odio (*I hate*) también el inglés porque el profe es muy antipático y nunca me ayuda cuando tengo problemas.

Me llamo Roberto, tengo trece años y vivo en Ceuta. Mi instituto se llama Instituto Clara Campoamor y es muy grande y bueno. Estudio muchas asignatura y me gustan todas. Me encanta el inglés porque la profe es muy amable y trabajadora y siempre está de buen humor. También me gustan mucho las ciencias porque el profe es muy gracioso y paciente, y siempre me ayuda cuando tengo problemas. Además, me encanta la historia, porque el profe es muy simpático y divertido y aprendo mucho en las clases. Nunca nos chilla.

1. Find the Spanish for the following in Marta's text

a. Good

b. Subjects

c. Funny

d. Homework

e. Also

f. Helps me

g. When

h. On the other hand

i. Mean

j. Shouts at me

k. Gets angry

2. Complete the statements below based on José's text

a. I study _____ subjects

b. I _____ like history and geography

c. The history teacher always _____ when I _____

d. The science teacher is _____ and _____

e. Neither do I like maths because the teacher is very _____ and _____ easily.

3. Correct the incorrect statements about Roberto's text

a. Roberto only likes English, science and history

b. The history teacher is boring

c. The science teacher is funny

d. The English teacher is a bit lazy

e. The history teacher tells him off often

4. Find someone who...

a. ...doesn't like science because the teacher is boring

b. ...has a hard-working English teacher

c. ...has a boring and mean art teacher

d. ...has a helpful history teacher

e. ...has a funny French teacher

f. ...learns a lot in the history lessons

g. ...goes to a school which is big and good

h. ...has an art teacher who always tells them off

i. ...hates English

j. ...has a geography teacher who's always in a good mood

k. ...has a fun history teacher

Unit 10. Describing my teachers: WRITING

1. Translate into Spanish
Please note: f = feminine, m = masculine

a. Nice [f]

b. Funny [m]

c. Mean [f]

d. Boring [m]

e. Interesting

f. Patient

g. Fun [f]

2. Complete with a suitable word

a. Me encanta la _ _ _ _ _ de ciencias

b. La profe de matemáticas _ _ graciosa

c. Me _ _ _ _ _ porque es simpático

d. _ _ me gusta porque es impaciente

e. Me gusta mucho el profe de _ _ _ _ _ _ _

f. No me gusta _ _ _ _ _ _ es muy antipático

g. La profe de inglés es _ _ _ divertida

h. _ _ profe de arte es muy aburrido

3. Broken words

a. La pro_ _ de cien_ _ _ _

b. Es diver_ _ _ _

c. M_ ch_ _ _ _

d. Se enf_ _ _

e. Es abur_ _ _a

f. Es grac_ _ _a

g. La _ _ _fe de fran_ _ _

h. Es muy inte_ _ _ _ _ _

i. Nos d_ pocos debe_ _ _

j. Nos _a much_ _ debe_ _ _

k. E_ profe e_ paci_ _ _ _

l. Siemp_ _ me ayu_ _

4. Complete the table

Masculine	Feminine
Aburrido	
Divertido	
	Graciosa
Paciente	
	Interesante
Trabajador	
Inteligente	

5. Spot and add in the missing word

a. La profe ciencias

b. Me gusta la profe de arte porque divertida

c. No gusta el profe de educación física

d. Profe de matemáticas es muy aburrido

e. El profe de francés siempre enfada

f. Me encanta la profe de alemán porque simpática

g. El profe de ciencias nos muchos deberes

6. Tangled translation: into Spanish

a. No me **like** la profe **of French**

b. Me **love the teacher** de **English**

c. **She gives us a lot of** deberes

d. El profe de ciencias **is patient**

e. Nos **gives little** deberes

f. El **teacher of maths** es muy **funny**

g. La profe de **Spanish** me **tells off**

h. **The teacher** (m) siempre **gets angry**

7. Translate into Spanish

a. I don't like the science teacher because she is boring

b. The French teacher gives a lot of homework

c. The German teacher always helps me

d. The maths teacher always gets angry

e. The art teacher is funny and understands me

f. The PE teacher is fun and gives us little homework

g. The music teacher is mean and impatient

h. The English teacher is interesting and hard-working

1. Me llamo Ofelia y tengo catorce años. Mi cumpleaños es el dieciséis de junio. Soy de Inglaterra pero ahora vivo en Oslo, la capital de Noruega, con mi familia.

2. En mi familia somos cinco personas: mi hermano mayor, Lucas, mi hermana menor, Marta, mi padre, Guillermo, mi madre, Carmen, y yo. Prefiero a mi madre porque es más relajada que mi padre. Mi padre es más estricto.

3. Mis abuelos se llaman David y Mary. David tiene sesenta y ocho años y Mary tiene sesenta y nueve. Son muy cariñosos y les gusta pasar tiempo con nosotros. Mi madre es tan cariñosa como mi abuela, pero mi abuelo es más gracioso que mi padre.

4. Mi hermano mayor se llama Lucas. A Lucas le gusta tocar el piano y jugar al rugby. Tiene dieciséis años y es muy rápido y fuerte. Su cumpleaños es el nueve de octubre. Lucas tiene el pelo castaño y los ojos azules. Lucas es más organizado que yo, pero yo soy más creativa que él.

5. Mi hermana menor es más artística que mi hermano. Tiene los ojos verdes y el pelo rizado. Le gusta pintar y bailar hip-hop. En el colegio, su asignatura favorita es la informática porque es útil para el futuro. No le gustan las matemáticas porque son un poco complicadas y aburridas.

6. Voy a un colegio bastante grande en mi barrio. Me encanta mi colegio porque los profesores son muy buenos. Son comprensivos y siempre nos ayudan cuando tenemos un problema. Además, me encanta la clase de música porque puedo explorar diferentes melodías en el piano y escribir canciones. Mi asignatura favorita es la ciencia porque aprendo mucho en clase. La profesora es muy severa y a veces me regaña, pero también es graciosa y explica las cosas muy bien. No sé (*I don't know*) si me gusta o no.

7. Mi profesor favorito es el profe de historia. Siempre me ayuda cuando no comprendo y siempre está de buen humor. Sin embargo, no me llevo bien con mi profesora de chino porque es un poco aburrida y siempre me chilla. No aprendo mucho en clase.

Ofelia, 14, Oslo, Noruega

1. Find the Spanish equivalent for the following in paragraphs 1 to 4

a. I am from England

b. We are

c. My older brother

d. Stricter

e. Are called

f. They are affectionate

g. To spend time

h. He likes to play

i. Strong

2. Complete the following translation of paragraph 5

My _____ sister is more artistic than my brother. She has _____ eyes and _____ hair. She enjoys _____ and dancing hip hop. At school, her favourite subject is _____ because it is _____ for the future. She doesn't like maths because it is a bit complicated and _____.

3. Answer the following questions about paragraph 6

a. Where is Ofelia's school located?

b. Why does she like her school?

c. What are her teachers like? (2)

d. Why does she like the music lesssons? (2)

e. What is her favourite subject? Why?

4. Translate the following phrases taken from paragraphs 6 and 7

a. Son comprensivos   f. Me ayuda

b. Nos ayudan   g. De buen humor

c. Escribir canciones   h. Sin embargo

d. Aprendo mucho   i. No me llevo bien

e. Me regaña   j. Me chilla

 **THE LANGUAGE GYM**

1. Me llamo Álvaro y tengo trece años. Mi cumpleaños es el dieciocho de julio. Soy de Gales y ahora vivo en Cardiff, la capital de Gales, con mi familia. Estoy muy tranquilo porque es domingo y hoy no tengo colegio.

2. En mi familia somos cinco personas: mi hermano mayor, Diego, mi hermana menor, Pilar, mi padre, Dante, mi madre, Guadelupe, y yo. Prefiero a mi padre porque es más gracioso que mi madre y siempre me ayuda. Mis abuelos se llaman Elías y Romina. Elías tiene sesenta y tres años y Romina tiene sesenta y cuatro. Son muy divertidos y les gusta ir al parque con nosotros. Mi madre es tan habladora como mi abuela, pero mi abuelo es más perezoso que mi padre.

3. A Diego, mi hermano mayor, le gusta tocar la batería *(drums)*. Toca en un grupo *(he plays in a band)* con sus amigos. Tiene quince años y es muy amable y tranquilo. Su cumpleaños es el once de abril. Diego tiene el pelo rubio y los ojos verdes. Él es más trabajador que yo, pero yo soy más fuerte que él.

4. Mi hermana menor Pilar es más baja que mi hermano. Tiene los ojos marrones y el pelo liso. Le gusta ir al centro comercial con sus amigas y comprar ropa. En el colegio, su asignatura favorita es la química *(chemistry)* porque la profe es muy buena y aprende mucho en clase. No le gusta el teatro porque dice que es aburrido.

5. Voy a un colegio muy grande en mi ciudad. Mi colegio es muy bueno porque los profesores son muy inteligentes, divertidos y trabajadores. Siempre me ayudan si no entiendo algo. Me encanta la clase de inglés porque me gusta leer y escribir historias *(write stories)*. Mi asignatura favorita es la música porque la profesora es muy divertida y siempre me ayuda. Es mi profesora favorita.

6. El profesor favorito de mi hermana Pilar es la profe de ciencias. Siempre le ayuda cuando no comprende algo y es muy graciosa. Sin embargo, no se lleva bien con su profesora de historia porque da muchos deberes y siempre le regaña *(porque no hace los deberes)*. Pilar dice que no aprende mucho en clase.

Álvaro, 13, Cardiff, Gales

5. Find someone who…

a. …is feeling calm today

b. …always helps Álvaro

c. …is 64 years old

d. …enjoys playing the drums

e. …has brown eyes and straight hair

f. …has fun and hard-working teachers

g. …is very kind and calm

h. …always helps Álvaro when he doesn't understand something

i. …likes buying clothes with friends

6. Find the Spanish in paragraph 4

a. Shorter

b. Straight hair

c. To buy clothes

d. Very good

e. She says that

f. It is boring

7. Correct the errors in the following translation of paragraph 5

I go to a very small school in my city. My school is very good because the teachers are very intelligent, understanding and helpful. They always listen to me if I don't understand something. I like the English class because I love to speak and to write stories. My favourite game is music because the teacher is very talented and always praises me. She is my favourite teacher.

8. Find out the 4 words on the list below, which are not included in paragraph 6

a. Is	e. Also	i. A lot
b. But	f. Always	j. My
c. However	g. Never	k. In
d. With	h. That	l. For

UNIT 11
Saying what I and others do
in our free time

In this unit you will learn how to say:

- What activities you do using the verbs 'jugar' (play), 'hacer' (do) and 'ir' (go)
- How to use these verbs in the present indicative
- Other free time activities

You will revisit:
- Time and frequency markers
- Weather
- Expressing likes/dislikes
- Adjectives
- Pets

UNIT 11
Saying what I and others do in our free time

¿Qué haces en tu tiempo libre?	What do you do in your free time?
¿Qué hace tu amigo en su tiempo libre?	What does your friend do in their free time?
¿Qué deportes haces?	What sports do you do?
¿Haces otra actividad?	Do you do another activity?
¿Con qué frecuencia haces deporte?	How often do you do sport?

A menudo *Often* **A veces** *Sometimes* **Casi nunca** *Hardly ever* **Cuando hace buen tiempo** *When the weather is good* **Cuando hace mal tiempo** *When the weather is bad* **Raramente** *Rarely* **Todos los días** *Every day* ***Dos veces por semana** *Twice a week*	**(yo) juego** *I play* **mi amigo/a juega** *my friend plays*	**al ajedrez** **al baloncesto** **a las cartas** **al fútbol** **al tenis** **con mis amigos /as**	*chess* *basketball* *cards* *football* *tennis* *with my friends*
	(yo) hago *I do* **mi amigo/a hace** *my friend does*	**ciclismo** **los deberes** **deporte** **equitación** **escalada** **esquí** **footing** **natación** **pesas** **senderismo**	*cycling* *homework* *sport* *horse riding* *rock climbing* *skiing* *jogging* *swimming* *weights* *hiking*
	(yo) voy *I go* **mi amigo/a va** *my friend goes*	**a casa de mi amigo/a** **a la montaña** **a la piscina** **a la playa** **al gimnasio** **al parque** **al polideportivo** **de marcha** **de pesca** **en bici**	*to my friend's house* *to the mountain* *to the pool* *to the beach* *to the gym* *to the park* *to the sports centre* *clubbing* *fishing* *on a bike ride*

*Author's note: *Most adverbs of frequency (always/never etc) can go either at the start or end of the sentence. E.g.* **Siempre hago deporte / Hago deporte siempre.** *However, some expressions, such as* **dos veces por semana** *(twice a week) work better at the end of the sentence.*

 **THE LANGUAGE GYM**

1. Complete with JUEGO, HAGO or VOY

a. _____ al ajedrez

b. _____ pesas

c. _____ a las cartas

d. _____ escalada

e. _____ a la piscina

f. _____ de marcha

g. _____ a casa de mi amigo

h. _____ con mis amigos

2. Complete with the missing syllables

a. Juego a los videojue_ _ _

b. Hago senderis _ _

c. Voy al polideporti_ _

d. Voy de mar_ _ _

e. Hago cicli_ _ _

f. Voy a la monta _ _

g. _ _ _ go al tenis

h. Voy a la pla_ _

i. Voy al par_ _ _

j. Hago nata_ _ _ _

3. Listening for detail: what activities does Amparo do each day? Tick the correct one

a.	Monday	▪ Cycling ▪ Chess ▪ Rock climbing
b.	Tuesday	▪ Going to the mountain ▪ Swimming ▪ Going clubbing
c.	Wednesday	▪ Going to the gym ▪ Playing basketball ▪ Playing tennis
d.	Thursday	▪ Jogging ▪ Homework ▪ Horse riding
e.	Friday	▪ Skiing ▪ Weights ▪ Chess
f.	Saturday	▪ Hiking ▪ Weights ▪ Bike riding
g.	Sunday	▪ Swimming ▪ Weights ▪ Fishing

4. Spot the intruder

Me llamo Tomás Weidner. Soy un alemán. Soy muy deportista. En mi tiempo libre hago mucho deporte. Mi deporte preferido es la escalada libre. Hago escalada casi todos los días. Cuando hace mal tiempo por lo general me quedo en casa y juego al ajedrez o juego a las cartas con mi hermano menor. También me gusta mucho hacer natación. Hago la natación casi todos los fines de semana en la piscina cerca de mi casa.

5. Faulty translation: correct the translation

a. My name is Laura. I am red-haired and am very friendly and talkative.

b. I am not very sporty. I prefer to read books, to play chess, play cards and go shopping.

c. When the weather is nice I like going hiking and from time to time…

d. …I go to the park with my boyfriend. I rarely go to the gym.

e. It is very boring in my opinion. I prefer to go jogging.

THE LANGUAGE GYM

6. Listen to Dylan talk about his friends and fill in the grid below - in English

Name	Age	Description	Favourite food	Favourite clothes	Favourite sport	How often they practise sport
a. Chris						
b. Aaron						
c. Arnoud						
d. Nico						

7. Narrow listening - Gapped translation

My name is _____ and I am _____ years old. I am _____ and I am a Canarian. I am not a

kind of _____, I am someone from the beautiful _____. I live there with my _____, two

_____ and one _____. My parents are very _____ and _____. My brothers are very

_____ and my sister is _____ __ _____ helpful. My favourite foods are _____ and

_____. I also eat _____ very often. In my free time I do a lot of _____. I play _____

at school _____. I often do _____ at the gym near my house. Three times a week I

_____ and from time to time I go to _____ with my brothers. Besides sport, I also play

_____ and go to _____ once a week. I love _____. Goodbye.

Author's note: Please note that the Canary Islands are actually named after the Latin word for dogs "canis" (not because of canaries). Canarians, or Canary Islanders are renowned for being one of the friendliest and most welcoming people in Spain.

 **THE LANGUAGE GYM**

Unit 11. Free time: VOCABULARY BUILDING

1. Match

Juego al ajedrez	I go horse-riding
Hago footing	I play chess
Hago equitación	I play basketball
Juego a las cartas	I go hiking
Voy en bici	I go swimming
Hago natación	I go biking
Hago senderismo	I go jogging
Juego al baloncesto	I play cards

2. Complete with the missing word

a. Mi amiga juega al _____   *My friend plays chess*

b. _____ equitación   *I go horse riding*

c. _____ a las cartas   *I play cards*

d. Mi amigo va en _____   *My friend goes cycling*

e. Juego al _____   *I play basketball*

f. Voy de _____   *I go fishing*

g. Mi amigo hace _____   *My friend goes hiking*

h. Hago _____   *I go rock climbing*

i. Hago _____   *I go jogging*

j. Hago los _____   *I do my homework*

juego	baloncesto	pesca	escalada	hago
deberes	bici	ajedrez	senderismo	footing

3. Translate into English

a. Mi amigo va en bici todos los días

b. Mi amiga hace senderismo a menudo

c. Hago escalada dos veces por semana

d. Casi nunca hago equitación

e. Cuando hace mal tiempo juego a las cartas o al ajedrez

f. Juego al baloncesto a menudo

g. Voy de marcha raramente

h. Voy a casa de mi amigo a menudo

i. Voy a la playa todos los días

j. Voy de pesca una vez por semana

k. Juego al golf cuando hace buen tiempo

4. Broken words

a. Mi amigo hace eq_____ *My friend goes horse riding*

b. Hago na_____ *I go swimming*

c. Voy de pe_____ *I go fishing*

d. Mi amigo va en bi_____ *My friend goes biking*

e. Juego al aj_____ *I play chess*

f. Voy de ma_____ *I go clubbing*

g. Mi amiga juega a las ca_____ *My friend plays cards*

h. Hago esc_____ *I do rock climbing*

5. 'Voy', 'Juego' or 'Hago'?

a. _____ al baloncesto

b. _____ en bici

c. _____ al ajedrez

d. _____ a las cartas

e. _____ natación

f. _____ de marcha

g. _____ al tenis

h. _____ pesas

i. _____ escalada

6. Bad translation – spot any translation errors and fix them

a. Nunca voy de marcha : *I often go clubbing*

b. Juego a las cartas a menudo: *I play chess often*

c. Hago escalada raramente: *I go swimming rarely*

d. Cuando hace buen tiempo mi amigo hace footing: *When the weather is nice my friend goes hiking*

e. Voy en bici una vez a la semana: *I go biking every day*

f. Casi nunca juego al ajedrez: *I hardly ever play cards*

g. Hago senderismo a menudo: *I never go hiking*

h. Hago natación a menudo: *I go swimming from time to time*

 **THE LANGUAGE GYM**

Unit 11. Free time: READING

Me llamo Thomas Weidner. Soy alemán. En mi tiempo libre hago mucho deporte. Mi deporte favorito es la escalada. Hago escalada todos los días. Cuando hace mal tiempo me quedo en casa *[I stay at home]* y juego al ajedrez o a las cartas. También me gusta mucho jugar a videojuegos o a la Play. Juego a la Play a menudo. Mi amigo Fran siempre juega a las cartas.

Me llamo Verónica Palacín. Soy española, de Barbastro. Soy pelirroja y muy simpática y graciosa, pero no soy muy deportista. Prefiero leer libros *[read books]*, jugar a videojuegos o al ajedrez y escuchar música. Cuando hace buen tiempo, sin embargo, a veces hago footing en el parque de mi barrio o juego al tenis con mi hermano. No me gusta ir al gimnasio ni a la piscina. Odio la natación porque no me gusta el agua.

Me llamo Olga. Soy de Chipre *(Cyprus)*. En mi tiempo libre me gusta mucho leer libros y periódicos. También me gusta jugar a las cartas y al ajedrez. No soy muy deportista. Pero, a veces voy al gimnasio y hago pesas. Además, en el fin de semana, cuando hace buen tiempo, hago senderismo en el campo con mi perro. Buddy es un perro salchicha y es pequeño y marrón. Siempre juega con una pelota *[ball]*.

Me llamo Jean. Soy francés. Me encanta ir en bici. Voy en bici todos los días con mis amigos. Es mi deporte favorito. A veces hago escalada, footing o senderismo. No me gusta el tenis ni el fútbol. También odio hacer natación. Hago natación muy raramente. Dos veces por semana voy de marcha con mi amigo, Julien Barrett. Él siempre hace deporte.

1. Find the Spanish for the following in Thomas' text

a. I do a lot of sport

b. My favourite sport

c. Rock-climbing

d. Every day

e. When the weather's bad

f. I play chess

g. Also

h. I play on the Playstation

2. Find the Spanish in Jean's text for

a. I love biking

b. with my friends

c. sometimes

d. I do swimming

e. I go clubbing

f. I go rock climbing

g. with my friend, Julien

3. Complete the following statements about Verónica

a. She is from _____

b. She is not very _____

c. She plays videogames and _____

d. When the weather is nice she goes _____

e. She also plays tennis with her_____

f. She doesn't enjoy the gym nor the _____

4. List 8 details about Olga

1.

2.

3.

4.

5.

6.

7.

8.

5. Find someone who...

a. ...enjoys reading newspapers

b. ...hates swimming

c. ...does a lot of sport

d. ...does weight lifting

e. ...goes clubbing twice a week

Unit 11. Free time: TRANSLATION

1. Gapped translation

a. **Nunca voy de marcha:** I _____ go clubbing

b. **Juego a la Play a menudo:** I often play _____

c. **No juego al tenis casi nunca:** I _____ _____ play tennis

d. **Mi amigo juega al _____:** My friend plays chess

e. **Juego a las _____:** I play cards

f. **A veces voy en bici:** _____, I go cycling

g. **Mi amigo nunca hago pesas:** My friend never does _____

h. **Cuando hace _____ tiempo hago footing:**
When the weather is nice, I go jogging

2. Translate to English

a. Casi nunca

b. A veces

c. Cuando hace mal tiempo

d. A casa de mi amigo

e. Nunca

f. Todos los días

g. Hago escalada

h. Mi amigo va de marcha

i. Voy de pesca

3. Translate into English

a. Nunca voy de pesca con mi padre

b. Juego a las cartas con mi hermano

c. Hago senderismo con mi madre

d. Juego al ajedrez con mi mejor amigo

e. Casi nunca juego a la Play con mi hermano

f. Voy a la discoteca todos los sábados

4. Translate into Spanish

a. *Bike*: B

b. *Rock climbing*: E

c. *Basketball*: B

d. *Fishing*: P

e. *Weights*: P

f. *Videogames*: V

g. *Chess*: A

h. *Cards*: C

i. *Hiking*: S

j. *Jogging*: F

5. Translate into Spanish

a. I 'do' jogging

b. My friend plays chess

c. I 'do' rock climbing

d. I 'do' swimming

e. I 'do' horse riding

f. My friend does weights

g. I go clubbing

h. I play videogames

i. My friend 'does' cycling

j. I 'do' hiking

THE LANGUAGE GYM

125

Unit 11. Free time: WRITING

1. Split sentences

Nunca	el parque
Juego al ajedrez a	deporte
Voy a casa	hago escalada
Hago footing en	menudo
Mi amigo	en bici
Hago mucho	de mi amigo Paco
Mi amigo va	gimnasio
Hago pesas en el	juega a las cartas

2. Complete the sentences

a. Nunca _____ footing

b. A veces _____ al ajedrez

c. _____ escalada de vez en cuando

d. Mi amiga _____ equitación a menudo

e. Juego al tenis _____ _____ días

f. Voy a _____ de mi amigo

g. En mi _____ libre

h. Hago _____ en el gimnasio

i. Mi amigo _____ los deberes

3. Spot and correct mistakes (note: in some cases a word is missing)

a. Mi amigo juego tenis:

b. Juego a las ajedrez:

c. Voy a casa mi amigo:

d. Casi nunca voy de bici:

e. Voy mis deberes:

f. Voy natación:

g. Mi amigo hago pesos:

4. Complete the words

a. Aje_____

b. Balon_____

c. Sende_____

d. Video_____

e. Equi_____

f. Nun_____

g. A men_____

5. Write a paragraph for each of the people below in the first person singular (I):

Name	Sport I do	How often	Who with	Where	Why I like it
Juanita	Hiking	Every day	With my boyfriend	In the countryside	It's fun
Dylan	Weight-lifting	Often	With my friend James	At home	It's healthy
Alejo	Jogging	When the weather is nice	Alone	In the park	It's relaxing

1. Me llamo Liam y tengo quince años. Mi cumpleaños es el veintitrés de septiembre. Soy de Irlanda pero ahora vivo en Manchester, en el noroeste de Inglaterra, con mi familia.

2. En mi familia somos cuatro personas: mi hermano mayor, Noel, mi padre, Tommy, mi madre, Peggy, y yo. Prefiero a mi madre porque es más tranquila que mi padre. Mi padre es más trabajador. Mis abuelos se llaman Thomas y Mary. Thomas tiene setenta y dos años y Mary tiene sesenta y nueve. Son muy cariñosos y buenos con nosotros.

3. Mi hermano mayor se llama Noel. A Noel le gusta tocar la guitarra y cantar. Tiene diecisiete años y es muy talentoso. Su cumpleaños es el catorce de noviembre. Noel tiene el pelo oscuro y los ojos verdes. Noel es más organizado que yo, pero yo soy mejor cantante *(better singer)* que él.

4. En el colegio, mi asignatura favorita es la música. Me encanta escribir canciones *(writing songs)* y cantar *(singing)*. No me gusta el arte porque es un poco aburrido y no sé si es útil para el futuro.

5. Me encanta mi instituto porque los profesores son muy buenos. Son apasionados y siempre están dispuestos *(willing)* a ayudar cuando tenemos un problema. Además, me encanta la clase de música porque puedo explorar diferentes ritmos en el piano y componer *(compose)* mis propias *(my own)* canciones. Mi asignatura favorita es la química porque me encanta aprender sobre las reacciones y hacer experimentos. Mi profesora de química es exigente *(demanding)* pero también divertida, y siempre me ayuda en las clases.

6. En mi tiempo libre hago mucho deporte. Mi deporte favorito es la escalada. Hago escalada todos los días. Cuando hace mal tiempo me quedo en casa y juego a videojuegos o a las cartas. También me gusta mucho jugar a la Play con mis amigos. Cuando hace buen tiempo, a veces hago footing en el parque de mi barrio o juego al tenis con mi hermano Noel. Además *(furthermore)*, me gusta ir al gimnasio y a la piscina. La natación es agotadora pero muy divertida.

Liam, 15, Manchester, Inglaterra

1. Answer the following questions in English

a. Where is Liam from?

b. Why does he prefer his mother to his father?

c. How old are his grandparents?

d. What is Noel's hair like?

e. Why does he not enjoy art at school?

f. Why does he like his school?

g. What's his favourite subject? Why? (2)

h. What is his favourite sport? How often does he do it?

i. What does he say about swimming? (2)

2. Find the Spanish equivalent for the following in Liam's text

a. But now I live (par. 1)

b. We are (par. 2)

c. They are very affectionate (par. 2)

d. He is very talented (par. 3)

e. He has dark hair (par. 3)

f. I don't know (par. 4)

g. The teachers are very good (par. 5)

h. I love to learn about (par. 5)

i. She always helps me in lessons (par. 5)

j. In my free time (par. 6)

k. When the weather is bad (par. 6)

l. Sometimes I go jogging (par. 6)

m. Swimming is tiring (par. 6)

3. Complete the translation of paragraph 6 below

In my free time I do a lot of _____. My favourite sport is _____. I go _____ every day. When _____ I stay at home and I play videogames or _____. I also _____ _____ to play PlayStation with my friends. When the _____ is _____, sometimes I go _____ in the park in my _____ or I play tennis with my _____ Noel. _____, I enjoy going to the _____ and to the _____. Swimming is _____ but very _____.

1. Me llamo Damian y tengo doce años. Mi cumpleaños es el veintiocho de marzo. Soy de Inglaterra pero ahora vivo en Valencia, en el sureste de España, con mi familia. Hoy estoy regular porque estoy un poco estresado.

2. En mi familia somos tres personas: mi padre Alan, mi madre Becky y yo. Me llevo muy bien con mi madre porque es más paciente que mi padre. Mi padre es más perezoso. Mis abuelos se llaman John y Louise. John tiene setenta y siete años y Louise tiene sesenta y ocho. Son muy simpáticos conmigo *(with me)* pero a veces mi abuelo me regaña. Mi abuelo es la persona más impaciente de mi familia, mucho más que mi padre y mi madre.

3. Mi mejor amigo se llama Chris. A Chris le gusta ir a la playa y hacer surf con su padre. También le gusta jugar a videojuegos en su tiempo libre. Tiene doce años, igual que yo. Su cumpleaños es el diecinueve de septiembre. Chris tiene el pelo rubio y los ojos azules. Chris es más guapo que yo, ¡pero un poco más tonto también!

4. En el colegio, mi asignatura favorita es el arte. Me encanta hacer dibujos y pintar. Sin embargo, no me gusta mucho la geografía porque es un poco aburrida. La verdad *(the truth)* es que no me interesa.

5. Mi colegio se llama St Mary's y los profesores son excelentes. Son muy inteligentes y siempre me escuchan cuando tengo un problema. Además, me encanta la clase de inglés porque puedo explorar diferentes autores y escribir mis propias historias. Mi asignatura favorita es la historia porque me encanta aprender sobre el pasado y personajes históricos famosos. Mi profesora de historia es muy divertida y siempre me ayuda, pero nos da muchos deberes.

6. En mi tiempo libre leo libros y escucho música. Mi grupo favorito es 'El canto del loco'. También me gusta cantar y tocar la guitarra. Lo hago todos los días. Cuando hace mal tiempo me quedo en casa y veo películas o leo tebeos *(comics)*. También me gusta mucho jugar a videojuegos con mis amigos. Cuando hace buen tiempo, a veces juego al fútbol en el polideportivo *(sports centre)* cerca de mi casa. Además *(furthermore)*, me gusta ir al estadio y ver partidos de fútbol. ¡El equipo de Valencia es bastante bueno!

Damian, 12, Valencia, España

4. Answer the following questions about paragraphs 1 and 2 in Spanish as if you were Damian

a. ¿Cómo te llamas?

b. ¿Cuántos años tienes?

c. ¿De dónde eres?

d. ¿Dónde vives ahora?

e. ¿Con quién vives?

f. ¿Cómo estás hoy?

g. ¿Cuántas personas hay en tu familia?

h. ¿Quién es más paciente que tu padre?

i. ¿Cuántos años tienen tus abuelos?

j. ¿Quién te regaña de vez en cuando?

5. Translate the following words from paragraphs 3 and 4

a. Mejor	h. Más
b. Ir	i. Asignatura
c. Hacer	j. Pintar
d. Su	k. Sin embargo
e. También	l. Aburrida
f. Tiene	m. Verdad
g. Igual	n. Que

6. Correct the following statements about Damian, based on paragraph 5

a. Los profesores de Damian no son buenos

b. Los profesores de Damian no le escuchan

c. A Damian no le gusta el inglés

d. Su asignatura favorita es la geografía

e. Su profesora de historia es muy aburrida

f. Su profesora de historia le da pocos deberes

7. Find the Spanish equivalents in paragraph 5 and 6

a. I read: L	f. To sing: C
b. Group: G	g. Good: B
c. Also: T	h. Team: E
d. Weather: T	i. Films: P
e. Comics: T	j. I see: V

TERM 2 - BRINGING IT ALL TOGETHER – QUESTION SKILLS

1. Fill in the missing question words

a. ¿C_____ personas hay en tu familia?

b. ¿ ___ _____ te llevas bien en tu familia?

c. ¿ __ _____ ___ con alguien? ¿ ____ ___?

d. ¿C_____ te llevas con tu padre?

e. ¿C_____ años tiene tu hermano?

f. ¿C_____ es tu hermano?

g. ¿C_____ es su cumpleaños?

h. ¿__ _____ tu profe de inglés? ¿ ____ ___?

i. ¿ _____ es tu profesor favorito?

j. ¿ ____ _____ profesor que no te gusta?

k. ¿ _____ profesor te ayuda siempre?

l. ¿ _____ es tu asignatura favorita?

m. ¿ ____ _____ en tu tiempo libre?

n. ¿ _____ deportes haces?

o. ¿ ____ _____ cuando hace mal tiempo?

2. Listen and choose the option that you hear

a. En mi familia hay **cuatro / cinco** personas

b. Me llevo mejor con mi **hermana / madre**

c. A veces no me llevo bien con mi **padre / hermano**

d. Me llevo **muy bien / muy mal** con mi padre

e. Mi hermano tiene **ocho / nueve** años

f. Es bastante **alto / bajo**, tiene el pelo rubio

g. Su cumpleaños es el diecinueve de **mayo / marzo**

h. Sí, me gusta **bastante / mucho**

i. Mi profesor favorito es el profesor de **historia / arte**

j. No me gusta mucho mi profesora de **arte / inglés**

k. Mi profesor de **inglés / tecnología**

l. Me encantan las **ciencias / matemáticas**

m. Voy a casa de mi mejor **amigo / amiga**

n. Hago **equitación / natación**

o. **Me quedo en casa / quedo con mis amigos**

3. Listen and write in the missing information to the questions for exercise 1

a. En mi _____ hay _____ personas, mis _____, mi _____ pequeño y yo

b. Me _____ mejor con mi _____ porque es muy _____

c. A veces no me _____ bien con mi _____ porque es un poco _____

d. Me llevo _____ _____ con mi _____ porque es muy _____

e. Mi _____ tiene _____ años

f. Es bastante _____, tiene el pelo _____ y los ojos _____

g. Su _____ es el _____ de _____

h. _____, me gusta _____ porque _____ las _____ muy _____

i. Mi profesor _____ es el profesor de _____ porque es muy _____

j. No me _____ mucho mi profesora de _____ porque es demasiado _____

k. Mi profesor de _____ siempre me _____ mucho

l. Me _____ las _____ porque _____ muy útiles para el _____

m. En mi tiempo _____, voy a _____ de mi mejor _____ y jugamos a _____ en línea

n. Hago _____ y juego al _____, y a veces juego al _____

o. Cuando hace _____ tiempo, me _____ en casa y _____ una serie o _____ un libro

 **THE LANGUAGE GYM**

TERM 2 - BRINGING IT ALL TOGETHER – QUESTION SKILLS

4. Fill in the grid with your personal information

Question	
1. ¿Cuántas personas hay en tu familia?	
2. ¿Con quién te llevas bien?	
3. ¿Cómo te llevas con tu padre/madre?	
4. ¿Cuántos años tiene tu hermano/a?	
5. ¿Cómo es tu hermano?	
6. ¿Cuándo es su cumpleaños?	
7. ¿Cuál es tu profesor favorito?	
8. ¿Hay algún profesor que no te gusta?	
9. ¿Cuál es tu asignatura favorita?	
10. ¿Qué haces en tu tiempo libre?	
11. ¿Qué deportes haces?	
12. ¿Qué haces cuando hace buen tiempo?	

5. Survey two of your classmates using the same questions as above– write down the main information you hear in Spanish

Q.	Person 1	Person 2
1.		
2.		
3.		
4.		
5.		
6.		
7.		
8.		
9.		
10.		
11.		
12.		

No Snakes No Ladders

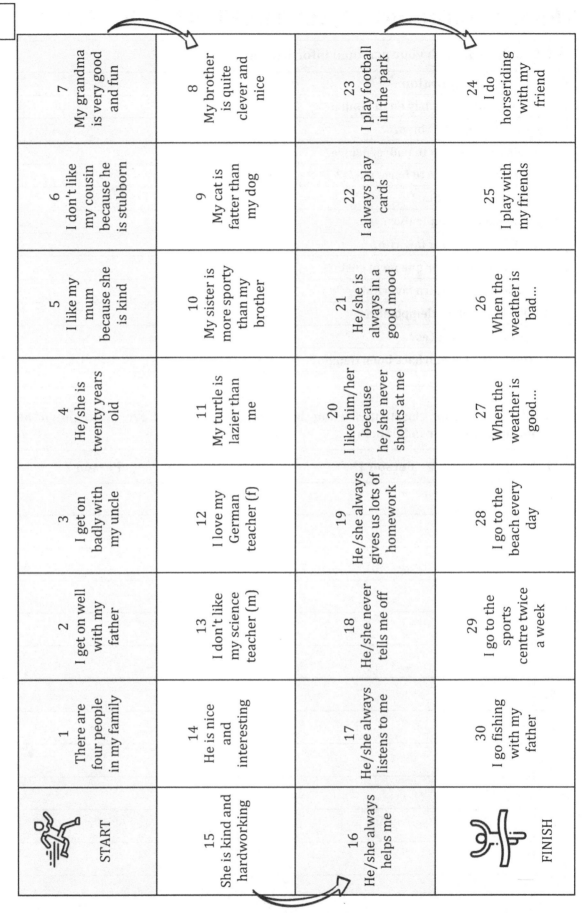

7 My grandma is very good and fun	6 I don't like my cousin because he is stubborn	5 I like my mum because she is kind	4 He/she is twenty years old	3 I get on badly with my uncle	2 I get on well with my father	1 There are four people in my family
8 My brother is quite clever and nice	9 My cat is fatter than my dog	10 My sister is more sporty than my brother	11 My turtle is lazier than me	12 I love my German teacher (f)	13 I don't like my science teacher (m)	14 He is nice and interesting
23 I play football in the park	22 I always play cards	21 He/she is always in a good mood	20 I like him/her because he/she never shouts at me	19 He/she always gives us lots of homework	18 He/she never tells me off	17 He/she always listens to me
24 I do horseriding with my friend	25 I play with my friends	26 When the weather is bad...	27 When the weather is good...	28 I go to the beach every day	29 I go to the sports centre twice a week	30 I go fishing with my father

START

15
She is kind and hardworking

16
He/she always helps me

FINISH

 **THE LANGUAGE GYM**

No Snakes No Ladders

SALIDA

1. Hay cuatro personas en mi familia
2. Me llevo bien con mi padre
3. Me llevo mal con mi tío
4. Tiene veinte años
5. Me gusta mi madre porque es amable
6. No me gusta mi primo porque es terco
7. Mi abuela es muy buena y divertida
8. Mi hermano es bastante inteligente y simpático
9. Mi gato es más gordo que mi perro
10. Mi hermana es más deportista que mi hermano
11. Mi tortuga es más perezosa que yo
12. Me encanta mi profesora de alemán
13. No me gusta mi profesor de ciencias
14. (Él) Es simpático e interesante
15. (Ella) Es amable y trabajadora
16. Siempre me ayuda
17. Siempre me escucha
18. Nunca me regaña
19. Siempre nos da muchos deberes
20. Me gusta porque nunca me chilla
21. Siempre está de buen humor
22. Siempre juego a las cartas
23. Juego al fútbol en el parque
24. Hago equitación con mi amigo
25. Juego con mis amigos
26. Cuando hace mal tiempo...
27. Cuando hace buen tiempo...
28. Voy a la playa todos los días
29. Voy al polideportivo dos veces a la semana
30. Voy de pesca con mi padre

LLEGADA

PYRAMID TRANSLATION

Term 2 - Recap - Free Time

Translate each part of the pyramid out loud with your partner, then write it into the spaces provided below.

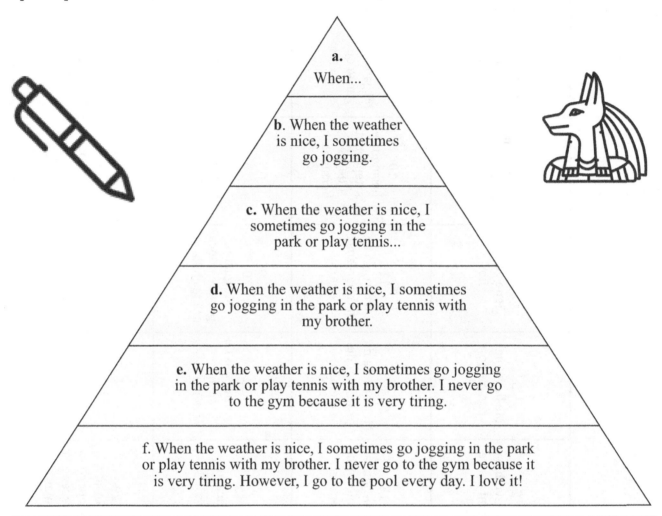

a.
When...

b. When the weather is nice, I sometimes go jogging.

c. When the weather is nice, I sometimes go jogging in the park or play tennis...

d. When the weather is nice, I sometimes go jogging in the park or play tennis with my brother.

e. When the weather is nice, I sometimes go jogging in the park or play tennis with my brother. I never go to the gym because it is very tiring.

f. When the weather is nice, I sometimes go jogging in the park or play tennis with my brother. I never go to the gym because it is very tiring. However, I go to the pool every day. I love it!

Write your translation here

THE LANGUAGE GYM

One pen One dice

Play in pairs. You only have 1 pen and 1 dice.
One person has the pen and starts translating the sentence into **English.** The other person rolls the dice until they roll a 6, they swap the pen and translate. The winner is the person who finishes translating all the sentences first.

1. Hay cinco personas en mi familia.	
2. Me llevo bien con mi madre.	
3. Tiene cuarenta años.	
4. Me gusta mi abuela porque es cariñosa.	
5. Mi perro es más gracioso que mi gato.	
6. Mi abuela es tímida, pero simpática.	
7. Mi profesor siempre me ayuda.	
8. Nunca me regaña.	
9. Cuando hace buen tiempo...	
10. Siempre voy a la playa.	

One pen One dice

Play in pairs. You only have 1 pen and 1 dice.
One person has the pen and starts translating the sentence into **Spanish.** The other person rolls the dice until they roll a 6, they swap the pen and translate. The winner is the person who finishes translating all the sentences first.

1. There are five people in my family.	
2. I get on well with my mother.	
3. She is forty years old.	
4. I like my grandma because she is caring.	
5. My dog is funnier than my cat.	
6. My grandmother is shy, but nice.	
7. My teacher (m) always helps me.	
8. He/she never tells me off.	
9. When the weather is good...	
10. I always go to the beach.	

TERM 3 – OVERVIEW

This term you will learn:

Unit 12 - How to talk about daily routine/school day
• What you do every day
• What time you do it
• Linking sentences using 'luego', 'después' & 'finalmente'

Unit 13 - How to talk about weekend plans
• To talk about your plans are for the weekend
• The immediate future structure "voy a + infinitive"
• How to use "al" and "a la" for masculine/feminine places
• To say what you are going to do using "para"

Unit 14 – How to talk about food – likes/dislikes
• How to say what food you like/dislike
• Why you like/dislike food
• Grammar: AR verbs – desayunar/cenar/tomar/almorzar

Unit 15 -How to talk about holiday plans
• Where you are going to go/stary
• How you will travel & who with
• What you will do there

KEY QUESTIONS

- ¿A qué hora te despiertas?	*What time do you wake up?*
- ¿Qué haces por la mañana?	*What do you do in the morning?*
- ¿Qué desayunas normalmente?	*What do you have for breakfast, normally?*
- ¿A qué hora sales de casa?	*What time do you leave the house?*
- ¿Cómo vas al colegio?	*How do you go to school?*
- ¿Qué planes tienes para el fin de semana que viene?	*What plans do you have for next weekend?*
- ¿Adónde te gustaría ir?	*Where would you like to go?*
- ¿Con quién vas a ir?	*Who are you going to go with?*
- ¿Qué más te gustaría hacer?	*What else would you like to do?*
- ¿Qué comida (no) te gusta? ¿Por qué?	*What food do you (not) like? Why?*
- ¿Te gusta el pescado?	*Do you like fish?*
- ¿Cuál es tu comida favorita?	*What is your favourite food?*
- ¿Hay alguna comida que odias?	Is there any food that you hate?
- ¿Adónde vas a ir de vacaciones este verano?	*Where are you going to go on hol this summer?*
- ¿Cómo vas a viajar?	*How are you going to travel?*
- ¿Cuánto tiempo vas a pasar allí?	*How long are you going to spend there?*
- ¿Dónde vas a quedarte?	*Where are you going to stay?*
- ¿Qué te gustaría hacer allí?	*What would you like to do?*

UNIT 12
Talking about my
daily routine/school day

In this unit you will learn how to say:

- What you do every day
- At what time you do it
- Sequencing events/actions (e.g. using 'then', 'finally')

You will revisit:
- Numbers
- Free time activities
- Nationalities
- Clothes
- Hair and eyes
- Food
- Jobs

UNIT 12
Talking about my daily routine

Háblame de tu rutina diaria	*Talk to me about your daily routine*
¿A qué hora te levantas?	*What time do you get up?*
¿Cómo vas al colegio?	*How do you go to school?*
¿Qué haces después del colegio?	*What do you do after school?*

Almuerzo *I have lunch*		***la una**	*1*	
Ceno *I have dinner*		**las dos**	*2*	
Desayuno *I have breakfast*		**las tres**	*3*	
Descanso *I rest*		**las cuatro**	*4*	
Hago mis deberes *I do my homework*		**las cinco**	*5*	
		las seis	*6*	
	a *at*	**las siete**	*7*	
Juego en el ordenador *I play on the computer*		**las ocho**	*8*	
Me acuesto *I go to bed*		**las ocho y cinco**	*8.05*	**de la mañana** *in the morning*
Me lavo los dientes *I brush my teeth*		**las ocho y diez**	*8.10*	
		las ocho y cuarto	*8.15*	**de la tarde** *in the evening*
Me levanto *I get up*		**las ocho y veinte**	*8.20*	
Me visto *I get dressed*		**las ocho y veinticinco**	*8.25*	
	a eso de *at around*	**las ocho y media**	*8.30*	**de la noche** *at night*
Salgo de casa *I leave my house*		**las ocho y treinta y cinco**	*8.35*	
		las nueve menos veinte	*8.40*	
Veo la tele *I watch television*		**las nueve menos cuarto**	*8.45*	
		las nueve menos diez	*8.50*	
Vuelvo a casa *I go back home*		**las nueve menos cinco**	*8.55*	
		las nueve	*9*	

Voy al colegio *I go to school*	**a pie** *on foot*	
	en autobús *by bus*	
	en coche *by car*	

las diez *11*

las doce *12*

luego... *then*	
después... *after*	
finalmente... *finally*	

mediodía	*midday*
medianoche	*midnight*

*Author's note: *"A la una" is the only time which has "la". Watch out for it!*

1. Listen and fill in the gaps

a. Son las seis y _ _ _ _ _ _

b. Es la _ _ _

c. Son las siete y _ _ _ _ _

d. Me levanto a eso de las _ _ _ _

e. Salgo de casa a las _ _ _ _ y media

f. Voy al colegio a las siete _ _ _ _ _ cuarto

g. Almuerzo a _ _ _ _ _ _ _ _

h. Hago mis deberes a _ _ _ de las cinco

i. Me acuesto a eso de _ _ _ nueve

2. Multiple choice quiz: daily routine times

	1	2	3
a.	6:00	7:00	9:00
b.	10:00	10:05	10:10
c.	2:45	3:45	2:15
d.	6:15	5:45	6:05
e.	11:05	10:55	10:25
f.	2:30	2:15	2:20
g.	3:15	2:45	2:35
h.	12pm	12am	1pm
i.	7:20	7:10	7:45
j.	8:15	7:45	2:35

3. Spot the differences and correct your text

a. Me llamo Federico. Soy francés. Siempre me despierto a eso de las seis y media.

b. Luego me ducho y me lavo los dientes enseguida.

c. No desayuno nada por la mañana, pero mi hermano Valerio desayuna cereales en el garaje.

d. Voy al colegio en bici a eso de las siete y cuarto.

e. Vuelvo a casa a eso de las cuatro y luego me relajo un poco.

f. Por lo general veo la tele en el salón.

g. Luego navego por internet, veo una serie en Netflix o veo videos de TikTok en mi habitación.

h. Luego, a las ocho, preparo la comida con mi madre en la cocina.

i. Me encanta preparar ensaladas porque son deliciosas.

j. Me acuesto tarde, a eso de las once.

4. Listen and write in English what Carmen does at each time

Time	Activity
6:30	
7:15	
8:00	
9:15	
3:30	
4:00	
6:30	
10:00	
11.00	

THE LANGUAGE GYM

5. Listening slalom: follow the speaker and number the boxes accordingly

a. Myriam	b. René	c. Paloma	d. Sofía
Me despierto	Me levanto	Me ducho	Salgo del colegio
Luego voy al gimnasio	Luego me levanto	Luego desayuno	Luego me visto
Después vuelvo a casa	Después me visto	Después preparo mi mochila	Después me ducho
Y luego salgo de casa	Y luego salgo de casa	Y luego me peino	Y luego descanso un poco
Finalmente, hago mis deberes.	Finalmente, me visto.	Finalmente, mi padre me lleva al colegio en coche.	Finalmente, voy al colegio.

6. Narrow listening: gapped translation

My name is Valentina. I am _____. I am from _____. My daily routine is very _____. Generally, I get up _____, at around five thirty. Then I shower and _____my uniform. _____, I have breakfast with my brothers. Then I _____and prepare my _____. At around _____ past seven I leave home and go to school. I _____ home at around four. Then I rest _____. Generally I read my _____comics. From six to _____I do my homework. Then, at eight, I have _____. I don't eat _____. Afterwards, I read a _____or go on the _____. Then I _____at 10:35.

7. Fill in the grid: What do the different people do?

	a. Me	b. My mother	c. My father	d. My sister
At 7:30				
At 8:15				
At 12:00				
From 3:00 to 4:00				
From 6:00 to 8:00				
From 8:30 to 11:00				

Unit 12. Talking about my daily routine: VOCAB BUILDING

1. Match

Me levanto	I have lunch
Voy al colegio	I have dinner
Me acuesto	I get up
Almuerzo	I have breakfast
Ceno	I rest
Desayuno	I go to school
Descanso	I go back home
Vuelvo a casa	I go to bed

2. Translate into English

a. Me levanto a las seis de la mañana

b. Me acuesto a las once de la noche

c. Almuerzo a mediodía

d. Desayuno a las seis de la mañana

e. Vuelvo a casa a las tres y media de la tarde

f. Ceno a eso de las ocho de la tarde

g. Veo la tele

h. Escucho música

i. Salgo de casa a las siete de la mañana

3. Complete with the missing words

a. _____ al colegio   *I go to school*

b. _____ de casa   *I leave the house*

c. _____ a casa   *I come back home*

d. _____ la tele   *I watch television*

e. _____ mis deberes   *I do my homework*

f. _____ música   *I listen to music*

g. _____ en el ordenador   *I play on the computer*

h. _____ a mediodía   *I have lunch at noon*

4. Complete with the missing letters

a. ____escanso   *I rest*

b. ____uelvo a ___asa   *I go back home*

c. ____scucho música   *I listen to music*

d. ____esayuno   *I have breakfast*

e. ____eno   *I have dinner*

f. ____oy al colegio   *I go to school*

g. Me ____evanto   *I get up*

h. Me ____cuesto   *I go to bed*

i. ___lmuerzo   *I have lunch*

5. Faulty translation – spot and correct any translation mistakes. Not all translations are wrong.

a. Descanso un poco: *I shower a bit*

b. Me acuesto a medianoche: *I go to bed at noon*

c. Hago mis deberes: *I do your homework*

d. Almuerzo: *I have lunch*

e. Voy al colegio: *I come back from school*

f. Vuelvo a casa: *I leave the house*

g. Veo la tele: *I watch television*

h. Salgo de casa: *I leave school*

i. Me lavo los dientes: *I wash my hands*

6. Translate the following times into Spanish (add de la mañana / tarde / noche where appropriate)

a. At 6.30 a.m.

b. At 7.30 a.m.

c. At 8.20 p.m.

d. At midday

e. At 9.20 a.m.

f. At 11.00 p.m.

g. At midnight

h. At 5.15 p.m.

 **THE LANGUAGE GYM**

Unit 12. Talking about my daily routine: VOCAB BUILDING

7. Complete the table

Me acuesto	
	I brush my teeth
Me levanto	
	I go back home
A las ocho y cuarto	
Almuerzo	
	I have dinner
Escucho música	
	I leave the house
Desayuno	
Descanso	
	I do my homework
Me visto	

8. Complete the sentences using the words in the table

a. A las siete y _____   *At seven thirty*

b. A _____ de las cinco   *At about 5.00*

c. A las ocho de la _____   *At 8.00 a.m.*

d. A _____   *At noon*

e. A las _____ y cuarto   *At 11.15*

f. A las tres _____ veinte   *At 2.40*

g. A _____   *At midnight*

h. A eso de _____ cuatro   *At about 4.00*

i. ____ eso de las siete   *At about 7.00*

j. A las ocho menos _____   *At 7.55*

cinco	media	las	mañana	mediodía
once	a	menos	eso	medianoche

9. Translate into English (numerical)

a. A las ocho y media _____ ***At 8.30*** _____

b. A las nueve y cuarto _____

c. A las diez menos cinco _____

d. A mediodía _____

e. A medianoche _____

f. A las once menos cinco _____

g. A las doce y veinte _____

10. Complete

a. A l____ c_____ y m_____   *At 5.30*

b. A l___ o_____ y c_____   *At 8.15*

c. A m_____   *At noon*

d. A las o_____ m_____ c_____   *At 7.45*

e. A m_____   *At midnight*

f. A las o_____ y m_____   *At 11.30*

g. A e_____ d____ l___ u_____   *At about 1.00*

11. Translate the following into Spanish

a. I go to school at around 8

b. I come back home at around 3

c. I have dinner at 7.30

d. I do my homework at around 5.30

e. I have breakfast at 6.45

f. I go to bed at midnight

g. I have lunch at midday

Unit 12. Talking about my daily routine: READING

Me llamo Hiroto. Soy Japonés. Mi rutina diaria es muy sencilla. Por lo general, me levanto a eso de las seis. Luego me ducho y me visto. Después, desayuno con mi padre y mi hermano menor. Luego me lavo los dientes y me peino. A eso de las siete y media salgo de casa y voy al colegio. Voy en bici. Vuelvo a casa a eso de las cuatro. Luego descanso un poco. Por lo general veo la tele. Entonces, voy al parque con mis amigos hasta las seis. Desde las seis hasta las siete y media hago mis deberes. Luego, a las ocho, ceno con mi familia. No como mucho. Solo una hamburguesa. Después, veo una película en la tele y, a eso de las once, me acuesto.

Me llamo Gregorio. Soy mexicano. Mi rutina diaria es muy simple. Por lo general, me levanto a las seis y cuarto. Luego me ducho y desayuno con mis dos hermanos. Después, me lavo los dientes y preparo mi mochila. A eso de las siete voy al colegio. Voy al colegio a pie. Vuelvo a casa a eso de las tres y media. Luego me relajo un poco. Por lo general navego por internet, veo una serie en Netflix o chateo con mis amigos en Whatsapp o Snapchat. Desde las cinco hasta las seis, hago mis deberes. Luego, a las siete y media, ceno con mi familia. Como arroz o ensalada. Después, veo la tele y, a eso de las once y media, me acuesto.

Me llamo Andreas. Soy alemán. Mi rutina diaria es muy sencilla. Por lo general, me levanto temprano, a eso de las cinco. Hago footing y luego me ducho y me visto. Después, a eso de las seis y media, desayuno fruta con mi madre y mi hermana. Luego me lavo los dientes y preparo mi mochila. A eso de las siete y cuarto salgo de casa y voy al colegio. Vuelvo a casa a eso de las tres y media. Luego, descanso un poco. Por lo general, veo la tele o chateo con mis amigos en internet. Desde las seis hasta las ocho hago mis deberes. Luego, a las ocho y cuarto, ceno con mi familia. No como mucho. Después, juego a la Play hasta medianoche. Finalmente, me acuesto.

1. Answer the following questions about Hiroto

a. Where is he from?

b. At what time does he get up?

c. Who does he have breakfast with?

d. At what time does he leave the house?

e. Until what time does he stay at the park?

f. How does he go to school?

2. Find the Spanish for the phrases below in Hiroto's text

a. At around eleven

b. With my friends

c. I go by bike

d. I go to the park

e. I shower and get dressed

f. I don't eat much

g. From six to seven

h. I do my homework

3. Complete the statements below about Andreas

a. He gets up at _____

b. He comes back from school at _____

c. For breakfast he eats _____

d. He has breakfast with _____

e. After getting up he _____ and then showers

f. Usually he _____ until midnight

g. After breakfast he brushes his teeth and then

_____.

4. Find the Spanish for the following phrases/sentences in Gregorio's text

a. I am Mexican

b. I shower

c. With my two brothers

d. I relax a bit

e. I eat rice or salad

f. I surf the internet

g. I have dinner

Unit 12. Talking about my daily routine: READING

Me llamo Yang. Tengo doce años. Soy chino. Mi rutina diaria es muy sencilla. Por lo general, me levanto a eso de las seis y media. Luego me ducho y me visto. Después, desayuno con mi madre y mi hermano, Li Wei. Luego me lavo los dientes y preparo mi mochila. A eso de las siete y media salgo de casa y voy al colegio. Vuelvo a casa a eso de las cuatro. Luego descanso un poco. Por lo general veo la tele, escucho música o leo mis tebeos favoritos. Desde las seis hasta las siete y media hago mis deberes. Luego, a las ocho, ceno con mi familia. No como mucho. Después, veo una película en la tele y, a eso de las once, me acuesto.

Me llamo Anna. Soy italiana. Mi rutina diaria es muy sencilla. Por lo general, me levanto a las seis y cuarto. Luego me lavo y desayuno con mi hermana mayor. Después, me lavo los dientes y preparo mi mochila. A eso de las siete voy al colegio en autobús. Vuelvo a casa a eso de las dos y media. Luego descanso un poco. Por lo general navego por internet, veo la tele o leo revistas de moda. Desde las cinco hasta las siete, hago mis deberes. Luego, a las ocho, ceno con mi familia. Como fruta o una ensalada. Después, leo una novela y, a eso de las once y media, me acuesto.

Me llamo Kim, soy inglesa. Tengo quince años. Mi rutina diaria es muy sencilla. Por lo general, me levanto temprano, a eso de las cinco y media. Hago ejercicio y luego me lavo y me visto. Después, a eso de las siete, desayuno con mi madre y mi hermanastra. Luego me lavo los dientes y preparo mi mochila. A eso de las siete y media salgo de casa y voy al colegio. Vuelvo a casa a eso de las tres. Luego, descanso un poco. Por lo general, escucho música o chateo con mis amigos en Internet. Desde las seis hasta las ocho hago mis deberes. Luego, a las ocho y cuarto, ceno con mi familia. Como bastante. Después, veo una película en la tele hasta medianoche. Finalmente, me acuesto.

1. Find the Spanish for the following in Yang's text

a. I am Chinese

b. My daily routine

c. I shower

d. Very simple

e. At around 7.30

f. I don't eat much

g. I watch television

h. I go to school

i. I do my homework

j. From six to seven

2. Translate these items from Kim's text

a. I am English

b. Generally

c. At around 5.30

d. With my mum and stepsister

e. I go back home

f. I have dinner with my family

g. I rest a bit

h. I brush my teeth

3. Answer the following questions on Anna's text

a. What nationality is Anna?

b. At what time does she get up?

c. What three things does she do after school?

d. How does she go to school?

e. Who does she have breakfast with?

f. At what time does she go to bed?

g. What does she eat for dinner?

h. What does she read before going to bed?

4. Find someone who…

a. …has breakfast with their older sister

b. …doesn't watch television at night

c. …reads fashion magazines

d. …gets up at 5.30am

e. …has breakfast with their brother and mother

f. …chats with their friends on the internet after school

g. …does exercise in the morning

THE LANGUAGE GYM

144

Unit 12. Talking about my daily routine: WRITING

1. Split sentences

Voy al colegio	casa
Vuelvo a	deberes
Hago mis	en autobús
Veo	la tele
Juego en el	a medianoche
Me levanto a	de casa
Me acuesto	eso de las seis
Salgo	ordenador

2. Complete with the correct option

a. Me levanto a _____ siete de la mañana

b. Hago _____ deberes

c. Veo _____ tele

d. Juego en el _____

e. Me _____ a medianoche

f. Vuelvo _____ casa

g. Salgo de _____

h. Voy al colegio _____ autobús

a	acuesto	las	en
la	mis	casa	ordenador

3. Spot and correct the grammar and spelling mistakes: in several cases a word is missing

a. Voy a colegio en bici

b. Me levanto a la siete y media

c. Salgo casa a las ocho

d. Vuelvo al casa

e. Voy colegio en autobús

f. Me acuesto a eso las once

g. Ceno a las ocho meno cuarto

h. Hago mi deberes a las cinco media

4. Complete the words

a. cu_____	*quarter*
b. me_____	*half*
c. a l____ di____	*at 10*
d. a e_____ d__	*at around*
e. a l_____ o_____	*at 8*
f. ve_____	*twenty*
g. l_____	*then*
h. a_____	*I have lunch*
i. v_____	*I come back*
j. j_____	*I play*

5. Guided writing: write 3 short paragraphs in the first person (I) using the details below

Person	Gets up	Showers	Goes to school	Comes back home	Watches TV	Has dinner	Goes to bed
Elías	6.30	7.00	8.05	3.30	6.00	8.10	11.10
Santino	6.40	7.10	7.40	4.00	6.30	8.15	12.00
Julieta	7.15	7.30	8.00	3.15	6.40	8.20	11.30

TERM 3 - BRINGING IT ALL TOGETHER – 12

1. Me llamo Aoife y tengo quince años. Mi cumpleaños es el siete de mayo. Soy de Irlanda y vivo en Dublín, la capital de Irlanda, con mi familia. Hoy estoy feliz porque hoy es mi cumpleaños, y de mi hermana gemela (twin) Órla también. Vamos a hacer una fiesta de cumpleaños.

2. En mi familia somos cinco personas: mi hermano mayor, Conor, mi hermana gemela, Órla, mi padre, Patrick, mi madre, Siobhán, y yo. Prefiero a mi madre porque es más paciente que mi padre. Mi padre es más interesante. Mis abuelos se llaman Sean y Maureen. Sean tiene setenta y tres años y Maureen tiene sesenta y nueve. Son muy amables y buenos.

3. Mi hermano mayor se llama Conor. A Conor le gusta tocar la batería y practicar artes marciales. Tiene diecisiete años y es muy inteligente y trabajador. Su cumpleaños es el veintidós de noviembre. Conor tiene el pelo castaño y los ojos verdes. Conor es más guapo que yo, pero yo soy más divertida que él.

4. Mi rutina diaria es muy sencilla *(simple)*. Por lo general, me levanto temprano, a eso de las seis y media. Hago ejercicio y luego me lavo y me visto. Después, a eso de las siete y cuarto, desayuno con mi madre y mi hermana Orla. Luego me lavo los dientes y preparo mi mochila. A eso de las siete y media salgo de casa y voy al colegio. Voy al colegio a caballo porque es rápido y divertido.

5. En el colegio, mi asignatura favorita es el español. Me encanta cantar canciones y hablar en español en clase. Tengo muchos amigos en clase y mi profesora es muy graciosa. No me gusta mucho la historia porque es un poco aburrida, pero creo que es bastante útil en el futuro.

6. Vuelvo a casa a eso de las tres. Luego, descanso un poco. Por lo general, escucho música o chateo con mis amigos en Internet. Desde las seis hasta las siete hago mis deberes y leo un libro. Luego, a las ocho y cuarto, ceno con mi familia. Me gusta la comida saludable *(healthy)* como la ensalada. Después, veo una película en la tele con mi hermano y mi hermana hasta las once. Finalmente, me acuesto a las once y cuarto.

Aoife, 15, Dublín, Irlanda

1. Complete the sentences below using paragraphs 1, 2 and 3 as reference

a. My name is Aoife and I am _____ years old

b. Today I am feeling _____

c. My mother is more _____ than my father

d. My grandparents are very kind and _____

e. Conor enjoys playing _____

f. Conor is very intelligent and _____

g. He is more _____ than Aoife

2. Find the Spanish equivalent for the following in paragraph 4

a. Simple: S

b. Early: T

c. Then: L

d. I get dressed: M

e. Around: A

f. I have breakfast: D

g. I brush my teeth: M

h. On horseback: A

3. Answer (in English) the following questions about paragraphs 5 and 6

a. What is Aoife's favourite subject?

b. Why? (4 details)

c. Why does she not like history?

d. What is good about history, though?

e. What does she do at 3:00 pm?

f. What does she do on the internet? (2 details)

g. What does she do from 6:00 to 7:00 pm?

h. At what time does she have dinner?

i. What kind of food does she like?

j. What does she do until 11:00?

k. Who with?

l. At what time does she go to bed?

1. Me llamo Órla y tengo quince años, ¡igual que mi hermana gemela, Aoife! Mi cumpleaños es el siete de mayo. Soy de Irlanda y vivo en Dublín, la capital de Irlanda, con mi familia.

2. En mi familia somos cinco personas: mi hermano mayor, Conor, mi hermana gemela, Aoife, mi padre, Patrick, mi madre, Siobhán, y yo. Prefiero a mi hermana gemela porque es más divertida que mi hermano. Mi padre es más severo que mi madre. Mis abuelos se llaman Sean y Maureen y son muy graciosos y cariñosos.

3. Mi mejor amiga se llama Ciara. A Ciara le gusta leer libros y ver la televisión. Tiene catorce años y es muy habladora. Es baja y fuerte. Su cumpleaños es el ocho de octubre. Ciara tiene el pelo negro largo y liso y los ojos verdes.

4. Mi rutina diaria es bastante sencilla *(simple)*. Normalmente, me levanto a eso de las siete menos cuarto. Es bastante temprano. Luego, me ducho y me peino. Finalmente, me pongo el uniforme. Después, desayuno con mi madre y mi hermana Aoife. Luego me lavo los dientes y preparo mi mochila. A eso de las siete y media salgo de casa y voy al colegio con Aoife. Vamos al colegio a caballo porque es rápido y divertido.

5. En el colegio, mi asignatura favorita es el alemán. Me encanta hablar en alemán en clase y mi profesora siempre explica las cosas muy bien. Tengo muchos amigos en clase y mi profesora es muy graciosa. No me gusta mucho la música porque es un poco difícil y complicada.

6. Vuelvo a casa alrededor de las tres y media. Luego, hago mis deberes enseguida. Por lo general, después de hacer mis deberes voy al gimnasio y hago escalada con mis amigos. Desde las seis hasta las siete me meto en internet y chateo con mis amigos. Luego, a las ocho y cuarto, ceno con mi familia. Me gusta la comida picante *(spicy)* como el curry de pollo *(chicken curry)*. Después, veo una película con mi hermano Conor y mi hermana Aoife hasta las once. Finalmente, me acuesto a las once y cuarto.

Órla, 15, Dublín, Irlanda

4. Find the Spanish equivalent in par. 1 to 3

a. Same as: I	h. Than: q
b. Birthday: c	i. To read: l
c. I live: v	j. Books: l
d. Older: m	k. To watch: v
e. Twin sister: h	l. Talkative: h
f. Funnier: m	m. Hair: p
g. Strict: s	n. Straight: l

5. Find the 13 mistakes in the following English translation of paragraph 4

My daily routine is very simple. Normally, I wake up at around seven-fifteen. It is quite late. Afterwards, I wash and I brush my teeth. Finally, I put on my uniform. Afterwards, I have lunch with my mother and my cousin Aoife. Afterwards, I brush my hair and prepare my lunch. Around eight-thirty I leave the house and go to school with Aoife. We go to school by bike because it is fast and comfortable.

6. Answer the questions below on paragraphs 5 and 6 in Spanish, as if you were Órla

a. ¿Cuál es tu asignatura favorita?

b. ¿Por qué te gusta el alemán?

c. ¿Por qué no te gusta la música?

d. ¿A qué hora vuelves a casa por lo general?

e. ¿Qué haces después de llegar a casa?

f. ¿Qué haces después de hacer los deberes?

g. ¿Qué haces entre la seis y la siete de la tarde?

h. ¿Qué tipo de comida te gusta?

i. ¿Con quién ves la tele después de cenar?

j. ¿A qué hora te acuestas?

7. Identify and translate into English the SEVEN items on the list below which are not included in paragraph 6

a. Entre	e. A eso	i. Divertido
b. Hermana	f. Un poco	j. Sencilla
c. Después	g. Película	k. Ceno
d. Desayuno	h. Me meto	l. Me pongo

 **THE LANGUAGE GYM**

UNIT 13 – Talking about weekend plans

In this unit you will learn:

- To talk about your plans are for the weekend
- To say where you are going using the immediate future structure "voy a + infinitive"
- How to use "al" and "a la" for masculine/feminine places
- Some activities with "de"
- To say what you are going to do using "para"

You will revisit the following:

- Places
- Activities
- Friends and family members
- Adjectives

UNIT 13
Talking about weekend plans

¿Qué planes tienes para el fin de semana que viene?	*What plans do you have for next weekend?*
¿Adónde te gustaría ir?	*Where would you like to go?*
¿Qué planes tiene tu hermano/a?	*What plans does your brother/sister have?*
¿Adónde va a ir tu hermano/a?	*Where is your brother/sister going to go?*

El fin de semana que viene *Next weekend*	**voy a ir** *I am going to go* **me gustaría ir** *I would like to go*	**al**	**centro comercial**	*shopping mall*
			cine	*cinema*
			estadio	*stadium*
			gimnasio	*gym*
			parque	*park*
			polideportivo	*sports centre*
El viernes *On Friday* **El sábado** *On Saturday*	**mi amigo/a va a ir** *my friend is going to go* **mi hermano va a ir** *my brother is going to go*	**a la**	**piscina**	*pool*
			playa	*beach*
	mi hermana va a ir *my sister is going to go*	**de**	**marcha**	*clubbing*
			paseo	*for a walk*
			pesca	*fishing*
			tiendas/ compras	*shopping*

...con *...with*	**mi** *my*	**mejor amiga** *best friend (f)* **mejor amigo** *best friend (m)* **hermana** *sister*	**para** *(in order) to*	**bailar**	*dance*
				comprar cosas	*buy things*
				comprar ropa	*buy clothes*
				hacer pesas	*do weights*
	su *his/her*	**hermano** *brother* **novia** *girlfriend* **novio** *boyfriend*		**jugar al fútbol**	*play football*
				montar en bici	*ride my bike*
				nadar	*swim*
				tomar el sol	*sunbathe*
				ver una película	*watch a film*
				ver un partido	*watch a match*

Será aburrido	**Será agotador**	**Será divertido**	**Será relajante**
It will be boring	*It will be tiring*	*It will be fun*	*It will be relaxing*

Unit 13. Talking about weekend plans: LISTENING

1. Sentence puzzle

a. fin de El semana viene que

b. Voy a cine ir al

c. a amigo va ir a piscina la Mi

d. gustaría Me ir al con mis estadio amigos

e. de Voy a paseo ir

f. Voy a parque ir montar al bici para en

g. a ir al cine para ver Voy una acción de película

h. Voy centro a ir al comercial cosas para comprar

2. Tick or cross

a. Piscina

b. Marcha

c. Cine

d. Estadio

e. Paseo

f. Deporte

g. Partido

h. Gimnasio

3. Listen and fill in the gaps

a. El _____ de semana _____viene voy a ir al _____

b. Voy a ___ al centro _____ para comprar _____

c. Mi _____ amigo va a ir a la _____ para _____ el sol

d. Voy ___ ir al parque_____ hacer _____

e. Me _____ ir al _____ para ver un _____

f. Voy a ir ___ cine para _____ una _____ de acción

g. Voy a ir al _____ para _____ en bici con ___ amigos

h. Voy a ir ___ marcha _____ mi _____ mayor

4. Break the flow

a. Voyairalparque

b. Voyairalcine

c. Voyairalaplaya

d. Miamigovaaairalapiscina

e. Voyairalcentrocomercial

f. Megustaríairalestadio

g. Voyairalparqueparamontarenbici

h. Voyairalestadioparaverunpartido

5. Spot and cross out the intruder in each sentence

a. El fin de semana que no viene voy a ir de marcha

b. Voy a ir al estadio para ver a un partido de fútbol

c. Mi amigo Pedro va a ir al la parque con mi hermano

d. El sábado mi hermana y va a ir a una fiesta

e. Mañana voy a ir a la piscina. ¡Será muy fenomenal!

f. El fin de la semana que viene voy a ir a la playa

6. Faulty translation: spot and fix the translation errors

a. I am going to go to the beach

b. I am going to go to the gym

c. I am going to go to the park

d. I am going to go clubbing

e. I am going to buy clothes

f. I am going to ride my horse

7. Gapped translation: word level

_____ _____ I am going to do many things. First of all, on _____, after school, I am going to go to the _____ _____ with my mother and _____ to buy clothes and other _____. It will be a bit _____. On Saturday I will go to the park to _____my _____ and after that I am going to play _____ with my friends. It will be _____. In the evening we are going to go to the _____ with my parents. On Sunday I will go to the _____ with my _____ to lift weights. It will be _____. After that, I will go _____with my _____ _____ Paco.

THE LANGUAGE GYM

8. Write which place each person is going to go to

a.	
b.	
c.	
d.	
e.	
f.	
g.	

9. Gapped translation: phrase level

a. On Saturday I am going to go to the _____

b. On Sunday I am going to go to the _____

c. Next weekend I am going to go to the _____

d. On Saturday I am going to go to the _____

e. On Sunday I am going to go to the _____

f. On Saturday I am going to go to the _____

g. Next weekend I am going to go to the _____

10. Arrange in the correct order

I'm going to go to the gym with my brother	
to watch a Real Madrid match.	
First, on Saturday	
I'm going to go to the stadium	
to do weights	
with my friends	
Next weekend	1
Then, on Sunday	
I'm going to do many things.	
and to the pool to swim.	

11. Broken words

a. V__ a ir al ci__ para v__ una pelí__la

b. El f__ de se__na que vie__ voy a ir al par__

c. El sába__ voy a i__ al est___

d. El domin___ voy a i_ al gim___sio

e. Se__ agota___ pero diverti__

f. V__ a ir al __tro com__cial pa__ compr__ cos__

g. Voy a i_ a l_ pis__na para __dar

h. Voy a ir al restaurant__ para cen__ con m_ famil___

12. Slalom listening

a.	b.	c.	d.
Next weekend	Next Saturday	Next Sunday	Today
I am going to go to the swimming pool	I am going to go to the gym	I am going to go to the park	I am going to go to the shopping centre
to do weights	to ride my bike	with my sister	to swim
with my best friend.	to buy clothes and other things.	with my friends.	with my older brother.
It will be great.	It will be fun.	It will be tiring.	It will be a bit boring.

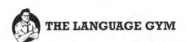

Unit 13. Talking about weekend plans: VOCAB BUILDING

1. Gapped translation

a. Voy a ir al parque   *I am going to go to the _____*

b. Voy a ir de paseo   *I am going to go for a _____*

c. Voy a ir a la piscina   *I am going to go to the _____*

d. Voy a ir al gimnasio   *I am going to go to the _____*

e. Voy a ir al centro comercial   *I am going to go to the _____*

f. Será agotador   *It will be _____*

g. Será relajante   *It will be _____*

h. Será aburrido   *It will be _____*

i. Será divertido   *It will be _____*

2. Match

piscina	bike
agotador	pool
playa	park
bici	walk
tiendas	tiring
paseo	shops
parque	gym
gimnasio	beach

3. Faulty translation

a. Voy a ir al centro comercial para comprar cosas.   *I am going to the mall to buy clothes.*

b. Voy a ir a la piscina para nadar.   *I am going to the swimming pool to play golf.*

c. Voy a ir al parque para montar en bici.   *I am going to go to the park to go jogging.*

d. Voy a ir a la playa para tomar el sol.   *I am going to the beach to play beach volley.*

e. Voy a ir al centro comercial para comprar ropa.   *I am going to the sports centre to swim.*

f. Voy a ir de paseo. Será relajante.   *I am going to go for a walk. It will be tiring.*

g. Mi hermana va a ir de marcha. Será divertido.   *My sister is going to go shopping. It will be fun.*

h. Mi mejor amigo va a ir al estadio.   *My best friend is going to go clubbing.*

4. Complete with the correct option

a. Voy a __ al parque   *I am going to go to the park*

b. El fin de semana __ viene   *Next weekend*

c. Voy __ ir a la playa   *I am going to go to the beach*

d. Voy a ir de _____   *I am going to go fishing*

e. Me gustaría ir de _____   *I would like to go for a walk*

f. Voy a ir __ tiendas   *I am going to go shopping*

g. para _____ el sol   *to sunbathe*

h. para montar en _____   *to ride a bike*

que	a	de	pesca
bici	ir	tomar	paseo

5. Sentence puzzle

a. ir Voy a parque al

b. amigo al estadio Mi va a ir

c. de a ir Voy tiendas

d. a Voy la piscina ir a

e. a Voy de paseo ir

f. ir va a Mi hermana de marcha

g. Voy a gimnasio ir al

h. centro Voy al a ir comercial

i. playa ir Me gustaría a la

j. Mi restaurante va a ir al hermano

THE LANGUAGE GYM

Unit 13. Talking about weekend plans: VOCAB BUILDING

6. Find the Spanish for the words/phrases below

a	r	d	a	r	u	n	p	a	s	e	o	l
b	i	c	i	e	p	l	a	y	a	s	t	i
n	t	i	c	n	i	a	h	o	r	a	e	s
d	g	r	i	o	s	r	r	e	a	z	r	l
e	l	l	a	b	c	g	b	q	o	a	g	a
t	o	m	a	s	i	k	i	l	u	m	r	h
s	a	y	o	e	n	l	o	r	g	e	a	o
a	l	e	j	l	a	p	e	p	a	d	t	r
n	e	w	t	i	e	n	d	a	s	y	n	a
o	a	g	o	t	a	d	o	r	t	o	o	d
m	e	g	u	s	t	a	r	í	a	h	m	e
e	s	t	v	i	d	u	x	o	n	e	r	t

1. go for a walk
2. bike
3. to ride
4. I would like
5. shops
6. park
7. swimming pool
8. to go
9. beach
10. tiring

7. Break the flow

a. Voyairdetiendasparacomprarcosas

b. Voyairalcentrocomercialparacomprarropa

c. Voyairalparqueparamontarenbici

d. Voyairdepaseo.Serárelajante

e. Voyairalgimnasioparahacerpesas.Seráagotador

f. Voyairalapiscinaparanadar.Serádivertido

8. Translate into English

a. Voy a ir de paseo

b. Voy a ir de compras

c. Voy a ir al gimnasio

d. Voy a ir al polideportivo

e. Voy a ir a la piscina

f. Voy a montar en bici

9. Tick the 3 sentences which are error free and cross & correct the ones which contain errors

a. Voy ir al parque

b. Voy a ir para comprar cosas

c. Voy a ir a paseo

d. Voy a ir de marcha

e. ...para montar in bici

f. El fin semana que viene

g. Será relaxante

h. Me gustaría a ir

i. Voy a ir de tiendas

10. Split sentences

Voy a ir al	paseo
Voy a ir de	parque
Voy a ir a la	de tiendas
Voy a ir	agotador
Será	piscina
Me gustaría	para ver una película
Me gustaría ir al cine	montar en bici
Voy a ir al parque para	ir a la playa

11. Complete with the missing letters

a. Voy a ir de pa___

b. Voy a ir de tien___

c. Será agota___

d. Me gustaría ir de mar___

e. No voy a ir al ci___

f. Será relaja___

g. Voy a ir al par___

h. Será divert___

| dor |
| das |
| nte |
| cha |
| seo |
| ido |
| ne |
| que |

THE LANGUAGE GYM

Unit 13. Talking about weekend plans: READING

Me llamo Yang. Tengo doce años. Soy chino. Por lo general, los fines de semana no hago mucho. Los sábados hago los deberes, me meto en internet y voy al centro comercial con mis amigos. Los domingos, escucho música, juego a la Play y a veces juego al ajedrez con mi hermano mayor. ¡Es muy divertido!

El fin de semana que viene, voy a hacer mucho deporte. El sábado, voy a ir al parque para montar en bici y al polideportivo para jugar al baloncesto con mis amigos. El domingo voy a ir a la piscina para nadar con mi hermano mayor y luego al gimnasio para hacer pesas. ¡Será agotador!

Me llamo Anna. Por lo general, los fines de semana son bastante aburridos. Voy de tiendas con mi madre, leo un libro o veo la tele.

El sábado que viene, voy a ir al centro comercial más grande de la ciudad para comprar ropa y un ordenador nuevo. Luego, voy a ir al cine con mis amigas para ver una película de humor. El domingo voy a hacer mucho deporte. Voy a ir al parque para correr y luego voy a ir al polideportivo para hacer gimnasia. Después voy a ir de paseo por el centro de la ciudad con mi mejor amiga. ¡Será divertido!

Me llamo Kim. Por lo general, los fines de semana hago mucho deporte. Por la mañana hago footing en el parque, juego al fútbol con mis amigos en el campo de fútbol cerca de mi casa y voy a la piscina para jugar al waterpolo.

La semana que viene, sin embargo, voy a hacer poco deporte. El sábado voy a ir de tiendas con mis padres para comprar unas camisetas y un móvil nuevo. Luego vamos a ir al restaurante italiano para almorzar pasta. Por la tarde voy a hacer mis deberes. El domingo voy a ir al parque para jugar al baloncesto con mis amigos y luego voy a ir al cine con ellos para ver una película de ciencia ficción. Luego voy a ir a casa de mi mejor amigo para jugar a la PlayStation.

1. Find the Spanish for the following in Yang's text

a. I don't do much

b. On Saturdays

c. I play chess

d. Next weekend

e. A lot of sport

f. To ride the bike

g. To play basketball

h. On Sunday

i. I am going to go

j. Older brother

k. Afterwards

l. To do weights

2. Complete based on Kim's text

a. On weekends I do a lot of _____.

b. In the morning I go _____ in the park.

c. The football pitch is _____ my house.

d. Next weekend I am going to do _____ sport.

e. On Saturday I am going _____ with my parents and I am going to buy a new _____.

f. On Sunday I am going to the park to _____.

g. After the cinema I am going to _____ _____ to play PlayStation.

4. Find someone who, next weekend, is going to...

a. ...buy a new computer

b. ...go to the city centre

c. ...do their homework

d. ...do weightlifting

e. ...do a lot of sport

f. ...buy T-shirts

g. ...swim with a sibling

3. Answer the following questions on Anna's text

a. What three things does Anna usually do at the weekend?

b. What is she going to buy at the shopping mall?

c. What is she going to watch at the cinema?

d. What is she planning to do at the park?

e. What is she planning to do at the sports centre?

f. What is she going to do in the city centre?

THE LANGUAGE GYM

154

Unit 13. Talking about weekend plans: WRITING

1. Broken words

a. Voy a ir al ci_ _ con mi_ amigo_

b. E_ fin d_ semana qu_ vie_ _

c. Me gusta_ _ _ i_ al par_ _ _

d. Vo_ a i_ al centr_ comercial con mi_ padre_

e. Voy a ir a_ gimnas_ _ para hac_ _ pesa_

f. Mi hermano v_ a ir de tiend_ _ con mi madre

g. Mi mejo_ amigo v_ a ir a la pla_ _ para tom_ _ el sol

h. Voy a ir a_ esta_ _ _ para v_ _ un partid_

2. Anagrams: unscramble the weird word

a. Voy a ir de daetins

b. Será verdidoti

c. Me gustaría ir de sepao

d. Voy a ir a la cipisan

e. Mi morej amigo va a ir al gimnasio

f. Mi hermano va a ir al estadio rapa ver un partido

g. Voy a ir a la playa para marto el sol

h. El fin de semana que venei voy a ir al parque

3. Tangled translation: into Spanish

a. Voy a **go** a la **swimming pool**

b. Mi **best** amigo **is going** a ir al **gym**

c. Mi hermano **older** va a ir al estadio **to watch** un partido

d. Voy a ir a la **beach** para tomar el **sun**

e. **The** fin de semana que **comes** voy a ir al **park**

f. **I would like** ir de **walk** por el **centre** de la ciudad

g. Voy **to go to the** centro **commercial** para **to buy** ropa **and** otras **things**

h. **It will be** divertido pero **tiring**

4. Spot and correct the errors

a. Voy a ir al piscina

b. La semana que viene voy ir al parque

c. Me gustaría ir a la playa por tomar el sol

d. Voy a ir al cine para ver una película acción

e. Mi mejor amiga voy a ir al gimnasion

f. Mi hermano vas a ir al estadio

g. Voy a ir a centro commercial para comprar cosas

h. Voy ir a la playa para nada en el mar

5. Translate into Spanish

a. Next weekend I am going to go to the park to ride the bike

b. Next Saturday I am going to the cinema to watch an action movie

c. Next Sunday I am going to the beach with my friends

d. I am going to the gym to do weights. It will be tiring

e. Next weekend my friend is going to go to the stadium to watch a match

f. I am going to go to the park to go for a walk

g. My friend is going to go to the shopping centre to buy clothes

h. I am going to the city centre to go shopping

i. I am going to go to the sports centre to swim

THE LANGUAGE GYM

TERM 3 - BRINGING IT ALL TOGETHER – 13

1. Me llamo Jonas y tengo dieciséis años. Mi cumpleaños es el siete de septiembre. Soy de Alemania y ahora vivo en Hamburgo, una ciudad grande, con mi familia. Estoy muy feliz porque después voy a ir al partido de fútbol de mi equipo favorito, el Hamburgo SV.

2. En mi familia somos cuatro personas: mi hermana mayor, Lisa, mi padre, Thomas, mi madre, Andrea, y yo. Me llevo muy bien con mi madre porque es muy cariñosa, un poco más que mi padre. Mi padre es más estricto que mi madre. Mis abuelos se llaman Wolfgang y Helga. Son muy amables y siempre vamos al parque y a la costa juntos *(together)*.

3. Mi hermana mayor se llama Lisa. A Lisa le gusta pintar y bailar. Tiene dieciocho años y es muy guapa y talentosa. Su cumpleaños es el veintidós de noviembre. Lisa tiene el pelo rubio y los ojos azules. Lisa es más artística que yo, pero yo soy más deportista que ella.

4. Mi rutina diaria es bastante sencilla. Por lo general, me despierto temprano, a eso de las siete de la mañana. Luego me lavo y me visto. Después, a eso de las siete y media, desayuno con mi padre y mi hermana, Lisa. Normalmente tomo cereales con leche. Mi padre toma una tostada y un café con leche. Luego, preparo mi mochila y salgo de casa.

5. En el colegio, mi asignatura favorita es la música. Me encanta tocar la guitarra y componer mis propias canciones. Todos los fines de semana toco con mi grupo *(my band)*.

6. Me encanta mi colegio porque los profesores son muy inteligentes y siempre me ayudan cuando tengo dudas *(doubts)*. Además, me encanta la clase de educación física porque puedo practicar diferentes deportes y mantenerme en forma *(stay in shape)*. Mi profesor de español es exigente *(demanding)* pero también inspirador, y siempre nos motiva.

7. El fin de semana que viene voy a hacer mucho deporte. El sábado, voy a ir al parque para montar en bici y al centro polideportivo para jugar al baloncesto con mis amigos. El domingo voy a ir a la piscina para nadar con mi hermano mayor y luego al gimnasio para hacer pesas. ¡Será agotador!

Jonas, 16, Hamburgo, Alemania

1. Find the Spanish for the following in the paragraphs indicated in brackets

a. A big city (1)

b. Happy (1)

c. Later (1)

d. Affectionate (2)

e. We always go (2)

f. To dance (3)

g. Beautiful (3)

h. More...than (3)

i. Simple (4)

j. I wake up early (4)

k. I have breakfast (4)

l. I go out of the house (4)

m. I love (5)

n. My own songs (5)

o. (they) Help me (6)

p. I am going to do (7)

q. I am going to go (7)

2. Complete the following translation of paragraph 4

My daily routine is quite _____. In general, I wake up _____, at around seven o'clock in the _____. Afterwards I wash and _____. Then at about seven-thirty, I _____ with my father and my sister, Lisa. Normally, I have cereal with _____. My father has a toast and a coffee with _____. After that I _____ my _____ and _____.

3. Correct the 10 mistakes in the following translation of paragraph 7

Next week I am going to do a lot of things. On Friday, I am going to go to the park to ride my horse and to the stadium to play handball with my friends. On Saturday I am going to go to the lake to swim with my younger brother and then to the gym to do some gymnastics. It will be fun!

1. Me llamo Annike y tengo quince años. Mi cumpleaños es el dos de mayo. Soy de Austria y ahora vivo en Viena, la capital, con mi familia. Estoy muy feliz porque después voy a ver un partido de fútbol. Juega mi equipo favorito, Austria Wien.

2. En mi familia somos cuatro personas: mi hermana mayor, Sonja, mi padre, Heinrich, mi madre, Heidi, y yo. Me llevo muy bien con mi madre porque es muy simpática. Normalmente es muy simpática, pero a veces puede ser un poco antipática cuando está estresada. Mis abuelos se llaman Wolfgang y Helga. Wolfgang tiene setenta y cinco años y Helga tiene setenta y tres. Son muy amables y siempre vamos al parque y a la costa juntos *(together)*.

3. Mi hermana mayor Sonja tiene dieciocho años y es muy guapa y trabajadora. Siempre saca buenas notas en el colegio. Su cumpleaños es el veinticinco de diciembre. Sonja tiene el pelo castaño y los ojos marrones.

4. Entre semana, me despierto temprano, a eso de las seis y media de la mañana. Luego me ducho y me lavo bien la cara. Después, a eso de las siete, desayuno en la cocina con mi familia. Por lo general, desayuno una tostada con miel y un café con leche. Mi padre no desayuna nada, pero mi madre siempre toma cereales. Salgo de casa a las siete y media y voy al colegio en coche.

5. En el colegio, mi asignatura favorita es la informática. Me encanta trabajar con el ordenador. En el futuro, me gustaría ser programador, igual que mi padre.

6. Mi colegio es bastante bueno. Los profesores son muy severos, en general, y siempre nos dan muchos deberes. Sin embargo, me gusta mi colegio porque aprendo mucho y tengo muchos amigos. Siempre me ayudan cuando tengo un problema. Además, me encanta la clase de español porque puedo aprender sobre muchos países donde se habla español. En el futuro, me gustaría visitar Cuba.

7. El fin de semana que viene voy a hacer muchas cosas con mis amigos. El sábado voy a ir al centro comercial para mirar escaparates e ir a mi restaurante italiano favorito. El domingo voy a ir al gimnasio para hacer pesas y luego voy a ir al cine para ver una película. ¡Será divertido!

Annike, 15, Viena, Austria

4. Answer the following questions about paragraphs 1 to 4 in Spanish, as if you were Annike

a. ¿De dónde eres?

b. ¿Cómo estás hoy? Por qué?

c. ¿Cuántas personas hay en tu familia?

d. ¿Cómo es tu madre?

e. ¿Cómo se llaman tus abuelos?

f. ¿Cómo son tus abuelos?

g. ¿Quién es guapa y trabajadora en tu familia?

h. ¿A qué hora te despiertas?

i. ¿Dónde desayunas?

j. ¿Qué come tu padre para el desayuno?

k. ¿Adónde vas a eso de las siete y media?

5. Find the Spanish equivalent for the following in paragraphs 5 and 6

a. My favourite subject

b. I love to work

c. In the future

d. Same as my father

e. Is quite good

f. They always give us

g. I learn a lot

h. They always help me

i. I can learn about

6. Paragraph 7 was copied incorrectly. Spot and correct the 10 mistakes

El fin semana que viene voy hacer muchas cosa con mis amigos. El sabado, voy a ir al centro commercial para mirar escaparates y a mi restaurante italiano favorita. El domingo voy ir al gimnasio para hago pesas y luego voy a ir al cine para veo una película. ¡Sera divertido!

7. Translate the following phrases from paragraph 7 into English

a. Hacer muchas cosas

b. Mirar escaparates

c. Hacer pesas

d. Ver una película

e. Será divertido

TERM 3 – MIDPOINT – RETRIEVAL PRACTICE

1. Answer the following questions in Spanish

¿A qué hora te levantas por lo general?	
¿Qué haces antes de ir al colegio?	
¿A qué hora sales de casa para ir al colegio?	
¿Cómo vas al colegio?	
¿Cuál es tu clase favorita? ¿Por qué?	
¿Qué haces después del colegio?	
¿Qué haces antes de acostarte?	
¿Cuál es tu comida favorita?	
¿Qué comes normalmente en la cantina del colegio?	
¿Qué haces normalmente el fin de semana?	
¿Qué vas a hacer el fin de semana que viene?	

2. Write a paragraph in the first person singular (I) providing the following details

a. Your name is Lionel. You are 12. You are from Argentina but live in London.

b. Your daily routine is simple: every day you get up at 6, then you shower, have breakfast with your brother and then go to school by bus at 7:30. You come back home around 4.

c. In the afternoon you eat bread and jam or honey and drink a cup of hot chocolate.

d. Later you play PlayStation, go on the internet and watch films on TV with your family.

e. You don't like school because the teachers are too strict and give too much homework. However, you love art class because the teacher is fun and always helps you.

f. Next weekend you will do a lot of sport: you will go to the gym, to the swimming pool and will also play tennis. You will also go shopping and buy clothes with your friends. Finally, you will go to the cinema to watch an action movie.

3. Write a paragraph in the third person singular (he/she) providing the following details about a real or fictitious friend

a. Brief introduction (10 words min)

b. Daily routine (20 words min)

c. Description of 2 family members (10 words min)

d. Food he/she likes and dislikes and what they eat at different meals (20 words min)

d. How he/she feels about school and teachers. Subjects he/she likes and dislikes and why (20 words min)

e. What he/she normally does at the weekend (20 words min)

f. His/her plans for the weekend (20 words min)

THE LANGUAGE GYM

UNIT 14
Talking about food:
likes, dislikes, reasons

In this unit you will learn how to say:

- What food you like/dislike and to what extent
- Why you like/dislike it (old and new expressions)
- New adjectives
- The full conjugation of 'comer' *to eat* and 'beber' *to drink*

You will revisit the following
- Time markers
- Providing a justification

UNIT 14
Talking about food: likes, dislikes, reasons

¿Qué te gusta comer y beber? ¿Por qué? *What do you like to eat and drink? Why?*

Singular

Me encanta *I love* **Me gusta** *I like* **Me gusta mucho** *I like a lot* **Me gusta un poco** *I like a bit* **Prefiero** *I prefer* **No me gusta** *I don't like* **Odio** *I hate*	**el arroz** *rice* **el café** *coffee* **el chocolate** *chocolate* **el pan** *bread* **el pescado** *fish* **el pollo asado** *roast chicken* **el queso** *cheese* **el zumo de fruta** *fruit juice* ****el agua** *water* **la carne** *meat* **la ensalada verde** *green salad* **la fruta** *fruit* **la leche** *milk* **la miel** *honey*	**porque** *because*	**es** *it is* **no es** *it is not*	**amargo/a** *bitter* **asqueroso/a** *disgusting* **delicioso/a** *delicious* ***dulce** *sweet* **duro/a** *tough* **grasiento/a** *greasy* **picante** *spicy* **refrescante** *refreshing* **rico/a en proteínas** *rich in protein* **sabroso/a** *tasty* **salado/a** *salty* **saludable** *healthy*

Plural

Me encantan *I love* **Me gustan mucho** *I like a lot* **Me gustan** *I like* **Me gustan un poco** *I like a bit* **No me gustan** *I don't like* **Odio** *I hate* **Prefiero** *I prefer*	**los champiñones** *mushrooms* **los huevos** *eggs* **los plátanos** *bananas* **los tomates** *tomatoes* **las fresas** *strawberries* **las gambas** *prawns* **las hamburguesas** *burgers* **las manzanas** *apples* **las naranjas** *oranges* **las verduras** *vegetables* **las zanahorias** *carrots*	**porque son** *because* *they are*	**asquerosos** *disgusting* **deliciosos** *delicious* **dulces** *sweet* **duros** *tough* **saludables** *healthy* **grasientas** *greasy* **refrescantes** *refreshing* **ricas en proteínas** *rich in protein* **sabrosas** *tasty* **saludables** *healthy*

Author's note: ** Adjectives ending in 'E' do not change from masculine to feminine.*
*** "Agua" is a **feminine** noun but takes the masculine article "el". This is because the **first 'a'** of 'agua' is stressed. Therefore there would be a phonetic clash if we had to say "l**a a**gua".*

THE LANGUAGE GYM

1. Listen and fill in the gaps

a. A mi hermano le encantan los _____.

b. Me encanta el _____.

c. A Rafa le gusta mucho la _____.

d. A mi padre le encanta la _____ de fresa.

e. A Paco no le gustan nada las _____.

f. Mi madre odia los _____.

g. A Alejandro le gusta muchísimo el _____.

h. Odio los _____.

i. A mi hermana le encanta el _____ _____ picante.

2. Mystery words: guess the words, then listen and see how many you guessed right

a. el a_ _ a

b. la m _e _

c. el _u_ v _

d. la _ a _n_

e. el p _ _ c_ _ _

f. la m _ _ z_ _ _

g. el _ _ n

h. el _ r _ _ z

3. Spot the differences and correct your text

a. Me encanta la fruta, sobre todo las fresas.

b. Odio las verduras, sobre todo los champiñones.

c. No me gusta el pollo frito.

d. Me gusta muchísimo el marisco.

e. Me gusta mucho la pasta.

f. Me encanta el zumo de manzana.

g. La carne roja no es picante.

h. El café es sabroso.

i. Las hamburguesas son sanas.

j. Las verduras son sabrosas.

k. Las manzanas son crujientes.

l. No me gusta mucho la leche.

4. Listen, spot and correct the spelling and grammar errors

a. Me gusta las verduras porque son sanas.

b. Me encanta las hamburguesas.

c. El pescado y la carne son sabrosas.

d. Me gustan bastante el zumo de naranja.

e. Como muy pescado porque es rico en proteínas.

f. No me gusta carne porque es grasienta.

g. Me encanta la pollo asado porque es sabroso.

h. Me gusta mucho los calamares fritos aunque no son muy saludables.

5. Faulty translation: spot the translation errors and correct them

My name is Felipe. What do I enjoy eating? I love fruit, especially bananas. I drink them every day. My favourite vegetables are tomatoes and potatoes because they are healthy. I also like jam because it is delicious and meat because it is tasty. I hate turkey and burgers. They are rich in protein but they are not spicy.

6. Why do they like/dislike these foods?

People and what they like/dislike	Reasons why they like/dislike
a. I like fruit	
b. My brother loves eggs	
c. Silvia hates vegetables	
d. Jaime likes fish	
e. Conchi loves oranges	
f. Rafa loves Indian food	
g. Ahmed dislikes pork	
h. Pilar dislikes tomatoes	
i. Susana hates carrots	

7. Listening slalom: follow the speaker from top to bottom and number the boxes

a	b	c	d
I love	I hate	I can't stand	I love
chocolate	meat	spinach	burgers
and cakes	sausages	because it is	and tomatoes
or French fries	because they are sweet	because they are	tasty
and delicious	disgusting.	and rich in protein.	because they are
not	I eat it with salad	I prefer	although they are
not very healthy.	healthy.	or French fries.	carrots.

8. Answer the questions below about Maite

a. How many people are there in Maite's family?

b. What do her parents love?

c. What does her mother hate?

d. What does her brother Rafa love?

e. What does her brother Jaime love?

f. What does Maite love?

g. What does she hate?

h. Why?

Unit 14. Talking about food: VOCABULARY BUILDING

1. Match

Los plátanos	Eggs
Las fresas	Apples
La carne	Prawns
El pollo	Milk
El agua	Fruit
La leche	Water
Los huevos	Burgers
Las gambas	Chicken
Las hamburguesas	Meat
La fruta	Bananas
Las manzanas	Strawberries

2. Complete

a. Me gusta mucho el _____   *I like chicken a lot*

b. Me encantan las _____   *I love prawns*

c. Me gustan las _____   *I like strawberries*

d. Me encanta la _____   *I love milk*

e. Me encantan los _____   *I love bananas*

f. Me encanta el _____ mineral   *I love mineral water*

g. No me gustan los _____   *I don't like tomatoes*

h. Odio el _____   *I hate chicken*

i. Me encanta la _____   *I love fruit*

j. No me gustan los _____   *I don't like eggs*

3. Translate into English

a. Me gusta la fruta

b. Odio los huevos

c. Me encanta el pollo asado

d. Me gustan las hamburguesas

e. Odio la carne

f. Prefiero las naranjas

g. No me gustan los tomates

h. Odio la leche

4. Complete the words

a. Los hu_____

b. Los pl_____

c. La fr_____

d. Las verd_____

e. Las hamb_____

f. Las ga_____

g. Las man_____

h. El a_____

5. Fill the gaps with either 'me gust*a*' or 'me gust*an*' as per your own preference

a. No _____los huevos

b. _____el agua

c. _____el pollo

d. _____las hamburguesas

e. _____las verduras

f. _____la carne

g. _____la fruta

h. _____las gambas

i. _____la pasta

6. Translate into Spanish

a. I like eggs

b. I love oranges

c. I hate tomatoes

d. I don't like prawns

e. I love fruit

f. I don't like vegetables

g. I hate milk

Unit 14. Talking about food: VOCAB BUILDING

1. Complete with the missing words. The initial letter of each word is given

a. Estos plátanos son a_____
These bananas are disgusting

b. Estas manzanas son d_____
These apples are delicious

c. Este pollo es muy p_____
This chicken is very spicy

d. No me gusta la c_____
I don't like meat

e. Este café es muy d_____
This coffee is very sweet

f. Las hamburguesas son m_____
Burgers are unhealthy

g. Las verduras son s_____
Vegetables are healthy

h. Me encanta la l_____
I love milk

2. Complete the table

Español	English
La leche	
	Roast chicken
El pescado	
Los huevos	
	Water
	Bread
Los cereales	
El pan tostado	
	Vegetables

3. Complete with 'me gusta' or 'me gustan' as appropriate

a. _____ las manzanas

b. _____ la leche

c. No _____ los cereales

d. _____ el pan tostado

e. _____ las verduras

f. No _____ la pasta

g. _____ el arroz

h. No _____ el café

4. Broken words

a. N__ m__ g_____ l____ h_____ *I don't like eggs*

b. M__ e_____ l_____ m_____
I love apples

c. O_____ l___ h_____ *I hate burgers*

d. M___ g_____ n m_____ l___ c_____
I like chocolates a lot

e. E__ c_____ e___ s_____ *Coffee is tasty*

f. E__ p_____ e__ s_____ *Fish is healthy*

g. E__ curry indio e__ p_____ *Indian curry is spicy*

5. Complete each sentence in a way which is logical and grammatically correct

a. Las _____ no son sanas

b. Los plátanos son _____

c. No me _____ la leche

d. Me _____ el pollo asado

e. _____ el pescado porque es sano

f. _____ la carne roja porque es malsana

g. _____ las verduras porque son sanas y deliciosas

Unit 14. Talking about food: READING

¡Hola! Me llamo Roberto. ¿Qué prefiero comer? Me encanta el marisco, entonces me gustan mucho las gambas y los calamares porque son deliciosos. Me gusta mucho el pescado también porque es sabroso y rico en proteínas. Sobre todo el salmón. Me gusta bastante el pollo asado. Además, me gusta bastante la fruta, sobre todo los plátanos y las fresas. No me gustan mucho las verduras porque no son sabrosas.

¡Hola! Me llamo Alejandro. ¿Qué prefiero comer? Me encantan las verduras. Las como todos los días. Mis verduras favoritas son las espinacas, las zanahorias y las berenjenas porque son ricas en vitaminas y minerales. También me gusta la fruta porque es sana y deliciosa. Odio la carne y el pescado. Son ricos en proteínas pero no son sabrosos.

¡Hola! Me llamo Violeta. ¿Qué prefiero comer? Me encanta la carne, sobre todo la carne de cordero, porque es muy sabrosa. Me gusta mucho el pollo asado picante porque es sabroso y rico en proteínas. Me gustan bastante los huevos. Son sanos y ricos en vitaminas y proteínas. Me gusta bastante la fruta, pero no me gustan nada las manzanas. Odio el marisco, especialmente los calamares.

¡Hola! Me llamo Juan. ¿Qué prefiero comer? Prefiero la carne. Me encanta porque es sabrosa. Me gustan mucho las hamburguesas porque son sabrosas. También, me gusta mucho la fruta porque es dulce. No me gustan las verduras. Odio los tomates y las zanahorias. No aguanto los huevos. Son ricos en proteínas y vitaminas, pero son asquerosos. No me gustan las patatas fritas porque no son muy saludables.

¡Hola! Me llamo Fernando. ¿Qué prefiero comer? Me encanta la carne roja porque es muy sabrosa y rica en proteínas. No como mucho pescado porque no me gusta. Me gustan bastante los calamares fritos, pero no son sanos. Me gusta muchísimo la fruta, sobre todo los plátanos, porque son deliciosos, ricos en vitaminas y no son caros. No me gustan las manzanas y odio las naranjas. No como verduras.

1. Find the Spanish in Roberto's text

a. I love seafood

b. I like prawns

c. Are delicious

d. I like fish a lot

e. Salmon

f. I quite like

g. Moreover

h. Above all

i. They are not tasty

2. Fernando or Roberto? Write F or R next to each statement below

a. I love seafood - *Roberto*

b. I hate oranges

c. I like fruit a lot

d. I don't like vegetables

e. I prefer salmon

f. I quite like squid

g. I prefer bananas

h. I don't eat much fish

i. I love red meat

3. Complete the following sentences based on Alejandro's text

a. Alejandro loves_____

b. He eats them _____

c. His favourite vegetables are _____ _____and _____

d. He also likes _____because it is _____and _____

e. He hates _____and _____

4. Fill in the table (in English) about Juan & Violeta

Loves	Likes a lot	Doesn't like	Hates

 THE LANGUAGE GYM

Unit 14. Talking about food: TRANSLATION

1. Faulty translation: spot and correct IN THE ENGLISH any translation mistakes you find below

a. Me encantan las gambas: *I hate prawns*

b. Odio el pollo: *I like meat*

c. Me gusta la miel: *I don't like honey*

d. Me encantan las naranjas: *I love apples*

e. Los huevos son asquerosos: *Eggs are tasty*

f. Los plátanos son ricos en vitaminas: *Bananas are rich in protein*

g. El pescado es muy sano: *Fish is unhealthy*

h. Prefiero el agua mineral: *I prefer tap water*

i. Odio las verduras: *I love vegetables*

j. Me encanta el arroz: *I love rice pudding*

k. No me gusta la fruta: *I quite like fruit*

l. Los calamares fritos son sabrosos: *Fried squid is salty*

m. Este café es delicioso: *This coffee is disgusting*

2. Translate into English

a. Las gambas son sabrosas:

b. El pescado es delicioso:

c. El pollo es rico en proteínas:

d. Me encanta el arroz:

e. La carne roja no es saludable:

f. Unos calamares fritos:

g. Los huevos son asquerosos:

h. Prefiero el agua con gas:

i. Me gustan bastante las gambas:

j. No me gustan las verduras:

k. Me gustan las zanahorias:

l. Este café es muy dulce:

m. Una manzana asquerosa:

n. Unas naranjas deliciosas:

3. Phrase-level translation En to Sp

a. Spicy chicken:

b. This coffee:

c. I quite like:

d. Very sweet:

e. A disgusting apple:

f. Some delicious oranges:

g. I don't like:

h. I love:

i. Tasty fish:

j. Mineral water:

k. Roast meat:

4. Sentence-level translation En to Sp

a. I like spicy chicken a lot

b. I like oranges because they are healthy

c. Meat is tasty but unhealthy

d. This coffee is very sweet

e. Eggs are disgusting

f. I love oranges. They are delicious and rich in vitamins

g. I love fish. It is tasty and rich in protein

h. Vegetables are disgusting

i. I prefer bananas

j. This tea is sweet

THE LANGUAGE GYM

166

Unit 14. Talking about food: WRITING

1. Split sentences

Me gusta el pollo	fruta
Odio las verduras porque	asado
Prefiero la	café es dulce
Este	son asquerosas
Me gusta bastante la	sabrosos pero no son saludables
Los calamares fritos son	los plátanos
Me encantan	carne

2. Rewrite the sentences in the correct order

e.g. el Me asado pollo encanta
Me encanta el pollo asado

a. las verduras Odio

b. café Este dulce es

c. fritos Los no saludables son calamares

d. el mineral Prefiero agua

e. asquerosas son verduras Las

f. mucho las gustan naranjas Me son porque deliciosas

3. Spot and correct the grammar and spelling (there may be missing words)

a. Me gusta las naranjas

b. No gustan las verduras

c. Los huevos asquerosos

d. Me encanta este cafe

e. Prefero las zanahorias

f. Odio el carne

4. Anagrams

a. sArosoque

b. erudVasr

c. rneCa

d. escaPdo

e. anSo

f. ulDec

g. cheLe

5. Guided writing: write 4 short paragraphs in the first person singular (I) describing the people below

Person	Loves	Quite likes	Doesn't like	Hates
Natalia	Chorizo because spicy	Milk because healthy	Red meat	Eggs because disgusting
Iker	Chicken because healthy	Oranges because sweet	Fish	Meat because unhealthy
Julieta	Honey because sweet	Fish because tasty	Fruit	Vegetables because boring

6. Describe this person in the third person (he)

Name: Rafa
Age: 18
Description: Tall, good-looking, sporty, nice
Occupation: Student
Food he loves: Chicken
Food he likes: Vegetables
Food he doesn't like: Red meat
Food he hates: Fish

TERM 3 - BRINGING IT ALL TOGETHER – 14

1. Me llamo Andrew y tengo catorce años. Mi cumpleaños es el dos de enero. Soy de Escocia y vivo en Edimburgo, la capital del país, con mi familia. Hoy estoy un poco cansado y estresado porque tengo demasiados *(too much)* deberes.

2. En mi familia somos cuatro personas: mi hermana mayor, Skye, mi padre, Angus, mi madre, Isla, y yo. Me llevo muy bien con mi madre porque es muy paciente y buena. Sin embargo, mi padre es un poco impaciente.

3. Mi hermana mayor se llama Skye. A Skye le gusta leer libros, escribir y cantar. Tiene veinte años y es muy creativa y talentosa. Su cumpleaños es el siete de mayo. Skye tiene el pelo castaño y los ojos verdes. A Skye le encanta la música, pero a mí me gusta estudiar. También soy más deportista. Hago deporte todos los días.

4. Mi rutina diaria es muy sencilla. Por lo general, me despierto muy temprano, a eso de las cinco de la mañana. Luego me ducho y me pongo el uniforme. Después, a eso de las seis, desayuno con mi hermana Skye en la cocina. Las dos desayunamos tostadas con miel y un vaso *(a glass)* de leche. Luego me lavo los dientes y salgo de casa. Siempre voy al colegio a pie. Me gusta ir al colegio a pie porque vivo muy cerca del colegio.

5. ¿Qué prefiero comer? Me encantan las verduras porque son ricas en vitaminas y minerales. Las como todos los días. También me gusta la carne, sobre todo la carne de ternera, porque es muy sabrosa. Pero no es tan saludable así que solo la como una vez a la semana. También me gustan mucho el pescado y los mariscos. No aguanto los huevos y la leche.

6. Me gusta mi colegio porque los profesores son buenos y tengo muchos amigos. Mi asignatura favorita es el arte porque soy una persona bastante creativa. Además, me encanta la clase de educación física porque me encanta hacer deporte y jugar con mis amigos. Mi profesor de educación física es muy severo, pero muy gracioso e inspirador también.

7. El fin de semana que viene voy a hacer muchas cosas. El viernes voy a salir con mis amigos al centro comercial. Vamos a ir de compras y a cenar en un restaurante italiano. Luego, el sábado voy a quedarme en casa y ver una película con mi hermana Skye. ¡Será divertido!

Andrew, 14, Edimburgo, Escocia

1. Complete the sentences below based on paragraphs 1-4 in Andrew's text

a. Andrew is _____ years old

b. Today he is a bit _____ and stressed

c. My _____ sister is called Skye

d. Skye enjoys reading books, _____ and singing

e. Skye has _____ hair and green eyes

f. Andrew is more _____ than her

g. He does sport _____

h. Andrew gets up very _____

i. He goes to school _____

2. Find the Spanish for the following in paragraph 5

a. Vegetables: V   i. What: Q

b. I eat: C   j. But: P

c. Also: T   k. Them: L

d. Above all: S   l. So: T

e. Veal: T   m. Of: D

f. Tasty: S   n. Only: S

g. Healthy: S   o. Once: U

h. Fish: P   p. Eggs: H

3. Some of the below statements about Andrew are incorrect. Spot them and correct the inaccuracies

a. Today, Andrew has no homework

b. Andrew is more hard–working than Skye

c. They have breakfast in the dining room

d. He goes to school by bike

e. He only eats meat twice a week

f. His teachers are good

g. His favourite subject is PE

h. His PE teacher is very strict

i. Next Saturday he will go shopping

j. He will also watch a movie at the cinema

1. Me llamo Angus y tengo dieciséis años. Mi cumpleaños es el ocho de octubre. Soy de Aberdeen, en el norte de Escocia. Vivo aquí con mi familia.

2. En mi familia somos cuatro personas: mi hermana mayor, Maisie, mi padre, Gordon, mi madre, Olivia, y yo. Me llevo muy bien con mi madre porque es muy tranquila, paciente y divertida. Mi padre también es muy divertido. Me llevo muy bien con él porque siempre me escucha.

3. A Maisie le encanta hacer deportes acuáticos. Sus deportes favoritos son el piragüismo y el esquí acuático. Tiene dieciocho años y es muy deportista y fuerte. Su cumpleaños es el doce de junio. Maisie tiene el pelo largo y rubio y los ojos azules. Ella es más deportista que yo, pero a mí me gusta más la música que a ella.

4. Entre semana mi rutina diaria es igual todos los días. Por lo general, me despierto a eso de las siete de la mañana. Luego me lavo la cara y los dientes y me visto. Después, a las siete y cuarto, desayuno con mi hermana Maisie en el comedor. Los dos desayunamos tostadas y cereales con leche. A veces también tomo un café con leche. Siempre voy al colegio en autobús. Me gusta ir al colegio en autobús porque puedo charlar con mis amigos.

5. ¿Qué prefiero comer? Me gusta mucho el pollo asado porque es sabroso y rico en proteínas. También me gustan bastante los huevos. Son sanos y ricos en proteínas. Me gusta bastante la fruta, sobre todo las manzanas. Son muy deliciosas y ricas en vitaminas. Sin embargo, no me gustan nada las naranjas.

6. Me gusta bastante mi colegio. Los profesores no son muy severos y nunca me chillan. Lo mejor *(the best thing)* es que tengo muchos buenos amigos. Mi asignatura favorita es las matemáticas porque soy una persona muy lógica. Además, me encanta la clase de ciencias. Mi profesor de ciencias es muy estricto, pero me gusta.

7. El fin de semana que viene voy a hacer un montón *(a load)* de cosas. El viernes voy a ir de excursión *(on a trip)* a la playa con mis amigos. En la playa vamos a nadar en el mar y tomar el sol. Luego, el sábado voy a ir al parque con mi familia. Vamos a hacer una barbacoa con mis tíos y mis primos. Vamos a comer hamburguesas y ensalada. Mi prima Clara va a comer una hamburguesa de tofu porque ella es vegetariana. Luego, el domingo voy a quedarme en casa para descansar.

Angus, 16, Aberdeen, Escocia

4. Translate the following phrases from paragraphs 1 to 3

a. Vivo aquí

b. Mi hermana mayor

c. Tranquila

d. Me escucha

e. Deportes acuáticos

f. Deportista y fuerte

g. El pelo largo y rubio

h. Más deportista que yo

5. Fix the 10 mistakes in the following English translation of paragraph 4

Every week my daily routine is the same every day. In general, I get up around 7 o'clock in the morning. Then, I wash my hair and teeth and I shave. Afterwards, at seven-thirty, I have breakfast with my sister Maisie in the kitchen. The two of us have toasts and cereals with juice for breakfast. I always go to school by bus. I like to go to school by bus because I can mess around with my friends.

6. Answer the questions below about paragraphs 6 and 7 in Spanish, as if you were Angus

a. ¿Te gusta tu colegio? ¿Por qué?

b. ¿Qué es lo mejor de tu colegio?

c. ¿Por qué te gustan las matemáticas?

d. ¿Cómo es el profe de ciencias?

e. ¿Adónde vas a ir de excursión el fin de semana próximo?

f. ¿Con quién vas a ir?

g. ¿Qué vais a hacer en la playa?

h. ¿Dónde vas a hacer una barbacoa el sábado que viene?

i. ¿Qué vas a comer?

j. ¿Quién es Clara?

k. ¿Por qué Clara no come hamburguesas?

l. ¿Adónde vas a ir el domingo próximo?

UNIT 15
My holiday plans
(Talking about future plans for holidays)

In this unit you will learn how to talk about:

- What you intend to do in future holidays
- Where you are going to go
- Where you are going to stay
- Who you are going to travel with
- How it will be
- Means of transport

You will revisit:
- The verb 'ir'
- Free-time activities
- Previously seen adjectives

UNIT 15
My holiday plans

¿Adónde vas a ir este verano?	*Where are you going to go this summer?*
¿Cómo vas a viajar?	*How are you going to travel?*
¿Cuánto tiempo vas a pasar allí?	*How long are you going to spend there?*
¿Dónde vas a quedarte?	*Where are you going to stay?*
¿Qué vas a hacer durante las vacaciones?	*What are you going to do during the holidays?*

Este verano voy a ir a *This summer I am going to go to* **Voy a ir de vacaciones a** *I am going to go on holiday to* **Vamos a ir de vacaciones a** *We are going to go on holiday to*	**Argentina** **Chile** **Cuba** **España** **México**	**en autocar** *by coach* **en avión** *by plane* **en barco** *by boat* **en coche** *by car*	
Voy a pasar *I am going to spend* **Vamos a pasar** *We are going to spend*	**una semana** *1 week* **dos semanas** *2 weeks*	**allí** *there* **con mi familia** *with my family*	**Será aburrido** *It will be boring*
Voy a quedarme en *I am going to stay in* **Vamos a quedarnos en** *We are going to stay in*	**la casa de mi familia** **un camping** **un hotel barato** *a cheap hotel* **un hotel de lujo** *a luxury hotel*		**Será divertido** *It will be fun*
Voy a *I am going to* **Vamos a** *We are going to* **Me gustaría** *I would like to* **Nos gustaría** *We would like to*	**bailar** **comer y dormir** **comer comida deliciosa** **comprar recuerdos** **descansar** **hacer buceo** **hacer deporte** **hacer turismo** **ir a la playa** **ir de compras/tiendas** **ir de marcha** **jugar con mis amigos** **montar en bici** **salir al centro** **tocar el ukelele** **tomar el sol**	*dance* *eat and sleep* *eat delicious food* *buy souvenirs* *rest* *go diving* *do sport* *go sightseeing* *go to the beach* *go shopping* *go clubbing* *play with my friends* *go biking* *go out into town* *play the ukulele* *sunbathe*	**Será guay** *It will be cool* **Será relajante** *It will be relaxing*

THE LANGUAGE GYM

1. Listen and fill in the gaps

a. Este verano _____ a ir de vacaciones a Cuba.

b. Voy a viajar en _____.

c. Vamos a _____ una semana allí.

d. _____ divertido.

e. Voy a _____ en un hotel de lujo.

f. Voy a _____.

g. Vamos a ___ ___ _____.

h. Me gustaría _____ _____.

i. Nos gustaría _____ _____.

2. Spot the differences and correct your text

a. Este invierno voy a ir de vacaciones a México.

b. Voy a pasar tres días allí.

c. Voy a ir con mi amigo.

d. Vamos a quedarnos en un hotel caro.

e. Voy a hacer mis deberes.

f. Mi hermana va a comprar regalos.

g. Vamos a ir a la piscina.

h. Voy a beber Zumosol.

i. Me gustaría ir al museo.

j. Nos gustaría ir de pesca.

3. Multiple choice quiz

	1	2	3
a.	He is Swiss	He is Swedish	He is Russian
b.	He is travelling by train	He is travelling by plane	He is travelling by boat
c.	He is travelling alone	He is travelling with his friend	He is travelling with his family
d.	He is staying in a cheap hotel	He is staying in a three-star hotel	He is staying in a luxury hotel
e.	He is staying there for two weeks	He is staying there for three weeks	He is staying there for ten days
f.	He is going to scuba dive	He is going to go clubbing	He is going to eat and sleep
g.	He will also go sightseeing	He will also go shopping	He will also sunbathe
h.	It will be fun	It will be cool	It will be expensive

4. Write in the missing words

(a) Este verano voy a ir _____ vacaciones a Roma, ____ Italia. (b) Voy ___ ir en avión. Vamos a pasar una semana _____. (c) Vamos _____ quedarnos en un hotel _____ lujo. (d) _____ voy a ir de marcha. Mis hermanas van a ir _____ compras (e) y mis padres van _____ comprar recuerdos. (f) Además, van a hacer turismo porque _____ muchos sitios históricos _____.

5. Listen, spot and correct the spelling and grammar errors

(a) Esto verano voy ir de vacaciones avión. (b) Voy pasar dos semana allí. (c) Voy a ir con mi toda familia.

(d) Vamos a quedarme en un hotel de luxo con piscina cerca de la playa. (e) Por manana vamos a ir a la

playa. (f) Por la tarde vamos a ir compras y a hacer turismo. (g) A eso de las ocho vamos cenar en

restaurants locales para comer platos típico. (h) Por la noche, mi hermana y yo voy a ir de marcha. (i)

También, me gusta aprender a bailar salsa. Lo pasaramos bomba.

6. Listen to Carlos and answer the questions below in English

a. Where is he going on holiday? (two details)

b. When does his holiday begin?

c. How long for?

d. How is he travelling?

e. Who with?

f. Who are they staying with?

g. What is the name of the town where they will stay?

h. What are they going to do there? (4 details)

1.   3.

2.   4.

7. Narrow listening: fill in the grid in English

	Carolina	Benicio	Sofía	Mateo
Destination				
Who with				
Departure date				
How long for				
Accommodation				
Location				
Activities				

Unit 15. My holiday plans: VOCABULARY BUILDING

1. Match

Voy a ir	I'm going to spend
Voy a pasar	a campsite
Voy a quedarme	I'm going to go
Un hotel barato	it will be cool
Un camping	I'm going to stay
Me gustaría	to buy
Comprar	a cheap hotel
Será guay	I would like to

3. Translate into English

a. Este verano voy a ir a Grecia

b. Voy a pasar tres semanas allí

c. Voy a ir a Cuba en avión

d. Vamos a ir de compras

e. Me gustaría salir al centro

f. Voy a jugar con mis amigos

g. Nos gustaría comer y dormir

h. Voy a descansar todos los días

i. Voy a hacer deporte con mi hermano

2. Complete with the missing word

a. Comer y _____   *To eat and sleep*

b. Voy a _____   *I am going to rest*

c. Me _____ ir a…   *I would like to go to…*

d. _____ con mis amigos   *To play with my friends*

e. _____ __ quedarme en…   *I am going to stay in…*

f. _____ aburrido   *It will be boring*

g. Vamos a _____   *We are going to spend…*

h. Voy a viajar en _____   *I'm going to travel by plane*

i. Voy a pasar dos semanas _____ con mi _____
I am going to spend two weeks there with my family

4. Broken words

a. Com___ y dorm____   *To eat and sleep*

b. Vamos a qu_____   *We are going to stay*

c. Voy a p_____   *I am going to spend*

d. Me g_____ ir a…   *I would like to go to…*

e. Ir a la p_____   *To go to the beach*

f. M_____ en bici   *To go biking*

g. T_____ el sol   *To sunbathe*

h. S_____ relajante   *It will be relaxing*

5. 'Ir', 'Jugar' or 'Hacer'?

a. _____ de compras

b. _____ al centro

c. _____ turismo

d. _____ al fútbol

e. _____ buceo

f. _____ de marcha

g. _____ en bici

h. _____ deporte

i. _____ al ajedrez

j. _____ a la playa

6. Faulty translation: correct the English

a. Este verano vamos a ir a…: *Last summer I am going to go to…*

b. Voy a ir a Argentina con mi padre:
I am going to go to Argentina with my mother

c. Voy a comer y dormir: *I am going to drink and sleep*

d. Me gustaría descansar mucho: *I would like to rest a bit*

e. Vamos a quedarnos en un hotel: *I am going to stay in a hotel*

f. Voy a pasar una semana allí: *I am going to spend one week here*

g. Vamos a viajar en coche y barco:
I am going to travel by coach and barge

h. Voy a quedarme en la casa de mi familia:
We are going to stay in my family's house

Unit 15. My holiday plans: READING

Me llamo Hugo. Soy de Oviedo pero vivo en Madrid. Este verano voy a ir de vacaciones al sur de España, a Cádiz. Voy a viajar en coche con mi novio Alejandro. Vamos a pasar cuatro semanas allí y vamos a ir a la playa todos los días. También vamos a comer comida deliciosa. No voy a ir al cine porque es muy aburrido. Prefiero tomar el sol en la playa.

Me llamo Deryk y soy de Canadá. En mi familia hay cuatro personas. Mis personas favoritas son mi mujer, Anna, y mis hijas Saskya y Ciella. Este verano vamos a viajar a Inglaterra y después a Quebec, en Canadá. Voy a descansar y leer libros en Inglaterra y luego voy a hacer esquí con mis amigos en Canadá. Anna va a montar en bici y comer comida deliciosa, como 'poutine' (similar a patatas fritas con queso). ¡Será guay!

Me llamo Dino. Soy italiano, de Venecia. Este verano voy a ir de vacaciones a México en avión, solo. Voy a pasar dos semanas allí y voy a quedarme en una caravana en la playa. Voy a visitar monumentos, museos y galerías de arte. No me gusta mucho el deporte, pero me encanta la cultura. Será interesante.

Me llamo Diana. Soy de Polonia pero vivo en Dubai. Allí tengo una tienda de curiosidades. Este verano voy a viajar a Chile con mis amigas Olivia y Natasha. Olivia vive en Berlín y tiene un bebé que se llama Nouriel. Voy a viajar en barco porque tengo mucho tiempo (porque nunca trabajo). El viaje dura 8 semanas. Luego, voy a pasar cinco semanas allí y voy a quedarme en un hotel de lujo. Me encanta bailar, así que voy a bailar todos los días. También voy a comer y dormir mucho. No voy a ir a museos porque es muy aburrido.

1. Find the Spanish for the following in Hugo's text

a. I am from

b. But I live in

c. I am going to travel by

d. With my boyfriend

e. We are going to spend

f. Every day

g. I am not going to

h. I prefer to sunbathe

2. Find the Spanish for the following in Diana's text

a. This summer

b. By boat

c. I have a lot of time

d. I am going to spend

e. I love to dance

f. So/therefore

g. Also

h. It is very boring

3. Complete the following statements about Deryk

a. He is from _____

b. His favourite people are called _____, _____ & _____

c. They will travel to _____ and _____

d. Deryk is going to _____ and _____ _____ in England

e. Anna is going to _____ and _____

f. "Poutine" is made up of _____ and _____

4. List any 8 details about Dino (in 3rd person) in English

1.

2.

3.

4.

5.

6.

7.

8.

5. Find someone who...

a. ...doesn't mind being out at sea for long periods

b. ...is going to rest and read books

c. ...loves learning about culture

d. ...prefers the beach to going sightseeing

e. ...has opposite interests to Dino

f. ...is going to travel by car

g. ...really loves his family

Unit 15. My holiday plans: READING

Me llamo Monserrat. Soy de Barcelona. Tengo una tortuga en casa. Es muy lenta y muy gorda pero me encanta. Es mi mejor amiga. Este verano voy a ir de vacaciones a Málaga, en el sur, con mi familia. Voy a viajar en avión y luego en coche. Vamos a pasar tres semanas en Torremolinos y vamos a quedarnos en un hotel de lujo. ¡Será muy divertido! Luego vamos a ir en coche a Granada y vamos a ver monumentos famosos, como La Alhambra (un palacio árabe muy antiguo). Voy a comer comida deliciosa; me encantan las tapas. También voy a ir de compras todos los días y voy a comprar ropa guay.

Me llamo Freddie. Soy de Buenos Aires, en Argentina. Este verano voy a ir de vacaciones a la ciudad de Cuzco en el sur de Perú, con mi hermano Brian. Vamos a viajar en avión y vamos a pasar dos semanas allí. En Perú vamos a visitar un sitio histórico muy especial: las ruinas Incas de Machu Picchu. Será muy impresionante y divertido. También, en Cuzco vamos a hacer senderismo en la montaña. Será duro pero muy guay. Un día me gustaría descansar y escribir canciones. Me encanta cantar y a mi hermano Brian le gusta mucho tocar la guitarra. Nuestro grupo favorito se llama Queen. Mi música favorita es la música rock.

Me llamo Josefina y vivo en Granada, en el sur de España. Este verano voy a viajar a Barcelona, en Cataluña, en el noreste de España. Voy a viajar en coche y luego en tren. Voy a pasar dos semanas allí y voy a quedarme en un hotel barato. En Barcelona me gustaría visitar un monumento muy famoso que se llama La Sagrada Familia. Es una catedral muy grande y bonita, diseñada por Antoni Gaudí. También voy a ir a la playa. La playa de Barcelona es un poco fea así que voy a ir en tren a un pueblo que se llama Sitges. ¡La playa allí es espectacular! Tengo una amiga en Sitges que se llama Alicia. Vamos a charlar en la playa y tomar el sol juntas. Será divertido y relajante.

1. Answer the following questions about Montserrat

a. Where is she from?

b. What animal does she have?

c. Who will she go on holiday with?

d. Where will they stay?

e. How will they get to Granada?

f. What is the Alhambra?

g. What will she do every day?

2. Find the Spanish in Josefina's text

a. This summer

b. And then

c. Which is called

d. A cathedral

e. Designed by

f. A bit ugly

g. The beach there

h. Sunbathe together

3. Find someone who...

a. ...is going to travel south

b. ...has a brother who is a musician

c. ...has a slow moving pet

d. ...is going to be walking in the mountains

e. ...is going to visit a famous religious monument

f. ...is going to visit a famous palace

g. ...is going to visit the oldest historical site

h. ...is planning to relax on the beach

4. Find the Spanish for the following phrases/sentences in Freddie's text

a. My brother Brian

b. The Incan ruins

c. It will be very impressive

d. It will be tough

e. I would like to rest

f. To play the guitar

g. Our favourite group

h. Rock music

THE LANGUAGE GYM

176

Unit 15. My holiday plans: TRANSLATION/WRITING

1. Gapped translation

a. *I am going to go on holiday:*
Voy a ir de _____

b. *I am going to travel by car:*
Voy a viajar en _____

c. *We are going to spend one week there:*
Vamos a _____ una semana _____

d. *I am going to stay in a cheap hotel:*
_____ __ quedarme en un hotel _____

e. *We are going to eat and sleep every day:*
Vamos __ comer y _____ todos los _____

f. *If the weather is nice I am going to go to the beach:*
Si hace buen _____ voy a ir a la _____

g. *I am going to go shopping:*
Voy a ir de _____

2. Translate to English

a. Comer

b. Comprar

c. Descansar

d. Hacer turismo

e. Ir a la playa

f. Todos los días

g. En avión

h. Hacer buceo

i. Salir al centro

3. Spot and correct the grammar and spelling mistakes note: in several cases a word is missing

a. Voy hacer deporte

b. Voy a paso una semana alí

c. Voy a quedarme un hotel lujo

d. Vamos quedarno en una hotel

e. Me gustaría jugar un fútbol

f. Vamos a sallir al centero

g. Voy a voy a la playa

h. Voy a jugar a mes amigos

4. Categories: Positive or Negative?
Write P or N

a. Será divertido: _____

b. Será aburrido: _____

c. Será agradable: _____

d. Será relajante: _____

e. Será interesante: _____

f. Será terrible: _____

g. Será curioso: _____

h. Será asqueroso: _____

i. Será fascinante: _____

j. Será impresionante: _____

5. Translate into Spanish

a. I am going to rest

b. I am going to go diving

c. We are going to go to the beach

d. I am going to sunbathe

e. I would like to go sightseeing

f. I am going to stay in...

g. ...a cheap hotel

h. We are going to spend 2 weeks

i. I am going to go by plane

j. It will be fun

 THE LANGUAGE GYM

TERM 3 - BRINGING IT ALL TOGETHER – 15

1. Me llamo Barri Mock y tengo dieciséis años. Mi cumpleaños es el veintitrés de marzo. Soy de Gales y vivo en Caerphilly, cerca de Cardiff, la capital del país, con mi familia. Hoy estoy muy feliz porque la semana que viene voy de vacaciones a España con mi familia.

2. En mi familia somos cuatro personas: mi hermana mayor, Rhiannon, mi padre, Gareth, mi madre, Elin, y yo. Me llevo muy bien con mi madre porque es muy paciente y amable. Sin embargo, mi padre es un poco impaciente. Normalmente nos llevamos bien, pero a veces es un poco antipático y me regaña si no hago los deberes.

3. Mi rutina diaria es bastante sencilla. Por lo general, me despierto un poco tarde, a eso de las ocho de la mañana. Luego me ducho, me peino y me visto. Después, a eso de las ocho y cuarto, desayuno con mi hermana Rhiannon en la cocina. Ambos tomamos *(we both have)* tostadas con mermelada y zumo de naranja.

4. ¿Qué me gusta comer? Me encantan las verduras, como las espinacas, las zanahorias y los calabacines porque son ricos en vitaminas y minerales. Sin, embargo, no como carne porque soy vegetariano. Mi comida favorita es la comida india, la como todas las semanas. Me gusta mucho la fruta, sobre todo las fresas.

5. Me gusta mi colegio porque los profesores son inteligentes y pacientes y explican las cosas muy bien. Mi asignatura favorita es el teatro porque soy una persona bastante creativa. Además, me encanta la clase de música porque me gusta cantar y tocar la guitarra.

6. El próximo fin de semana empiezan las vacaciones de verano. Voy a ir de vacaciones a Málaga, en el sur de España, con mi familia. Voy a viajar en avión y luego en coche. Vamos a pasar tres semanas en Fuengirola y vamos a quedarnos en un hotel de lujo. Luego vamos a ir en coche a Córdoba y vamos a ver monumentos famosos, como la Mezquita-Catedral y el puente romano. Voy a comer comida deliciosa. También voy a ir de compras todos los días y voy a comprar ropa guay.

Barri Mock, 16, Caerphilly, Gales

1. True (T), False (F) or Not Mentioned (NM)?

Today, Barri is quite sad	
He doesn't get on well with his mother	
Barri has a girlfriend	
He has breakfast in the dining room	
For breakfast he has toast with honey	
He loves vegetables	
He doesn't eat fish	
He likes Indian food but has it rarely	
He likes strawberries a lot	
He can't stand his school	
He enjoys singing	
He is going on holiday to northern Spain	
In Fuengirola he'll stay in a luxury hotel	
He will go shopping every day	

2. Find the Spanish equivalent for the following phrases/sentences in the text

a. I am very happy (par. 1)

b. I am going on holiday (par.1)

c. I get on well (par. 2)

d. However (par. 2)

e. A bit (par. 2)

f. Tells me off (par. 2)

g. I wake up (par. 3)

h. I love vegetables (par. 4)

i. I don't eat meat (par. 4)

j. They explain things (par. 5)

k. I like singing (par.5)

l. I am going to go (par.6)

m. We are going to spend (par. 6)

n. I am going to go shopping (par. 6)

o. I am going to buy (par. 6)

1. Mi nombre es Federica y tengo diecisiete años. Mi cumpleaños es el veintitrés de junio. Soy de Italia y vivo en San Felice Circeo, un pueblo pequeño en la costa del Lacio, con mi familia. Hoy estoy muy feliz porque estoy de vacaciones con mi familia.

2. En mi familia somos cuatro personas: mi hermana mayor Francesca, mi padre Gennaro, mi madre, Gabriela, y yo. Mi madre es mucho más estricta que mi padre. Él hace ciclismo con sus amigos todos los días. Hay una montaña cerca de donde vivo. Mis abuelos se llaman Gabriele y Alessia. Gabriele tiene ochenta y tres años y Alessia tiene ochenta y dos. Los dos son muy amables y cariñosos.

3. Mi hermana mayor se llama Francesca. A ella le gusta pintar y cantar. Tiene dieciséis años y es muy creativa y talentosa. Su cumpleaños es el nueve de mayo. Francesca es muy guapa. Tiene el pelo castaño y los ojos azules. Francesca es más artística que yo, pero mis amigos dicen que yo soy más graciosa que ella.

4. ¿Qué me gusta comer? Me encantan las verduras, como la lechuga, los tomates y los pepinos porque son ricos en vitaminas y minerales. Mi comida favorita es la comida china. La como dos veces a la semana. Me gusta mucho la fruta, sobre todo la sandía. Odio la carne.

5. Me gusta mi colegio porque los profesores son muy amables y graciosos. Siempre me ayudan cuando tengo un problema. Mi asignatura favorita es la música. Mi profesor de música toca muy bien la batería y el piano, pero su instrumento principal es el violín. Él toca en la orquesta de Roma y del Lacio. En el futuro me gustaría ser músico profesional como él.

6. El próximo fin de semana empiezan las vacaciones de verano. Voy a ir de vacaciones a Atenas, la capital de Grecia, con mi familia. Voy a viajar allí en avión y luego en tren. Vamos a pasar una semana en Atenas y vamos a quedarnos en un hotel barato. ¡Será muy interesante! Luego vamos a ir en barco a una isla que se llama Santorini. Vamos a quedarnos en una casa típica, de color blanco y azul. Voy a comer platos locales deliciosos y nadar en la piscina todos los días. ¡Será increíble!

Federica, 17, San Felice Circeo, Italia

3. Read paragraphs 1 to 3 and complete the following statements correctly

a. Federica lives in a _____ town

b. Federica's dad cycles _____

c. There is a mountain near _____

d. Her grandparents are called _____ and _____

e. Her _____ sister is called Francesca

f. Francesca likes _____ and _____

g. Federica's friends say she is _____ than Francesca

4. Correct the 14 mistakes in the following translation of paragraphs 4 and 5

What do I like to eat? I like vegetables, such as carrots, tomatoes and mushrooms because they are rich in vitamins and minerals. My favourite is Indian food. I eat it twice a month. I like fruit a lot, apart from pineapple.

I love my school because the pupils are very kind and helpful. They often help me when I have a problem. My favourite subject is music. My music teacher plays the guitar and the piano quite well, but his minor instrument is the violin. He plays in the Roma and Lazio orchestra. In the future I would like to be a music teacher like him.

5. Answer the questions below in Spanish as if you were Federica

a. ¿Dónde está situado tu pueblo?

b. ¿Qué deporte hace tu padre?

c. ¿Qué le gusta hacer a tu hermana Francesca?

d. ¿Cómo es Francesca?

e. ¿Cuál es tu comida favorita?

f. ¿Qué opinas de la carne?

g. ¿Cómo son tus profesores?

h. ¿Qué trabajo te gustaría hacer en el futuro?

i. ¿Qué empieza la semana que viene?

j. ¿Adónde vas a ir de vacaciones?

k. ¿Cómo vas a viajar?

l. ¿Adónde vas a quedarte en Santorini?

m. ¿Qué vas a comer allí?

TERM 3 - BRINGING IT ALL TOGETHER – QUESTION SKILLS

1. Fill in the missing question words – Daily life

a. ¿ ___ _____ _____ te despiertas?

b. ¿ _____ _____ por la mañana?

c. ¿ _____ _____ normalmente?

d. ¿ ___ _____ _____ sales de casa?

e. ¿ _____ vas al colegio?

f. ¿ ___ _____ _____ para el fin de semana que viene?

g. ¿ _____ te gustaría ir?

h. ¿ _____ _____ vas a ir?

i. ¿ _____ _____ te gustaría hacer?

2. Sentence Puzzle – Food: listen and re-arrange the sentences

a. ¿ desayunas Qué normalmente?

b. ¿ te comida Por gusta Qué? ¿ qué?

c. ¿ pescado gusta Te el?

d. ¿ comida Cuál es favorita tu?

e. ¿ alguna Hay odias comida que?

f. ¿ la las Prefieres o carne verduras?

g. ¿ fruta es tu Cuál favorita?

3. Tangled translation – Holidays: into Spanish

a. ¿**To where** vas a ir de **holidays** este **summer**?

b. ¿**How** vas a **travel**? **Why**?

c. ¿Cuánto **time** vas a **spend** allí?

d. ¿Dónde **you're going** a quedarte?

e. ¿**What** te gustaría **do** allí?

4. Translate, then listen and check

a. To where?

b. How?

c. When?

d. At what time?

e. What do you do?

f. With who?

g. Do you like...?

h. How much time?

5. Listen and write in the missing information to the questions: Daily life

a. ¿A _____ hora te despiertas? *Me _____ a eso de las _____ de la _____*

b. ¿Qué _____ por la mañana? *Por la mañana, casi siempre _____ con mi _____ en la _____*

c. ¿Qué _____ normalmente? *Normalmente _____ un zumo de _____ y una tostada con _____*

d. ¿A qué _____ sales de _____ ? *_____ de casa a las _____ y _____*

e. ¿ _____ vas al _____ ? *Voy al _____ a _____ con mi mejor _____*

f. ¿ _____ planes _____ para el fin de _____ que viene? *Este _____ de semana voy a ___ ___ _____ con mi _____ al parque y después voy a _____ una _____*

g. ¿ _____ te _____ ir? *Si hace _____ tiempo me _____ ir a la _____*

h. ¿ _____ _____ vas a ir? *Voy a _____ con mis _____ porque me _____ pasar _____ con ellos*

6. Listen and write in the missing information to the questions: Food & Holidays

a. ¿ _____ comida te _____? ¿Por _____? *Me _____ mucho la comida _____ porque es _____*

b. ¿Te _____ el _____? *Me _____ el _____, pero lo que más me _____ es el _____*

c. ¿ _____ es tu comida _____? *Mi _____ favorita es la _____*

d. ¿ _____ alguna _____ que _____? ¿ _____ que? *Sí, _____ los _____. Son _____.*

e. ¿ _____ vas a ir de _____ este _____? *Este _____ voy a ir a _____ de _____*

f. ¿ _____ vas a _____? *Primero voy a _____ en _____ y después en _____*

g. ¿ _____ _____ vas a pasar _____? *Voy a pasar _____ semanas _____*

h. ¿ _____ vas a _____? *Voy a _____ en un _____ en las _____*

i. ¿ _____ te gustaría _____ allí? *Me _____ hacer _____ y _____ porque me _____ los deportes al _____ libre*

THE LANGUAGE GYM

TERM 3 - BRINGING IT ALL TOGETHER – QUESTION SKILLS

7. Fill in the grid with your personal information

Question	Answer
1. ¿A qué hora te despiertas?	
2. ¿Qué haces por la mañana?	
3 ¿A qué hora sales de casa?	
4. ¿Cómo vas al colegio?	
5. ¿Qué planes tienes para el fin de semana?	
6. ¿Adónde te gustaría ir?	
7. ¿Qué comida (no) te gusta? ¿Por qué?	
8. ¿Cuál es tu comida favorita?	
9. ¿Hay alguna comida que odias?	
10. ¿Adónde vas a ir de vacaciones este verano?	
11. ¿Cómo vas a viajar?	
12. ¿Cuánto tiempo vas a pasar allí?	
13. ¿Dónde vas a quedarte?	
14. ¿Qué te gustaría hacer allí?	

8. Survey one of your classmates using the same questions as above– write down the main information you hear in Spanish

Q.	Person 1
1.	
2.	
3.	
4.	
5.	
6.	
7.	
8.	
9.	
10.	
11.	
12.	
13.	
14.	

No Snakes No Ladders

	7 I am going to go to the cinema	6 Next weekend...	5 I go back home at four	4 I leave the house at eight	3 I have breakfast in the kitchen	2 I get dressed at seven thirty	1 I get up at seven
	8 I would like to go to the park	9 My friend (m) is going to go to the pool	10 In order to swim	11 In order to watch a match	12 It **will** be fun	13 What do you like to eat?	14 I love cheese because it is tasty
	23 I am going to stay in a luxury hotel	22 I am going to stay in a cheap hotel	21 I am going to spend one week there	20 I am going to go on holiday to Cuba	19 I prefer vegetables	18 Hamburgers are not healthy	17 I hate oranges!
	24 I am going to eat delicious food	25 We are going to buy souvenirs	26 We are going to do diving	27 I would like to sunbathe at the beach	28 I would like to go shopping	29 We would like to go to the beach	30 We would like to do sightseeing

START

15
I like roast chicken because it is delicious

16
Meat is rich in protein

FINISH

THE LANGUAGE GYM

182

No Snakes No Ladders

TERM 3

7 Voy a ir al cine	6 El fin de semana próximo / que viene	5 Vuelvo a casa a las cuatro	4 Salgo de casa a las ocho
8 Me gustaría ir al parque	9 Mi amigo va a ir a la piscina	10 Para nadar	11 Para ver un partido
23 Voy a quedarme en un hotel de lujo	22 Voy a quedarme en un hotel barato	21 Voy a pasar una semana allí	20 Voy a ir de vacaciones a Cuba
24 Voy a comer comida deliciosa	25 Vamos a comprar recuerdos	26 Vamos a hacer buceo	27 Me gustaría tomar el sol en la playa

3 Desayuno en la cocina	2 Me visto a las siete y media	1 Me levanto a las siete	15 Me gusta el pollo asado porque es delicioso SALIDA
12 Será divertido	13 ¿Qué te gusta comer?	14 Me encanta el queso porque es sabroso	16 La carne es rica en proteínas
19 Prefiero las verduras	18 Las hamburguesas no son saludables	17 ¡Odio las naranjas!	
28 Me gustaría ir de compras	29 Nos gustaría ir a la playa	30 Nos gustaría hacer turismo	LLEGADA

THE LANGUAGE GYM

183

Translate each part of the pyramid out loud with your partner, then write it into the spaces provided below.

a.
This summer

b. This summer I am going to go on holiday with my family.

c. This summer I am going to go on holiday with my family to Spain.

d. This summer I am going to go on holiday with my family to Spain. We are going to spend 2 weeks there.

e. This summer I am going to go on holiday with my family to Spain. We are going to spend 2 weeks there and we are going to stay in a campsite.

f. This summer I am going to go on holiday with my family to Spain. We are going to spend 2 weeks there and we are going to stay in a campsite. I am going to do sightseeing and go to the beach. It will be fun.

Write your translation here

SOLUTION: *Este verano voy a ir de vacaciones con mi familia a España. Vamos a pasar dos semanas allí y vamos a quedarnos en un camping. Voy a hacer turismo y voy a ir a la playa. Será divertido.*

TERM 3 – BRINGING IT ALL TOGETHER

One pen One dice

Play in pairs. You only have 1 pen and 1 dice.
One person has the pen and starts translating the sentence into **English.** The other person rolls the dice until they roll a 6, they swap the pen and translate. The winner is the person who finishes translating all the sentences first.

1. Me levanto a las ocho.	
2. Me ducho y me visto.	
3. Salgo de casa y voy al colegio a pie.	
4. El próximo fin de semana voy a ir al cine.	
5. Voy a ir a la piscina para nadar.	
6. Me gusta la carne pero no me gusta el pescado.	
7. Me gusta la ensalada porque es saludable.	
8. Voy a ir de vacaciones a Francia.	
9. Voy a pasar una semana allí.	
10. Voy a comprar recuerdos.	

One pen One dice

Play in pairs. You only have 1 pen and 1 dice.
One person has the pen and starts translating the sentence into **Spanish.** The other person rolls the dice until they roll a 6, they swap the pen and translate. The winner is the person who finishes translating all the sentences first.

1. I get up at eight.	
2. I shower and I get dressed.	
3. I leave the house and go to school on foot.	
4. Next weekend I am going to go to the cinema.	
5. I am going to go to the pool (in order) to swim.	
6. I like meat but I don't like fish.	
7. I like salad because it's healthy.	
8. I am going to go on holiday to France.	
9. I am going to spend one week there.	
10. I am going to buy souvenirs.	

The End

We hope you have enjoyed using this workbook and found it useful!

As many of you will appreciate, the penguin is a fantastic animal. At Language Gym, we hold it as a symbol of resilience, bravery and good humour; able to thrive in the harshest possible environments, and with, arguably the best gait in the animal kingdom (black panther or penguin, you choose). In Spanish, it is also the best example of the ü (dieresis); this is a symbol that helps distinguish "gui" (pronounced like the 'gi' in English "gift) and "güi"(pronounced like the 'gui' in "penguin"). The same occurs with 'gue' (ge) and 'güe' (gue).

Join us again on Spanish Sentence Builders – TRILOGY – Part II

Made in the USA
Middletown, DE
03 June 2024

55236324R00110